WITHDRAWN
FOR SALE

103522519

For Adventure and for Patriotism

ONE HUNDRED YEARS OF
The Legion of
FRONTIERSMEN

Lt Col D.P. Driscoll, D.S.O. from the painting by Abe Turner.

For Adventure and for Patriotism

ONE HUNDRED YEARS OF

The Legion of FRONTIERSMEN

*Soldiers, Spies and Counter-Spies,
Sacrifice and Service to the State*

GEOFFREY A. POCOCK

Phillimore

2004

Published by
PHILLIMORE & CO. LTD
Shopwyke Manor Barn, Chichester, West Sussex, England

© Geoffrey Pocock, 2004

ISBN 1 86077 282 X

Printed and bound in Great Britain by
MPG BOOKS
Bodmin, Cornwall

WEST SUSSEX LIBRARY SERVICE	
3522519	
Macaulay	04 Nov 2004
3SS	£ 25.00

'They had joined into a kind of Buffalo Bill army, for adventure and for patriotism ... '

BRIAN GARDNER (GERMAN EAST)

*'There's a legion that never was listed
That carries no colours or crest,
But, split in a thousand detachments,
Is breaking the road for the rest.'*

RUDYARD KIPLING

Contents

List of Illustrations	ix
Acknowledgements	xi
List of Subscribers	xiii
Preface	xiv
Foreword	xv
Introduction	xvii
1. Canada	1
2. Accusations of Murder	17
3. 'Listing the Legion	28
4. The Secret Government Subsidy	51
5. The War in East Africa	75
6. The World Flight Expedition	97
7. Upsetting the Americans	116
8. Success, then Failure Again	133
9. Dwindling Influence	159
Notes	177
Bibliography	182
Index	183

List of Illustrations

Frontispiece: Lt Col D.P. Driscoll, D.S.O.

1. Church Parade in Leeds, Yorkshire, *c.*1930 xviii
2. Royal Fusiliers, Armistice Day Parade, 7 November 1937 xix
3. Annual Parade, 17 November 1935 xxi
4. Evelyn ffrench who also toured the music halls as 'Jeffrey Silant' 2
5. Roger Pocock in Frontiersmen uniform, 1905 19
6. H.S.H. Prince Louis of Battenberg 30
7. Early Legion of Frontiersmen badges 40
8. Roger Pocock and Lt Col D.P. Driscoll, *c.*1907 41
9. Frontiersman William D. Kemp 52
10. One-man outfit for the Legion of Frontiersmen 59
11. Frontiersmen acting as Mounted Police Reserves in London 65
12. Manchester Frontiersmen with 3rd Belgian Lancers 68
13. Manchester Troop with 3rd Belgian Lancers near Dixmude, 1914 69
14. Manchester Frontiersmen with Belgian Lancers attack a farmhouse 70
15. *War Illustrated* 76
16. Frontiersmen working with remounts, 1914 77
17. The card sent out by Driscoll to all Frontiersmen 78
18. William Reginald Wilson prior to leaving for campaign in East Africa 80
19. *Nyanza* as she is today 81
20. Lieutenant F.C. Selous, and his Platoon at Kajiado, East Africa, *c.*1915 83
21. Capt. F.C. Selous 88
22. Mail arriving at camp, East Africa 89
23. Programe: rest camp for 25th Fusiliers in South Africa 92
24. Breaking camp, East Africa 93
25. Officer's badge and other ranks badge, 25th Service Bn. Royal Fusiliers 96
26. The S.Y. *Frontiersman* 98
27. The S.Y. *Frontiersman* 99
28. Lord Loch talking to the Captain and Dr Thompson 102
29. Lord Loch with the Captain 103
30. Captain Geoffrey Malins among the visitors to the ship 105
31. Loading stores donated by sponsors 107
32-3. Frontiersmen on board the ship 108
34. Visitors from the public on board the ship in London, 16 June 1923 110
35. Mellon, who was described as the ship's comedian, juggling 111
36. Guy Eardley-Wilmot and G.E. Heaton 111
37. Silver, the expedition photographer 111
38. Mellon fooling around again on board ship 112
39. Silver the photographer, Heaton and Captain Spalding 113
40. Heaton at work trimming coal 113
41. The sail bath 114
42. Eardley-Wilmot, Bromley, O'Dell, Mellon, Pearce, Masterson and Perry . . . 117
43. The membership certificate of the Adventurers Club of Los Angeles 117

44. The party at Mr Wooden's ranch at Beverley Hills, California 118
45. Mr Wooden with his thoroughbred horses and his daughters 118
46. The menu of the Dinner given at the Thos. Ince Motion Picture Studios . . .119
47. Menu of the lunch given to notable Los Angeles citizens. 120
48-9. Goldwyn stars on board the ship 121
50. Marshal Bill Finn poses by the writ for debt that he attached to the ship . .122
51. Eardley-Wilmot crewing for American millionaire William B. Leeds. 123
52. The first mail received at anchor in California 124
53. Vancouver Command outside the Armoury which is still in use 130
54. The Mayor of Vancouver inspecting the Frontiersmen 131
55. Stanley Park during the First World War. 132
56. Badge of 210th (Frontiersmen) Bn. C.E.F. 133
57. 210 Battalion Canadian Expeditionary Force, Moose Jaw, 1915 134
58. Maritime Division, Portsmouth, c.1930. 137
59. Captain E.C. Edwards Carter 138
60. Harborne Troop in camp, South Midlands, 1936 .140
61. March-past, Horse Guards Parade, 1935. 141
62. A Frontiersmen event of the 1930s 142
63. Mounted camp, South Midlands area, November 1935 143
64. Inspection by Major General Sir Edward Perceval. 143
65. The Legion of Frontiersmen on Horse Guards Parade. 144
66. Coronation Parade, 15 May 1937, Bombay 144
67. Lord Derby with the Liverpool Legion of Frontiersmen. 145
68. This spoof advertisement appeared in the *Frontiersman* magazine 147
69. Roger Pocock, Commandant Colonel J. Findlater and Captain W. Palmer 149
70. Hong Kong Squadron in camp, 12 October 1935. 150
71. Collage used in *Frontiersman* magazine 153
72. Collage from the *Frontiersman* magazine 154
73. Lord Mountbatten inspecting the Rhodesia Command 155
74. Inspection by Field Marshal Viscount Slim. 157
75. Photograph of an unknown Frontiersman 160
76. Captain Robert Moyse, M.C., D.C.M., B.E.M. 160
77. Manchester Frontiersmen with Robert Moyse 160
78. Brigadier Morton, C.B.E., Late Commandant General 161
79. Major General Sir John Duncan, Chief Commandant of St Johns. 162
80. Glasgow Troop, 1937. 166
81. Bognor Regis Frontiersmen, 1935. 166
82. The South Sussex Squadron kit inspection at Arundel Park, 1934 167
83. Captain Robert Moyse. 169
84. Gas warfare lecture on respirators. 170
85. Major Jack Gallagher, B.E.M. 170
86. Quebec Frontiersmen 1950s to mid-1960s. 170
87. Badge of the Canadian Division of the Legion of Frontiersmen 171
88. Roeslare, Belgium, May 1972. 172
89. The Legion Colours marching through London 172
90. Frontiersmen escort the Belgian Colours on Belgian Day. 172
91. Presentation of two lances carried into action by Frontiersmen, 1914 172
92. Colour Squadron Mounted Troop, Petts Wood, 1967. 173
93. Major Philip Shoosmith laying a wreath at the Cenotaph in London 173
94. Belgium Day, 1980. 173
95. Rough-rider Sgt. Mike King, Peace River, British Columbia, 1980. 174
96. Members of British North America and Eastern Canada Commands 174
97. Frontiersmen march on to Horse Guards Parade, Belgian Day, 2004. 175
98. Prince Philippe of Belgium takes the Salute from the Frontiersmen. 175
99. Cdt.-General Ronald J. Potter lays a wreath at the Cenotaph, 2004 175
100. The Frontiersmen on Horse Guards Parade. 176

Acknowledgements

Twenty-five years of research have gone into this book. Over the time I have been given generous help by so many people that it will be impossible to acknowledge everyone here. Sadly, many of those who have helped and supported me have since died. When I first started my research and contacted the Frontiersmen, they put me in touch with the charismatic Jack Gallagher who had led a life of adventure and who had been responsible for the resurgence of the Frontiersmen in West Sussex. The then Commandant-General, Brigadier Shoosmith was the first of a line of Commandants-General through to Ronald J. Potter in 2004 to give unstinting support. Colonel Edgar Vigay of the Canadian Division referred me on to Brigadier A. Mack of Regina who commanded Canadian Division. Until he died, Brigadier Mack gave me great help and generously gave me permission to quote from the History of Canadian Division that he had edited. As Roger Pocock never married, I traced, with the help of the American Press, his nephew Kennedy Pocock living in New Jersey. Again, I could not have wished for more whole-hearted support than I received from Ken and, since his death, his daughter Mrs Laurie Leonard. The noted naval historian, Tom Pocock, gave me much help and advice as some years ago he had begun research into the subject. The late Peter Lewison, C.B.E., undertook some research for me in Canada and through him I was able to make contact with British Columbia journalist Cecil Clark and towards the end of Clark's long life we were able to answer many of the questions regarding the disappearance of Sir Arthur Curtis.

Much of the Legion records were destroyed in the bombing of London in 1940 but the acquisition of personal albums and files have enabled the story to be pieced together. For many years my good friend Graham Burling supplied me with information from New Zealand where there are fuller archives and, on Graham retiring from the Legion, the New Zealand history duties were taken over by Bruce Fuller who continued supporting my work wholeheartedly. Since the death of Brigadier Mack, the Legion has been fortunate to secure the services of B.W. (Will) Shandro who has been ably assisted by Dean Bruckshaw. Will Shandro has delved into lesser-known Canadian records to improve vastly our knowledge of the Legion's early days in Canada. Jeff Henley of Queensland has always been most helpful regarding

Legion Australian history and I have had the help of Brian Tarpey of Malta. I was also fortunate to meet Capt. Charles Dudley who died at a tragically early age. Capt. Dudley held the Roger Pocock Canada papers and could not have been more supportive and helpful in granting me access to the papers and permission to quote where necessary. Similar praise must be made for Frank Ransley, O.B.E., M.C., who was probably the last surviving member of the 1923 World-Flight Expedition.

Tribute must also be paid for their help to the following, in no particular order (some of whom have now passed away): William Green, G.M.; Colonel K.F. Herbert; Sir John Eardley-Wilmot; Ernest F. Meacock, M.M.; Mrs G. Heaton; Bob Moyse Junior; Dr Peter Lovatt; Michael Kemp; Alec Coleman; Paul Murray-Hoodless; Alastair Cowan; Vincent Reed; George Hall; Mrs Shelagh Gregory; Susan Hora; Col. A. Patrick Hall, T.D.; Colin Rickards; Brian Roorda; Colin McDonald; Valerie Brooking of the Sunbury and Shepperton Local History Society; Mrs Betty Sheale; W.A. Main; Mrs Rita Gill; Frederick Scott; June Tobin and family; Henry and Ron White; Jim Grundy; Mrs M. Lawson; Mrs F. Hansford; Ron Rainbow; Dollina C.M. Lias, Mrs M. Holliday, Mr Tom Tappenden and the volunteers of the Printing Museum at Amberley Museum for their skill in transforming an old box of printing blocks into some most informative pictures; the staff of the Public Record Office, Kew (now the National Archives); The Royal Canadian Mounted Police and their historians; the generous people who have allowed photographs to be used and are credited elsewhere; Sir Patrick Moore for reading the draft and for writing his kind preface; The Rt. Hon. The Countess Mountbatten of Burma, Patron of the Legion of Frontiersmen of the Commonwealth (Countess Mountbatten's Own) for her Foreword and encouragement.

To those whose names do not appear I offer my grateful thanks and apologies that it has not been possible for reasons of space to mention every name. I am exceptionally grateful to every one of the large number of people who have been unstinting in their generous help and information. Every contribution and snippet of information has been important in celebrating the many thousands who served their fellows through the Legion of Frontiersmen, including some who made the greatest possible sacrifice.

ILLUSTRATION ACKNOWLEDGEMENTS
Alastair Cowan (son of Pat Cowan), 12; Mrs E. Featherstone of Felpham, 81; Legion of Frontiersmen archives, 5, 8, 10-11, 13-17, 20, 62, 68, 73-4, 78, 89-4; Legion of Frontiersmen archives, Canada, 53-5; Legion of Frontiersmen archives, New Zealand, 69; Legion of Frontiersmen, Yorkshire Command, 1 (22 and 24 photographed by W.R. Wilson); Mrs Frances Gallagher, 85; Shelagh Gregory, 18; Michael Kemp, 9; Mike King, 95; Mrs M. Lawson, 67; W.A. Main, 58; Moose Jaw archives, 57; The Countess Mountbatten of Burma, 6; Bob Moyse junior, 76-7, 83, 88; Natural History Museum, London, 21; Roger J. Pocock, 97-100; Vincent Reed, 23; Brian Roorda, 96; Eric Schoute, 19; James Shortt, 7, 25, 56, 87; Roger Tremblay, 86.

List of Subscribers

David Alexander-Fleming, JP
Lt Bill Anderson
Col TCR Armstrong-Wilson, TD
Brigadier DJ Baker
Richard Melville Ballerand
A M Banks
Cpl Jesse J Bargholz (LF)
Trooper Shane Bartley of Countess Mountbatten's Own Legion of Frontiersmen
Lt Col Anthony Bateman, LOF (IOC) Rtd
Carl Bellanca
Capt Dean Bruckshaw (LF)
Sergeant Michael Carmel ESM
Stuart Anthony Clewlow
Commissioner Alec Coleman LCH AMM CDM(CAN) LF
Prof. Joseph F Connolly II
Alastair Cowan
Geoffrey Cuthill
James Devonshire
Nigel Driscoll (Great-grandson of D P Driscoll)
Maj. T Eccles Adjutant, UK Command, Canadian Div.
Hon Colonel, Lt General Peter S Fitchett
Edward Fothergill
Bruce G Fuller
Capt B G Fuller LF(CMO)
Gail Fynes
RSM S A Gallard aka Sticks
Lt Col R Harreson Garner SSM CD ESM
Danny W Gill (Frontiersman)
Douglas J Gillies
Richard Gillies
Jane E Gjerde
Peter J Gorman
Lt Col Paul Grant LF
Russ Gregory, in memory of your grandfather
Colonel A P Hall TD RE (V), Ex Commandant General, LF of the Commonwealth, 1984-89
Captain George J Hall CDM LF
Major Stephen Allan Hensley
Capt Peter Hildebrand
Susan Hora
Troop Major R Howard, LF
Robert J Jones
Roger Kearin
Glyn Kemp
John Kemp
Mike Kemp
Nina Kemp
Sian Kemp
Andrew Kerr
Lawrence Andrew King
Earl Kitchener
Stephen John Klimczuk
LOF RSM R Kurelo 4 Para Canada
Pte Bruce C Laker 724 090 840
Jason Legere, in memory of your great-grandfather
Sue Legere, in memory of your grandfather
Colonel A H Lennan NZ Division LOF
Ann C Leonard
Laura A Leonard
Dollina Macfergus Lias
Dr Peter Lovatt
Kerry Luckey
Finian Manson
Carol Miller
Lt Col John T Minarik CDM
Rex Morgan AM MBE
Commissioner Paul Murray-Hoodless LF
John Naldrett
Edward Paice
Paritutu 'L' Troop LOF
Lieutenant Colonel Nigel Peel MFH
Tom Pocock
Victor John Pocock
Ronald J Potter
Major Larry P Ransom LF
Mrs R.V. Richards
Staff Sergeant Brian Roorda CMOF 4 Para/'P'Coy. Airborne
Frederick Scott
Lt Col D Sewell Canadian(Eastern) Command
Scott James Augustus Seymour
Frontiersman Barry William Shandro
Betty E Sheale
Major The Baron James Shortt of Castleshort LOF
Richard B Sturrock
Roy Swales 2LT LOF
Nina Helen Tapping
Lieut. B.N. Tarpey, CO. Malta Command, LF
R Marc Tremblay
Major Tanky Turner OC Wellingborough Troop
Wally Wake
Lt Col Wayne Buffett Warlow LF
Edward H. Watkins, Major LF, Deputy Commandant, HQ UK Command
Robin Weatherall
S/Sgt Greg White
Pat Whiteley
James G Willson
Monika Wilson
Rafal Wilson

Preface

The Legion of Frontiersmen is uniquely British. It could not have originated anywhere except in Britain and the old Commonwealth, and could not have survived to play a rôle far greater than its limited numbers would have indicated. At its heyday, almost a century ago now, it was a force to be reckoned with; had it received the support to which it was entitled, it could have achieved far more than it actually did.

Its founder, Roger Pocock, typified the entire movement. Eccentric, adventurer explorer, amateur spy, mildly successful novelist, and – above all – a patriot, he too was uniquely British. That he had his faults is not in doubt; he was wilful, egoistic and capable of appalling errors of judgement, but always his love of his country shines through; he was very much a man of his time. It is surely fitting that the story of the Frontiersmen should be written by a member of his clan, and Geoffrey Pocock has succeeded brilliantly.

He says, in his Introduction, that 'over the years, its eccentricities have steadily whittled away its fundamental support, until now it is but a pale shadow of its former self'. This is true enough, and at the moment it has to be said that Legion is in eclipse. But does not this mirror the whole state of the world? Yet we have faced crises before, and we have always won through in the end. The pendulum will swing – and when it does we will have desperate need of patriots and fighters such as the Frontiersmen.

I am proud to have been enrolled as a member of the Legion, though circumstances entirely beyond my control prevented me from playing a useful rôle. At least we know that, though they are small in numbers and lack the official backing which they merit, the Frontiersmen are still there – and in the hour of need they will be ready, just as they have always been ready in the past.

Sir Patrick Moore, CBE, FRS

Foreword

I am very pleased to be Patron of the Legion of Frontiersmen of the Commonwealth and able to continue the family association which started when my Grandfather, Prince Louis of Battenberg, became one of the Founders in 1905.

I also have another close link because many of the first soldiers to join Princess Patricia's Canadian Light Infantry in August 1914 at the beginning of the Great War, came from the Frontiersmen; and I have been Colonel-in Chief of the 'Patricias' since 1974.

I am very pleased that the Legion of Frontiersmen are now 'Countess Mountbatten's Own'.

The Frontiersmen continue to provide a valuable service across the British Commonwealth in support of the Services and Local Authorities and the Community in general.

The Right Honourable The Countess Mountbatten of Burma, CBE, CD, JP, DL.

In these days when the sense of community is not always very strong this commitment is an important aspect of the work, and allows opportunities for the younger generation to continue the tradition of being of help to those in their environment.

I wish all Frontiersmen well in their varied endeavours,

Mountbatten of Burma

Introduction

At 3 p.m. on 11 June 1909, the founder of the Legion of Frontiersmen called by appointment on Lord Esher as Chairman of the Esher Committee. Lord Esher told him that, subject to the abolition of the Governing Council of the Legion and the appointment of Esher's nominee as Commandant-General, he would grant the Legion £500 a year for one year's trial, with the founder to have £300 a year.[1]

The strength of Great Britain throughout the years has been in its individualists: men who have chosen to think their own ideas and not necessarily follow a lead without question. The Great British Eccentric has also been a feature of this race and we have been all the richer for such people. The Legion of Frontiersmen has always attracted its share of individual thinkers and of eccentrics. In its early days it attracted a few men of power but a far greater number of men of influence. Over the years, its eccentricities have steadily whittled away its influential support until now it is but a pale shadow of its original self. Its decline has mirrored the decline of British influence abroad. As Britain lost its colonies, so the Legion lost members. Its strength in the U.K. is small and it is probably strongest of all in Canada where it still flourishes as a symbol of old values, which have diminishing worth in Britain. A note in a Colonial Office file (CO323) from the 1930s about the Legion of Frontiersmen, Hong Kong, written by Col. H.R. Pownall, tells us quite a bit about the members of the Legion:

> I have some knowledge of the Legion of Frontiersmen in this country. They are mostly, but not entirely, men of middle age – or older, who have 'Knocked about' a good deal and like the glamour of a Stetson hat, boots and breeches, and a revolver holster, who, to their great credit, wish to have a useful function in emergency but are of too independent a spirit to stomach the bonds of army discipline in peace.[2]

As to the men of influence and, in some cases, of power who belonged to, or passionately supported, the Legion in its halcyon days before 1939, they read like pages from *Who's Who*. Names from Prince Louis of Battenberg to General Smuts, from Arthur Conan Doyle to Edgar Wallace, politicians such as Leo Amery, newspaper tycoons such as Viscount Burnham, all served

1 *Church Parade in Leeds, Yorkshire, c.1930.*

the Legion. They attracted adventurers, authors and naturalists, such as F.C. Selous, Cherry Kearton, Rider Haggard, Erskine Childers. Some of the names and stories will surprise. Before the Second World War, The Happy Valley set in Kenya were keen on the Frontiersmen. The victim of the murder scandal, the Earl of Erroll was a Captain in the Legion and commanded a Troop. All of this came from the idea of a minor author, keen adventurer, patriot but great dreamer: a man forgotten today but in his lifetime a nationally known figure. This man never received honour from the country he loved with an undying passion, mainly because he took to his death the suspicion that he may have murdered a man in the wilds of Canada at the 1899 Gold Rush. It was not until 40 years after his death that, working with a journalist in Canada, I was able to unearth enough facts to exonerate him completely and suggest what did happen to the disappeared baronet, Sir Arthur Curtis, on one tragic day.

Much writing has centred on Baden-Powell. The Boy Scout movement was a great success, but it owed this to the nationally honoured 'Hero of Mafeking' at its head. The Legion of Frontiersmen had ideas for service to the State that were far wider-ranging than those of the Boy Scouts, but they lacked a nationally admired hero at its head. Who was the founder? He was merely a minor author from a minor branch of a landed family. Invalided as a humble constable from the North-West Mounted Police, he had later served in a most irregular band of Scouts in South Africa, leaving as a corporal. Throughout his life, he was closest to his sister. She was far better known as an extremely good actress and an actor/manager. The 'O divinely-gifted Lena Ashwell', as George Bernard Shaw described her, had access to the royal set.[3] Later, even as a divorcee, she married Sir Henry Simson, the Duke and Duchess of York's doctor, who saw the Queen and Princess Margaret into the world. In those strictly class-conscious days, however much support the Legion attracted and however hard Pocock worked at drumming up that support, society was suspicious of this ex-corporal, particularly when national papers re-ran the story of the mystery of the missing baronet with more than a hint that Pocock had murdered him. Pocock had persuaded Lord Lonsdale to be the first President, but, although respected, he was no national hero – in fact, as Lonsdale's biographer said, he 'was never happier than when he was playing at soldiers. Brass bands, waving flags and colourful uniforms could bring tears to his eyes.'⁴ There could be no more exotic uniform worn by a volunteer than that of the Legion of Frontiersmen. In the popular view a 'frontiersman' was a colourful and exotic figure.

> Though this image was quintessentially American, by 1908 it had entered popular British culture. The explorer, the miner, and the frontier policeman belonged to a brotherhood whose loyalty to the clan was testament of loyalty to the Empire, whose very wanderings were token of the Empire's far-reaching bond. He seemed to revive the spirit of the Elizabethan seaman; he was virile, a true Englishman, one of the 'sons of a roving breed'. His adventures filled thousands of fictions for men and for boys, and in the hands of writers such as Rudyard Kipling, Rider Haggard, Robert Service, and John Buchan, he began to symbolize the imperial dream. Fact fed on fiction, history turned into myth: the frontiersman became a type that carried the meanings of a world still in flux. He proved his courage by panning gold in the Klondike, fighting pirates in the South Seas, running guns in South America, or killing Zulus in South Africa – and he came home to yarn about his experiences with other old frontier hands in the cosy camaraderie of London's Savage Club.⁵

2 *Frontiersmen at Royal Fusiliers, Armistice Day Parade, 7 November 1937.*

Robert H. MacDonald wrote this in his book on the frontier and the boy scout movement. The Frontiersmen could perhaps be described as not-quite-grown-up boy scouts. These were clubbable men and indeed the Savage Club was often their meeting place where the affairs of the world were discussed, although not with such power to influence those affairs as was held by those who met at, say, the Carlton Club. These men were what could often be described as the second sons of the families of power: those who had been sent out to the far-flung outposts of Empire to strengthen Britain's grip on the world.

First of all, we need to know about the man whose enthusiasm and effort set the Legion into being. In November 1941 we read in his obituary in *The Times*: 'Roger Pocock was so modest that few except his closest friends could guess that life to him was, and always had been, a splendid adventure.'[6] This gives us some idea of the man's character before we begin to chart his adventures. Of course, obituaries never speak ill of the dead but concentrate on a man's good points. Roger Pocock was all the more likeable for having been so human in his failings. For a start he trusted too easily. Every Englishman was a gentleman to be taken at his word. Even in Victorian times that could not have been wise. Roger Pocock had little respect for authority and yet expected Authority, in the shape of Government and the War Office, to back his Legion of Frontiersmen, the majority of whose members in foreign parts shared his contempt for officialdom as it then existed.

In its review of his autobiographical tales of the early Legion of Frontiersmen and its members *Chorus to Adventurers*, in the issue of 17 February 1931, *The Times* had some telling comments to make about him:

> As founder, closely involved in the curious activities of those who investigated schemes devised to the detriment of his beloved British Empire ... As he hates officers and officials and all who represent routine as cordially as he loves the Empire which the routine is presumably devised to serve, his tales do not lack piquancy; but the mellow that goes to their composition greatly exceeds the acid. There may have been something of the mountebank in the legionaries whose 'tribal customs' Capt. Pocock delights to recall, but he can afford to admit certain extravagances in these foster children of his, for they went with a death roll in the War of 6000 from a membership computed at 17000 down to the present time.[7]

Pocock knew many famous men who will come into our story. On one occasion he met and interviewed Butch Cassidy. He had a multitude of friends and acquaintances, but it is difficult to point to many really close life-long friends. He never married; his was not the sort of life that would have brought happiness to any wife. With advancing years he became more lonely. He achieved greater contentment when he was accepted as a Brother at Charterhouse in 1928 but in the spring of that year a lady who met him at Amiens remarked on his loneliness. The lady had been on a pilgrimage with her daughter to a cemetery at Albert to visit the grave of a relative. At their hotel table they looked up from their menus to see an elderly man approaching. They described him as a 'very courtly man'. He was of medium height, inclined to stoutness and with a pronounced limp. His Imperial beard made them think immediately of the late King Edward VII to whom he bore a certain resemblance. He had the air of a man who had spent much of his life in the open air and his right arm was held slightly unnaturally and had obviously been damaged at some time. 'May a very lonely Englishman sit at your table?', he enquired. 'Of course', replied the lady. They struck up an interesting conversation and she said he was able to give them many 'travellers

3 *Annual Parade, 17 November 1935, marching through Piccadilly, London preceded by Legion Band.*

tips'. He had come over from Rouen to see the cathedral at Amiens. After the meal he offered the lady a cigarette from a silver case. Engraved on the case was the name 'Roger Pocock' and he told her that the case had been given to him by Royal Flying Corps pilots during the 1914-18 War.

The name meant nothing to the 15-year-old daughter, but later on her mother remembered that the name of Roger Pocock was known nationally before the First War as the founder of the Legion of Frontiersmen, an organisation of roguish patriots who did all they could to ensure that Britain was prepared to defend itself.[8] They were the men who had called themselves 'the eyes and ears of the Empire'.[9] During the War many had belonged to the 25th Fusiliers (Frontiersmen) who had served with great valour in East Africa. The Frontiersmen were also famous as the first British troops into action in 1914, when the Manchester Troop had sailed with their own horses and at their own expense to serve with distinction with the Belgian army. When the Frontiersmen saw a need and a service to be fulfilled they seldom paused to ask permission from authority.

Why was this man so lonely? Why was he ignored and, in his own words, 'forgotten as becomes a Frontiersman'[10] by the country he loved with a fierce patriotism. He founded the Legion of Frontiersmen and nursed it through its earliest years with great love and care and yet it brutally expelled him once, and twice more before his death he would himself resign. He had an unusually active and adventurous life, during which he engaged in a multitude of activities, from being a constable in the North-West Mounted Police to being accused of murder on an expedition. He claimed experience of 28 trades but certainly could not have been considered an expert at more than a few. To him 'Civilization is a poor thing to one who has lived the spacious life of the West.'[11] He was one of that body of Victorian gentlemen-adventurers who helped secure the boundaries of the British Empire, but whose activities were little noted by others. Roger Pocock was different from the majority of other gentlemen-adventurers because he was a thinker, a man who dreamed dreams, but whose dreams and whose attempts at their realisation too often ruled his head and turned him into a Don Quixote, tilting at windmills.

He studied many subjects in depth and could discuss most things intelligently. He was a real expert on horses and wrote about them knowledgeably if individually in his much praised book *Horses*.[12] A friend saw him as a knight, jousting through life, helping lost causes and saving damsels in distress, demanding entrance at the castle gate, but happy so long as he had a good horse under him.[13] Geology was a great passion from an early age and he thought deeply on mysticism and the occult. If his meditations led him along independent and solitary paths to his conclusions, he was not one to shirk from publicising his arguments so that they could be debated.

Not only has the Founder of the Legion been unjustly forgotten, but the effect of the Legion of Frontiersmen on the history of Great Britain, the old Empire and the Commonwealth has been ignored. It is a startling fact that Britain came very close to handing to the amateurs of the Legion some of the tasks that were undertaken by what became MI5 and MI6. In the years between the two World Wars, it was impossible to see any parade in any substantial town or city throughout Britain (and many of its overseas Dominions) without the strong presence of the Frontiersmen in their distinctive uniform.

The Frontiersmen were also influential in the formation of the L.D.V. (Home Guard). Writers have regularly commented how the Home Guard in its early days rebelled against the authority of the War Office, often wishing to go its own way and even electing its officers by democratic ballot. This independence was a direct result of the methods of the Frontiersmen. Certainly in the first half of its life, the whole principle of the Legion of Frontiersmen sprang from the ideas and ideals of one unsung patriot, but was then taken up by a growing number of men and, to a lesser extent, women. These men, whose power in the world about them varied from considerable to insignificant, all shared the same aims of the Legion, of 'mutual fellowship and service to the State in times of need'.[14] The great majority were Royalists, but all were patriots. Many thousands of Frontiersmen made the ultimate sacrifice and were content in that sacrifice to be 'forgotten as becomes a Frontiersman'.[15] This book remembers them and pays the tribute for their sacrifices that has been owed to them for far too long.

GEOFFREY A. POCOCK

Lavant, Sussex
April 2003

One

CANADA

It is important to look into the life of the Founder of the Legion of Frontiersmen and try to understand what events in his early life led him to form this organisation. It could be said that others had parts of the same idea, but he was the one who set it into being and who stuck to his task grimly during the first difficult year when others decided that the proposition was too flawed to succeed. Pocock's early life and the events of his first thirty-nine years, particularly in Canada and America, brought together a combination of circumstances and experiences that made him the right man at the right time.

Roger Pocock was one of seven children, six of whom survived into adulthood, of Commander Charles Ashwell Pocock and Sarah Margaret Stevens. The Stevens were an old Cornwall family, related to the Coles who claimed descent from the old Cornish kings, so Pocock was inclined to jest on occasion that he was descended from Old King Cole. Charles had served in the suppression of the slave trade, which is slightly ironic as earlier generations of Pococks had made their money in Bristol, trading to a greater or lesser extent in slaves. The most famous ancestor was Nicholas Pocock, the marine watercolour artist. The Ashwells were a wealthy family into which a son of Nicholas married. The use of the name for Pocock children brought dividends in the form of several welcome legacies and the name was used by Lena when she went on the stage as Lena Ashwell, although the family always called her Daisy. According to Roger, when he wrote to his nephew in 1927, 'an aunt of Miss Ashwell was the local poetess at Bath during the eighteenth century and wrote bosh for eighty-five years'.[1]

Commander Pocock's main problem was his eyesight, which forced him to retire from the navy on half-pay and seek employment where he could around the world. His first son, Francis, who became an American citizen and a specialist in electric traction particularly in mines, was born in New Zealand. A second child, Lillian, was born in New Zealand but died in infancy, and then a second daughter, Rosalie, was born. The harsh pioneer life and child-bearing were affecting Sarah's health and unwise investments had lost much of Charles' money and they returned to England. Seaside air was recommended for Sarah so they took lodgings at Tenby where Roger was

4 *Evelyn ffrench who also toured the music halls as 'Jeffrey Silant' stock-whip artist. This was used in the* Frontiersman's Pocket Book *and also in* Frontiersman *magazines.*

born on 9 November 1865 and christened Henry Roger Ashwell Pocock. In later life he was to say he was born at Cookham where the senior branch of the family lived, presumably because it was more impressive. Two years later, in 1867, a daughter, Ethel, was born at Ashford Carbonel in Shropshire. A new training ship for boys was being started on the River Tyne and Charles was given the command, which he held for 13 years. This was the TS *Wellesley*, a wooden-walled ship that had originally been the *Boscawen*. The *Wellesley* was for the training of boys 'unconvicted of crime'. This was perhaps a suitable description for Roger (who had dropped the Henry) and here he received his early education.[2] As the captain's son, he was treated with a certain amount of respect, which was not really the most sensible upbringing for a boy who was somewhat inclined to a swollen head. Ethel was a baby when Charles took command of the ship and two more daughters, Lena and Hilda, were born on board. It was not the healthiest of places to bring up children, an ancient wooden battleship on the busy, dirty Tyne, all three younger girls were inclined to delicacy. Poor Ethel damaged a hip from a fall, and was to suffer from doctors whose ministrations made her worse rather than better, so that she had to be nursed for much of her life. She bore the ill-health uncomplainingly until she died in 1923 at the age of fifty-six.

As the captain's daughters, the girls were treated as little princesses by the boys on the ship. This certainly appealed to Lena, or Daisy, as she was always known to the family. She was a self-confident little tomboy. The two youngest girls were very different in character. Hilda hated being the youngest and yearned to grow up. Eventually she agreed with Lena to switch around the 18-month gap between them in public so that Lena Ashwell could be the ever-young actress and Hilda could gain a little age as she went on to distinguish herself as a nurse and later a hospital matron. She also went on to lecture in eugenics, a subject of interest at the time, but one that went on to be unacceptable.

In her autobiography *Myself a Player*, Daisy gave her impression of her brother as a boy:

> My brother Roger was a strange little being with an inexhaustible desire for personal knowledge; it was never enough to say that a fact was a fact because people said it was. He had to find out for himself. When he was shown the big gun which fired the one o'clock signal from Edinburgh Castle he put his head in to find out what was at the other end, and as his head was large it took time and patience to get him out. Even now (1936) he is apt to flop down on all fours to examine the pavement to find out what strata the stone has come from. When I was very small he took me off to Marsden Rock to search for troche. His interest in geology was a passion. But I was much more interested in a young couple engaged in a lingering embrace on the green edge of the white cliff. Roger, however, held a newspaper before my face and told me I must not look.[3]

This gives an insight into how the characters of the adults would develop. Roger was in for a very rude awakening when he was sent away to school, to Ludlow Grammar School, now known as Ludlow College, where his brother had earlier spent a short time. This school took many sons of Navy and Army officers. The school's history has never mentioned either boy, but Roger's fate since his death has been to be all but forgotten. He commented about the school in *A Frontiersman*:[4]

> When I was old enough, and went to school in the Midlands the big boys, with a healthy instinct of something wrong, did their best to put me out of my misery; and I survived, but with a broken nerve, a coward.
>
> Yet that was not so disastrous as the grammar school tuition which still prepares the modern boy to be a scrivener for the sixteenth century. We asked for bread and they gave us a stone – the bones of dead languages to gnaw instead of living speech of living nations; the useless abstractions of Euclid and the syntax instead of commercial mathematics; the squalid biographies of English Kings instead of the history of our freedom; the names of counties to us who were citizens of an Empire; dogmatic theology to cut us off from Christ; and no training whatever of the hands in craftsmanship, or of the eye in aiming rifles to defend our homes.
>
> Having missed an education, I came forth blinking into the modern world with an apologetic manner appealing for kindness, and large useless hands, as fit for earning wages as a nine days puppy.[5]

This irritating style of writing was all too evident in many of his books. At times he was capable of good and vivid descriptive writing, but the above passage makes it clear that he did not like school at all. Being a weedy youth with a prominent Pocock nose and a weak chin, he was an obvious target at school, particularly as he was never backward in making his opinions known. These opinions could be odd and sometimes revolutionary. He was conscious of his facial imbalance and wasn't happy with his face until he was old enough to adopt a generous beard. He was an individualist but was so friendly and disarming in the way he ploughed his own furrow that not many people could be cross with him for long.

There was no way he could do what most of the other boys were doing – follow his father into the services – as by now Father was trying to exist more or less on his pay. Roger was found a job in the Submarine Telegraph Service but it did not take him long to get the sack from that. Father was very depressed about his income and decided to make a move to see if he could improve matters. His moves were never short ones and this time the family moved across the Atlantic to Canada where he thought there would be more opportunities for his children. Father went first and the children with their mother followed when he had found a house. The ship on which the family sailed had a terrible journey and got caught in the ice entering the St Lawrence River, damaging its propeller.[6]

Francis had little problem making his way in America but as usual Roger was the problem. He was sent to work on a farm, but it was not long before a letter arrived from the farmer to tell Commander Pocock to take his son away as he had a mania for imparting information and a general distaste for such tasks as cleaning the stables.[7] Father still remained convinced that agriculture was the right career for his awkward son and thought he might be better at it after a spell at college, so he was sent to Guelph Agricultural College. This also failed, as Roger Pocock's great dislike of any conventional education remained unabated. He had received a legacy from a distant relative, Ashwell Curry, and was spending this with little thought for the future. He took a job working in the office of the Canada Life Assurance Company. After five months with Canada Life he got the sack for idleness so he lost his 'magnificent salary'.[8]

It was now September 1883 and Roger had spent the last of the legacy enjoying himself. The prodigal son returned home to his father who referred him to 'Various burning texts in the Holy Scriptures, and would have cut me off with a shilling but for the painful fact that he was short of change'.[9] Commander Pocock had been ordained as a Church of England deacon and set to help out in the very large parishes of Canada with a shortage of clergy. After a battle he managed to retain his Naval pension. Elder sister Rosalie married Mr Keefer, a comfortably well-off widower many years her senior. Keefer was the designer of the first footbridge at Niagara Falls.

A family friend wrote to Commander Pocock referring to Roger as 'a proper knight errant',[10] but there were no dragons to slay in 19th-century

Canada and no call for knights, so Roger was sent, armed with a letter from Mr Keefer, well away to the far side of Lake Superior. There, the Canadian Pacific Railway was hewing out the road bed of the railway. What Mr Keefer's relative, who was the engineer in charge, thought about being sent this puny youth without even his own blankets, one can only guess. However, the engineer, Mr Middleton, lent Roger blankets. Next day, Roger was sent off to the wild frontier country of Gravel Bay to help the surveyor there. He found many more interesting things to do than fetch and carry, and for his own safety had to be kept well away when dynamite was in use. He made a collection of geological specimens, but chose to store them outside the surveyor's tent, who one dark night fell over this spiky pile. Even on Sunday, the day of rest, young Pocock went off exploring and got himself lost, needing a search party. At the end of a month Mr Middleton arrived to inspect the site to be told in full frontier language just what they thought of Mr Keefer's protégé. Roger packed and left with Mr Middleton who deposited him by steam launch at the Hudson's Bay trading post at Fort Nipigon and paid him off.[11]

This was a considerable shock as he had been dumped in a real frontier settlement with a construction camp outside as home to some rough and tough construction gangs and an unsavoury tented brothel. Fort Nipigon did have a hotel of sorts, but not the sort he was used to. His money was fast running out and the alternative to paying the hotel bill was to receive a bullet. Winter was drawing in and soon ice would prevent any boat coming or leaving. A steamer did arrive and deposited 375 men, but would take no passengers out. Evidently a fraudulent contractor in Toronto had taken high fares from the men, promising lucrative employment at Camp Nipigon. As there was no food or work for them and no hope of more food arriving before spring, Roger did earn some gratitude from the Camp by getting there in advance to warn of the arrival of this horde. Work was found for the first 12 but the rest had to camp hungrily in the woods to be faced with a gun barrel if they tried to seek help in the Camp. Eventually, faced by certain death if they stayed, they began to disperse.

Knowing his money would not last through winter, Roger decided to follow them and make for the boom town of Port Arthur. He made it, but claimed he was one of the last to get through alive. He joined up with a party of Swedish navvies who had hitched a ride on a gravel train. In the bitter cold he claimed that it was only the sparks from the wood-burning engine which regularly caught their clothes and made them smoulder that kept them from dropping into a sleep from which they would never awaken. He eventually made a crowded Port Arthur and slept uncomfortably on a makeshift bed on a hotel billiard table. He said that the bodies of 23 men were buried under the gravel of the growing railroad track. They could not defeat the intense cold and trains still speed over their bones today. Roger had experienced his first personal taste of the life of a true frontiersman. Port Arthur was a fascinating town to him, so for a week or so he just enjoyed the scene before taking on a succession of odd jobs. The idea that he might some day take to professional writing begun to germinate. One job was at a Port Arthur hotel where he had such engaging tasks as cleaning out spittoons and chopping through the ice in the water hole to draw the 40 buckets a day that were needed, with an extra forty if the hotel caught fire. This was a regular happening. Finally, when the proprietor told him to change beds with a customer who had complained that his bed was too bug infested to sleep in, Roger decided he had had enough.[12] The work had hardened him up and filled him out sufficiently to take a job as labourer on the C.P.R. This did not last long, but encouraged him to boast in 1897, when writing for *Lloyds Weekly Newspaper,* 'I helped build the Canadian Pacific Railway'.[13]

When the summer came, he was able to move out of the town and camp in the woods. Always ready to talk to anyone, he began to study and respect the Canadian First Nations and pick up Native Canadian lore.[14] He also heard tales of the North-West Mounted Police and of the reputation they had built for themselves in only eleven years. Deciding to try to make his way to the central recruiting office at Winnipeg, he took a steamer to Duluth on Lake Superior. There he was living rough for a few days to try to find the money for the rest of the journey, and a letter from father caught up with him: 'Have you heard of the North-West Mounted Police?', asked father, 'Would you care to join?'[15]

Father was most unhappy at the life his son had adopted and was of the opinion that a good dose of military discipline would work wonders. The Police would give him this discipline, yet still allow him to indulge his taste for adventure and excitement. Money was enclosed with the letter for the train fare to Winnipeg. Roger Pocock lost no time in boarding the next available train. He arrived in Winnipeg on 3 November 1884, six days before his 19th birthday and about to start on a brief period of his life that was to have an effect on him which lasted to the end of his days. This experience was to lead eventually to the formation of the Legion of Frontiersmen and influence the way that it was organised, the discipline, the comradeship, the uniform, and the way it served Britain and the Dominions.

The North-West Mounted Police was founded in 1873 for the essential task of ensuring peace in the wildest parts of Canada with its far-flung settlements. It did not become the Royal Canadian Mounted Police until 1920. In 1872, Colonel Robertson Ross, Adjutant-General of the Canadian Militia, went on a tour of inspection of the plains and brought back the recommendation that some form of armed force was essential. The new force was originally to be called the North-West Mounted Rifles, but discretion caused the name to be altered to Police to avoid upsetting the Americans across the border, as it was thought that the Americans might be unhappy to have a military body on its frontier. Its duties were that of a frontier police force, but in every other way it was a quasi-military body with strict military discipline. Although always few in number, they soon established good relations with the population, especially the First Nations who had received bad treatment at the hands of American whiskey traders purveying a bad liquor. The Police also kept the American Army out of the country. Despite the pride with which America has held its army, Canadian opinion of them was poor, and some of the American Army's ways were considered inhuman. The Cree and the Blackfoot became peaceful and their leaders were wise enough to realise that the world was changing. There is a much-publicised statement by Crowfoot, the paramount chief of the Blackfoot: 'If the Police had not come to the country, where would we all be now? Bad men and whiskey were killing us so fast that few indeed of us would have been left today. The Police have protected us as the feathers of the bird protect it from the frosts of the winter.'[16] The North-West Mounted Police had quickly achieved a good reputation, but their very limited numbers meant that they had to cover great distances, often in the piercing cold of the Canadian winter. Death was always around the corner for the careless constable and the pay was not high.

As Roger Pocock approached Fort Osborne, he was struck by the sight of the sentry outside. He appeared to be an enormous man, wearing a white helmet and crossbelt over a scarlet tunic. The revolver hung from a belt carrying brass cartridges. He had gleaming white gauntlets, breeches with broad yellow stripe and long boots with spurs. Roger found out later that the sentry was a German Baron, and the Mounted Police in those days had a similar attraction to the French Foreign Legion. The official records note that when he took the oath of allegiance, Constable Pocock was 5ft 9ins in height and weighed 140 pounds. They fed him, issued him with blankets, gave him a bed for the night, and sent him next day on the noon train to Regimental Headquarters at Regina. On the train he boasted to whomever would listen that he was a Mounted Policeman, but the only young men who would listen to him warned of a hard life and an early death. Winter was approaching and snow appearing on the plains, but the barracks at Regina were warmer than he was used to. For some days he revelled in the strange happenings of regular meals and a reasonably comfortable bed. He put on weight and was full of patriotism when he donned the Imperial scarlet. Although in later years he was not known as a good man for time-keeping and strict discipline, he took readily to all the disciplines he had to follow at Regina. He was once put on a charge for fighting – with billiard balls.[17]

The Constables, or Troopers, were well fed and clothed. Out on the prairie on active service, rations were always increased. Through his life, Roger was always recalling the comradeship of his days in the N.W.M.P. and extolling its virtues to Frontiersmen. This was a general feeling expressed by all who served with the Mounted Police. Trooper John Donkin, writing in 1889 said:

> My comrades of the Corps were more like a band of brothers than merely a chance medley of individual atoms, thrown together to serve a stated term, and then fly apart again. This feeling is doubtless fostered in a great measure by the fact that we were in exile together and in danger often by ourselves, far from any extraneous aid. So the sense of interdependence became dominant.[18]

Here in the N.W.M.P. also was to begin Pocock's deep and lasting affection for the horse. Donkin again expresses the feeling: 'I myself can speak of the tacit understanding that exists on the lone prairie between man and horse.'[19] Before the First War the Legion of Frontiersmen was arranged as a mainly mounted organisation. Pocock was sufficiently far-sighted between the Wars to see that, although the horse had its uses, other forms of transport were becoming more important and was regularly recommending young men to seek adventure in flying. The Legion also carries on to this day the idea from the N.W.M.P. that officers and other ranks meet together informally off duty and only on parade and in action does strict military separation occur. Writers heralded this as an innovation when practised by the S.A.S., but the Frontiersmen carried it out in Edwardian days and the N.W.M.P. many years earlier. It is quite logical for small active units when they are different from the norm and also are likely to be outnumbered to an exceptional degree.

Donkin records a time, quite early in his service, when he was sent with an officer and his wife to catch up a detachment going to Prince Albert. Orders were changed and only the officer and Donkin went on to Prince Albert, the remaining twenty or so men being used to strengthen the Fort Carlton contingent. Stopping at a hotel at Qu'Appelle, the officer ordered Donkin to have his dinner at the hotel.

> He and his wife, his servant and myself all sat down together at the same table. This anomalous state of affairs would not be quite the thing in the British service; but such mixing of ranks in social and military life is quite common out here; nor is it at all subversive of discipline. The rank and file of course are of somewhat different material to the average linesman.[20]

They often were. Donkin records several in the ranks who had held commissions 'at Home'. There were many related to English families 'of good position', an ex-officer of Militia and of Volunteers, a son of a Major-General, an Oxford B.A., the son of the Governor of one of the smaller colonies. There were many who could be called 'gentlemen' and these outnumbered the shady types that interested Roger Pocock. Charles Dickens' son Francis rose to the rank of Inspector and commanded Fort Pitt at the time of the Second Riel Rebellion. After the Riel debacle, however, the N.W.M.P. recruited more tough characters to try to strengthen the Force and counteract the unjustified slurs of softness that were to be directed at the N.W.M.P. Some of the 'gentlemen' did not approve of the new recruits who came in.

There were many rich characters in the barracks. Tom the whisky-runner (prohibition was in force), Dutchy Koerner the self-confessed horse thief, and at the other end of the social scale a naval officer who was the son of an English peer. These men were to turn up over the years in Roger's short stories and fictional books, some under disguised names and some, like Mutiny the teamster, under their own names. Mutiny appears slightly altered in 'Curly', one of Roger's more successful fictitious tales which was Lord Mountbatten's favourite boyhood book.[21] Many of these men were later to meet a violent death, one or two made fortunes and Roger even claimed that one was awarded the Victoria Cross. His brief period in the Mounted Police had a lifelong effect on him and he tried to keep in contact with all those he met during his happy time there.

Winter on the Canadian plains can be exceptionally cold. Temperatures of 40 degrees fahrenheit below zero on still cold days are not uncommon. Roger was soon to be plunged into the Riel Rebellion, a revolt of mixed race French/First Nations, who nursed the customary grievances of minorities over land, electoral and governmental rights. They had some justification for their grievances, but under Louis 'David' Riel, a fanatic who suffered delusions, they looked to armed rebellion to gain their demands. Riel and his supporters had their centre at Batoche. Not far from Batoche was the settlement of Prince Albert, which was very much under threat and was in a very difficult strategic position.

Colonel Irvine, one of Roger's great heroes, although later the subject of much criticism by the army, set off from Regina at 6 a.m. on 18 March with 96 men to go to the aid of Superintendent Crozier at Prince Albert. One of those men was new constable Roger Pocock. They had three hundred miles to travel in bitter cold and across unbroken snow. There was no food or forage to be had and everything had to go with them. They made 42 miles a day and over sixty on the last day in the most intense cold. Roger, as a 'ring-tailed snorter', as the recruits were called, travelled with the transport. Citizen volunteers at Prince Albert were armed, Riel's Metis sacked the Hudson's Bay Company store at Batoche and Riel sent a demand that Fort Carlton and all the garrison should surrender. An intrepid Englishman called Gordon was sent to meet Col Irvine and warn him that he must avoid Batoche as there was an ambush prepared for him there. Gordon travelled on snow shoes and caught up with Irvine crossing the desolate Salt Plains just as Irvine was setting up camp for the fifth night. Irvine had camped on both the fourth and fifth night on the Salt Plains and it was on the fourth night that fate struck unkindly at Roger.

In this part of Canada in March, the intense cold was not continuous and it had actually rained at Prince Albert on 15 March. As the men were setting up the tents for the fourth camp there was a sudden and squelching thaw. Within minutes, all the men were dripping wet. They did not undress to sleep; 14 days without the opportunity to change day or night was not unusual for the Troopers. They rose at 3.30 a.m. to find that the weather had changed again just as suddenly and the temperature was now 25 degrees below zero fahrenheit. Every man had moccasins for such weather and these should have been in the pockets of his buffalo skin overcoat. Roger was a raw young recruit and was careless. He had left his with the packs on the sleighs. In his hurry to get on parade he spent minutes dragging on his frozen cavalry boots. In the rush to get ready, none of the older and more experienced men noticed in the dark what he had done. The moccasins were made of dressed moose skin. They were soft and pliable brogues, light yellow in colour, and reached just above the ankles. Two pairs of wool socks were worn, covered by a pair of wool stockings, which went over the legs of the riding breeches as far as the knee. Over these, the moccasins were as pliable as a glove and the blood could circulate freely through the feet. Roger Pocock was foolish enough to try to set off on the next stage of the march in stiff and frozen cavalry boots. The Trooper was well equipped for the cold, but in that sort of climate, trying to march for any distance in those frozen cavalry boots can be described as little short of insane. Unfortunately, throughout his life Roger Pocock was often thoughtless about the consequences of his actions:

> When we marched I thought it was cramp which gripped me from the knees to the heels, and though it was difficult to move, I trotted beside a sleigh, wondering what caused me so much pain. My little growls would have done no good to anybody, and where all were uncomfortable it was better not to complain. After about eighteen miles I lay on the sleigh and the fellows told me it would serve me right if I froze. Would I freeze like a man rather than run behind like a dog? Then they belaboured me with advice.
>
> At the noon halt I was told off on picket to guard camp but, not feeling well enough, went sick. The Hospital Sergeant found that the chafing of the frozen leather as I ran has almost severed the toes of the right foot, and that I was solidly frozen up to the calves – of no more use to the Colonel.
>
> Chafing with snow would have rubbed away the tissues, heat would have resulted in death by gangrene; so for seven hours of the afternoon march I sat on a sleigh-box luxurious, with six ounces of brandy inside, and my feet in a bucket of water kept cool with snow. After supper came a general collapse from shock, and the pain which results from a scalding. That night the officers gave their tent to the sick, for despite the use of goggles we had several men already totally blind from the glare on the ice-crusted snow. Next day there were sixty-five of us blind because of a hot mist rising from the snow glare. I went blind that day.[22]

Roger owed much of his thanks for not losing both his legs or even his life to the Hospital Sergeant attending the column. He was really a Veterinary Sergeant, only later to become Doctor A.E. Braithwaite. He did not meet Roger again until more than fifty years later, when Roger unveiled the Legion of Frontiersmen's Cenotaph at Fort Scott, Hastings Lake, Alberta in November 1935. That reunion was quite a celebration. Dr Braithwaite gave his own version of the incident to Colonel Louis Scott, who commanded the Canadian Frontiersmen in the 1930s:

> In March 1885, the Senior Surgeon sent for me, and told me that he had put me in medical charge of Colonel Irvine's column up to the frontier of the Rebellion. I said I was neither qualified nor competent for the assignment. He said that if I would not go, then he would have

to send a civilian doctor. At that time there were only eleven doctors in the whole of the North-West Territories, and the only one that would be available was a man who never drew a sober breath. I thought that I could not leave my comrades in the care of such a man, so agreed to take the assignment myself.

We had twenty-two men go snow blind and Constable Pocock had both his legs frozen from the knee down. I got a horse bucket, put his legs in it, and filled it with snow, and covered him with horse blankets, every now and then going to his sleigh and putting more snow in the bucket. I was very lucky in being able to save all but his toes.[23]

Veterinary Sergeant or not, if it had not been for Braithwaite, Roger Pocock would never have been able to lead such an adventurous life. There is a discrepancy between Roger's 65 snow blind and Braithwaite's 22, but, as Roger was often inclined to exaggerate, Braithwaite's figure must be taken as the correct one.

As they rode in to Prince Albert, the local Volunteers on guard presented arms. Donkin, who never knew Roger personally, was watching the column arrive. He was horrified by the sight of Roger: 'One young fellow was carried into the barracks with both feet a huge black mass; and his toes had afterwards to be amputated.'[24] Roger was put into the care of Doctor Miller, and his toes on the right foot were amputated. As these had been almost severed by his marching in frozen boots, the doctor had little alternative. Fortunately, his legs had shown a marked improvement and this saved him facing leg amputation in a somewhat basic hospital. Roger became a mere spectator to the frantic action going on and probably gathered more material for future use in his books from that short spell in his life than from any other single adventure. Irvine decided not to counter-attack but to remain in defence at one spot. On 20 May a relief column under General Middleton marched into Prince Albert. Irvine received much criticism for his conduct of the affair and for some time afterwards the Mounted Police were held in very low regard by the Canadian public and it took them a long time to live this down. They were left to lick their wounds and send out long patrols to carry out justice and try to restore some of their standing.

By spring 1886 Roger Pocock had recovered sufficiently to wear boots and do full duties. Roger's troop, F Troop, commanded by Supt. A. Bowen Perry – later to be Commissioner, or Colonel, and command the Police detachment at the 1897 Diamond Jubilee celebrations – was called on for 30 men to go to Battleford, where there had been unrest. That summer patrol was a delight to Roger. It was the life of the true frontiersman, living in the open with nature all around. In *A Frontiersman* his skill at descriptive writing was to be seen:

Clear down the years comes the especial memory of Eagle Creek, where, sunk three hundred feet below the Plains, there is a chain of pools, and an acre or so of meadow starred with the ashes of old camp fires. The little foxes played there while it was cool before bedtime, a crane stood on one leg hoping for a fish by way of supper, and the rim of the shadowed canyon glowed orange against the sky. But when a cloud of dust arose behind the rim of the high plains, and the tramp of our horses sounded soft thunder notes of warning, the little foxes crept away with their mother to earth, and the crane flapped lazily away into the blue gloom of evening.[25]

When he formed the Legion of Frontiersmen, Roger attracted the many who shared the opinion he wrote in *The Rules of the Game* that 'Civilization is a poor thing to one who has lived the spacious life of the West'. These men wanted to be part of an organisation like the Mounted Police where, as Roger wrote in *A Frontiersman*:

Ours were hard-featured weather-beaten, dusty, great big men, with such clear, far-searching eyes, such pride of bearing, swaggering gallantry, and wild grace in the saddle that one despairs of ever, with words or colours, making a picture worthy of the theme.

A bell tent was pitched for the officer commanding; the horses were watered, groomed and fed; then, at a merry call from the bugle, there was a general dash to the wagons for plates and cups, while knives were whipped from belt or boot leg, ready for a general assault on fried bacon, hard biscuit and scalding tea. After the meal there was a lively cross-fire of chaff, a cutting and burning of plug tobacco, and delicate grey smoke lifting towards the white stars which stole softly out of the twilight.[26]

The intense loneliness of the wilds made an impression on all those who had to spend much of their time in the North-West Territories. Trooper Donkin, a Border Scot, also reported the effect of this solitude and the utter vastness of the country:

One would wonder often in this far away seclusion of the night watches, if there actually existed a busy world ... One seemed to have died and to be walking in a spirit land of dreams ... The mysterious stillness brought strange fancies ... across the frozen prairie ... a phantom view would rise before me of a certain bonnie glen hidden in my own romantic borderland.[27]

Over the years, Frontiersmen tried to recapture that camaraderie and romance of life far from civilisation around the camp fire. Every summer until 1939 Frontiersmen units everywhere would arrange their tented camps with mounted exercises and competitions with evenings round the fire where tall tales were told. Roger Pocock was always greatly in demand to tell the younger men of his adventures while the camp fire burned and the men drew on their pipes. Frontiersmen, often past the days of their youth, were wishing to recreate and recall from the past the scenes that Pocock described of summer life with the R.C.M.P.

Roger's foot still refused to heal properly and, after a spell at base camp, it was decided that he was in no fit state to do full duties in the rigours of another Canadian winter. So, despite his protests, he was told with kindness that he was to be discharged on medical grounds and he was sent by train to Regina. The civilised life he encountered for the first time in a long while came as rather a shock. He was very upset by the reaction he received from a pretty young gentlewoman with whom he tried to strike up a conversation. She was just the type of young lady he had experienced such success with when he had been at Guelph, but he was hurt when she snubbed him as a common soldier. The smart uniform had received respect and admiration in the wilds but in polite company even this gentleman's son was considered unsuitable to mix with the gentler classes. In addition to this, it was the first time he had come across the reaction of the public to the Police following the Riel Rebellion. In Edwardian England also, there was to be no understanding for the status of the N.W.M.P. Constable from the frontier. When Roger Pocock formed the Legion of Frontiersmen, ex-officers objected to serving under a man who had never held the Queen's or King's commission, but had only been what they considered a lowly Trooper. This was to become one of the major causes of problems for him in England where social status still held considerable importance. The end of his short term of service came when an Orderly Sergeant read General Orders to confirm that Constable Pocock, having been invalided, was struck off the strength of the Force. His conduct at discharge was recorded as 'Very good'. As the frost tightened its grip on the evening air, a lonely ex-trooper, very near to tears, left Headquarters to stand some way away and listen in solitary misery to the Regimental Call and Lights Out. He would never forget the North-West Mounted Police. His future activities meant that the Police never forgot him and were to record his name with some pride as one of their members.

He was not completely abandoned, for the Canadian Government had given him a lifetime pension of 23 cents a day and had found him a job in the Civil Service at Ottawa. Before taking up the job, he took a holiday with his family. They had moved again, this time to Toronto. While at Toronto, Roger Pocock wrote his first published book, *Tales of Western Life*, a collection of anecdotes and poetry. A few copies have survived in Canada and one of his stories, 'The Lean Man', was considered good enough to be included in a 1994 anthology *Crime in a Cold Climate*.[28] It is a well written little story which shows considerable knowledge of and sympathy for the First Nations Canadian. His later experiences and travels brought him a deeper love and understanding of their way of life and he brought this into the Frontiersman ethic. In fact, both the Boy Scout movement and the Frontiersman influence on it bore some First Nations touches as explained by Professor MacDonald:

> The imagined Indian made a very definite impact on the Scout movement ... The Indian's champions pictured him as a stoical warrior superior even to the white frontiersman, a pagan more religious than a Christian, a child of nature more manly than a the sternest Puritan ... Yet the heroic brave, the real scout of scouting, had enormous appeal.[29]

After a short spell trying the Government job at Ottawa while his wounded foot healed to the stage when he yearned for the wide open spaces again, Roger gave it up and bought a horse.

Tragedy then hit the family. Hilda was struck down with diphtheria and her mother with erysipelas. When both recovered, mother travelled to Rosalie's house where there were servants and greater comfort. On her first outing to town with Rosalie, something frightened the horse, which bolted, both women were thrown out of the trap and while Rosalie got up with hardly a scratch, mother was killed instantly. Father never recovered from the shock and within two years had moved from Canada. The girls went to finishing school in Switzerland and the family moved to London when their education was finished. The Commander only returned to Canada once more, in 1891 when the elderly Mr Keefer died, to help clear up affairs.

Roger had the idea for a horseback ride, which he eventually achieved in 1899, from Canada to Mexico. It would be a record ride and give him much material for his writing, which he decided should be his main source of income from then on. He thought he would be able to earn his living on the way, doing any odd job that came along. He was one of a number of what today we would call 'backpackers' who wrote the stories of their adventures, such men as Morley Roberts, later one of Roger's Frontiersman friends, whose *Western Avernus*[30] became a best-seller running into many editions.

Roger took the train to Kamloops in British Columbia and used some of his little money to buy wares to set himself up as a peddler. Unfortunately the horse Roger bought from a Native Canadian turned out to be a man-hater with a bad reputation in the area. Sixteen miles from town the horse made its first serious move, running off and scattering Roger's wares and smashing his elbow as well. Roger staggered to a nearby farm where the farmer got him to hospital. He spent two months there, although his smashed elbow could not be properly set and he carried the noticeable injury for the rest of his life. When he was recovering he heard news of a minor uprising on the Skeena River some way to the north. In an area the size of Germany there were only about twenty-five whites living among the Gaetkshian Indians. The gentleman in charge of the Hudson's Bay Trading Post had taken to doctoring his provisions and some 250 Indians died, but no whites suffered. Roger persuaded a friend to send a telegram to a Montreal paper, the *Witness*, which had reviewed his *Tales of Western Life*, telling them that war was on the way in the Skeena valley and offering his services as correspondent. An offer came back of up to a hundred dollars for the story, but no cash in advance. Undeterred by this, the budding War Correspondent had to get to the Skeena. This was not easy, as nobody seemed to know where it was, until it was found on an old map about a thousand miles to the north. Roger took train to Victoria and coastal steamer to the Skeena.

Although he did not yet know it, by the time the War Correspondent had made his arrangements the 'war' was over, thanks to the British Columbia Police. He arrived at Spukshuat, a small canning settlement, known to the

Canadian Artillery as Fort Essington, and was disappointed to find there was no war, only the customary simmering discontent of the Indians. There were rumours that the Indians intended to vent their grievances on the Church and kill their missionary. The resident missionary at the main village, Gaetwangak, had newly married, but on hearing these rumours decided that he did not want his wife to suffer early widowhood. The Mission Synod was looking for a temporary missionary to take over for one nervous winter. Roger was keen to get some sort of story, so he volunteered, pointing out that his father was an ordained Minister, and he was therefore appointed missionary for one winter. Despite a few nervous moments, the winter passed without bloodshed and Roger's simple frontier Christianity apparently resulted in the conversion of the tribal chief. Spring came and with it the end of Roger's term. He wrote that the Diocesan Synod were pleased with him and offered him more training and a position as a full-time missionary. In fact, it seems that the Church quietly let it be known that they made no such offer due to Roger's 'indiscretions' with the Indian maidens.[31] Roger's writings make his fondness for Indian girls very clear.

For a while Roger settled in Victoria B.C. to engage in writing and exploring. He became a regular contributor to the *Victoria Times*. He carried on his studies of Indian life and came to the conclusion that the Indians were getting a raw deal. He put his opinions into print and so added the Indian Department to a growing list of enemies.

In later life he liked to list 'Skeena Indian War' among his experiences, and apparently no-one ever queried this non-existent war. He also liked to say that he served with the 'Yokohama Pirates'. Probably he would have liked people to imagine him swinging from the rigging with a cutlass between his teeth, but the truth was far from that. He stowed away in a scruffy sealer, the *Adele*. This was captained by a small-time crook, Capt. C.E. Hansen, known locally as the Flying Dutchman. Hansen was an unlicensed sealer, which raided the Pribiloff Islands, north of the Aleutians. Roger did get much information, which he intended to put to use in 1923 on the Frontiersmen World Flight Expedition. He also got enough material from the trip to write a story in the *Victoria Times*. When Hansen found out about this he waylaid Roger in an alleyway and gave him a bloody nose. Roger had also acquired one of the new Eastman Kodak cameras, which proved very useful. In the following spring, Roger was asked to go to the Kootenay district to try to persuade some of the prosperous silver miners to invest in Victoria. He did better in Spokane, in Washington State, but soon moved on to try his luck as a commercial photographer at the Couer d'Alene Mines. Further adventures took him to the boom town of Wallace, a town of some 1,500 people in the Bitterroot Mountains of Idaho. A little money came in, but winter was approaching and he needed to survive. He then came up with an ingenious idea. Every inch of the town's street was used by someone trading in one way or another, but the boardwalk continued as a bridge across the Couer d'Alene River to the far side where the railway line ran. Hundreds of men wandered on to that bridge every day, even if only for the simple pleasure of spitting into the river. The bridge was not straight but took a dog-leg bend. Roger saw that it would be easy to run a plank across the angle and there to trade with the public from the finest unused business spot in Wallace. The one possible objection could come from the Chairman of the Public Safety Committee, who happened also to be a wholesaler of cigars and confectionery. He was amused, told Roger that the air above the river was out of their jurisdiction, and sold him some stock. Roger prospered. The one plank across the angle became a platform, it grew counters, walls and a roof. Sliding glass windows were followed by a stove, bedding and kitchen equipment. At the end of six weeks both Roger and his wholesaler were pleased with their profits. Roger's artistic talents and ability to write bad verse were used to drum up more business. Among the strangest items to survive to this day are the actual advertisements that he pinned up around the town of Wallace to take down later and store away. One picture showed an unshaven tough. 'This durn'd seegar's got no strength to it – I'm just going down to the BRIDGE to get a good one.'[32]

His success began to be a problem as there was considerable lawlessness in the town. He moved on again rather aimlessly, but continued studying the ancient lore and beliefs of the First Nation's tribes. He scratched a meagre living travelling about and doing a little writing. He acquired an old but willing horse and spent an idyllic period:

> The cowboys rode miles to show me the way, prospectors took offence unless I stayed overnight, sheep herders were slighted if a leg of mutton proved too much for my supper. The Old Gentleman [his horse] took me from the white crests into purple-red fiery-heated canyons, where down in the bases of the world the rattlesnakes lay drowsily hoping for incautious flies.[33]

When Roger returned to town, he found that his writing had produced some success and also money in the bank. *Tales of Western Life* had been approved by a major British critic and two of his short stories had been accepted by an English national publication.

Two

ACCUSATIONS OF MURDER

Roger Pocock returned to England with plenty of ideas for books in his head. Until they could be written and published he had to make a living from journalism. He had great difficulty writing about places he had not seen, and was always far better at describing events based on experiences he had lived through or at least heard of from someone involved. Therefore, he spent much of his time and what little money he had in travelling. It was 1891 when he returned to England. He based himself on London, but as soon as possible went to visit Spain and Portugal. This trip gave him the background information for his Spanish Grandee hero in *The Blackguard*, a highly successful book based on his experiences in the Riel Rebellion.

Sister Hilda had started her nursing career and Ethel attended the Slade Art School when she was fit enough. Lena, known to the family as Daisy, was working her way towards success and had plenty of young and pretty actress friends who were keen to meet this brother of hers, going grey before his time, weatherbeaten and bearded, full of tales of the native tribes and the wild frontier lands of Canada and America. Always a self-publicist, Roger was a well-known figure in London, where he liked to be known as the 'Mysterious Pocock' and was to be seen around the city wearing riding breeches and western garb. Some of Lena Ashwell's friends made a great impression on Roger. Marriage to any of the young ladies was out of the question as he was seldom better off than penniless. Lena Ashwell made her first and disastrous marriage to actor Arthur Wyndham Playfair, who later turned out to be a drunkard. She had further problems when another actor introduced her to the pleasures of cocaine one evening when she was troubled by a sinus infection. She came close to becoming addicted. Commander Pocock was living a simple and religious life, although he died of Bright's Disease in 1899.

By the end of 1896, Roger Pocock was well represented on the booksellers' shelves. He had two adventure books, *The Blackguard* and *The Rules of the Game*; *The Dragon Slayer*, which he described as a fantasy and also something of an exercise in sociology, *Rottenness, a study of America and England*, all on sale. If not the best of his fiction, *The Blackguard* was the most successful, being re-issued as *The Cheerful Blackguard* in 1905 and *The Splendid Blackguard* in 1915. Even *The Dragon Slayer* earned a re-issue in 1909 as *Sword and*

Dragon. This was the period of expansion of reading for the masses. So many more working people than in previous years were literate and hungry for basic reading, particularly if it gave them tales of exotic places and deeds. Daily papers multiplied and weekly magazines and papers with names for the most part long forgotten were being produced. Roger wrote for such publications as *Household Words* (edited by Charles Dickens Jnr), *Black and White, Penny Pictorial Magazine, Country Gentleman,* and *Pearsons Magazine.* Publishers blossomed and then faded and some of those that Roger used, such as the New Vagabond Library and the Tower Romance Library, were absorbed or went into liquidation. Anyone who could write a little and who could tell a story would make a few pounds. From the many who, like Roger Pocock, made sufficient reputation to have their names published with their journalistic efforts and were then forgotten for years, some writers such as Conan Doyle were good enough to be permanently remembered.

They were clubable men and various clubs both little and large sprang up. In 1896, Roger was a member of the New Vagabond Club, a literary club that attracted some of the best. According to Douglas Sladen, Vagabond dinners could have an attendance of anything up to six hundred and attracted some excellent speakers.[1] Pocock's *The Rules of the Game* was rejected by most of the better known publishers, but Douglas Sladen and William le Queux, who later comes into the story of the early years of the Legion of Frontiersmen, recommended the book to the Tower Romance Library. The recommendations of these noted writers were sufficient for the publishers (who went into liquidation not many years later) to accept the book.

Roger made his first contact with Rudyard Kipling when he went down to Sussex to ask the great man's permission to quote a poem of Kipling's in *The Rules of the Game*:

> There's a legion that never was listed,
> That carries no colours or crest,
> But, split in a thousand detachments,
> Is breaking the road for the rest.
> Our fathers, they left us their blessing,
> They taught us and groomed us and crammed,
> But we've shaken the clubs and the messes,
> To go and find out, and be damned, dear boys,
> To go, and get shot, and be damned!

Those words made a great impression on Roger. This was the 'Lost Legion' he would talk about; the men working their solitary ways on the frontiers around the world for the benefit of the British Empire. This poem described exactly the men he called for later, when the time came for 'the 'listing of the legion' and the formation of the Legion of Frontiersmen, and Kipling was to be forever the favoured poet of Frontiersmen. Kipling is believed to have resented this cocky fellow marching in un-announced without bothering to write first. He may never have heard of Roger Pocock or his writings.

After a period of telling Roger exactly what he thought of him for his cheek, Kipling softened – many found it difficult to be cross with Roger for long – and gave him some advice. Roger had been back in civilisation for several years; was it not time he started his travels again like the true frontiersman he claimed to be?[2]

In any case, Roger Pocock was becoming bored with London and his feet were beginning to itch for more travel and perhaps to return to Canada again. There must have been frustrations in his relationships with young ladies. In *Rottenness* he makes a plaintive cry: 'Bourgeois Englishmen may not marry until they can support their wives in comfort. Before they are earning sufficient income they reach the average age of thirty-six years. From the age of sixteen to the age of thirty-six they must be monks or satisfy their natural desires by making or having harlots …'[3] This sounds like the cry from the heart of a penniless young man who had been bowled over by a pretty face and turned down as an unsuitable husband for their daughter by a respectable Victorian family. Some of the First Nations girls might have been still in his mind, but he wouldn't have passed over the chance of marriage into a well-to-do family. We can assume that he would have told some of his friends of his adventures with the Native Canadian girls (whose attitude to life was not as straight-laced as British girls in Victorian times) and rumours of these stories would have come to the ears of the fathers of the young British girls to whom Roger Pocock paid attention.

He went off on more travels about the world to pick up more experiences to aid his writing. He sailed in the most economical way he could, by tramp steamer. Where possible, he worked his passage as steward or purser, but as he wasn't a very good steward he did much of his travelling as a fee-paying passenger at between half-a-crown and five shillings a day. It was during one of his brief spells as a steward that Roger made his first attempt at espionage. By doing so, he realised that the lone Englishman doing his job in the distant corners of the world could serve his country by bringing back little scraps of information. All that was needed was an organisation to collect and collate these trifles. During the last twenty years of the 19th century, Baden-Powell was an active freelance British agent. By the time that Roger thought of the idea, Baden-Powell claimed to have done much work in this sphere. His efforts are well documented, including his trip to the Dalmatian fortress of Cattara disguised as an entomologist, bringing back plans on the wings of butterfly sketches. In 1908 Baden-Powell was warning of the 'German menace'.[4] When Pocock's ship docked at Sebastopol, most of the crew were too busy to go ashore. The few men who had time for shore leave had no interest in exploring such an unfriendly place, which was unwelcoming to foreigners particularly from Britain. Roger wanted to look around and made himself known to the British Consul. He let the Consul know he was a journalist and the Consul told him that, despite the Russian promise after the Crimean War not to re-arm, he was sure that they were putting in gun batteries. With time to kill, Roger made a decision that was more foolhardy than brave. He would have a good look round to see what he could discover. A lone Englishman was certain to attract attention, but, dressed as he was in a steward's black coat and striped trousers crowned with a straw hat, he was the typical eccentric Englishman.

His large nose was sniffing well and his luck was in as he stumbled on a new masked battery. He decided he must find the calibre of the guns. In front of these guns was a small parade ground, so he wandered openly across it, stopping regularly to pick up flints, which he pounced on with squeals of delight. Darting here and there with increasing feigned excitement, he finally grabbed one just under one of the guns, only to be confronted by a large Russian corporal, quickly followed by his guard. In very fast English, Roger told him all about his prize flints, chattering on about the Mezozoic Age and pressing some of the best on the corporal as valuable presents. When the corporal, who knew not a word of English, consulted his men about how deranged Roger actually was, it was time to satisfy the corporal's mind. Roger clutched him by the arm and in his best clerical English recited 'Mary had a little lamb'. That decided the Russians and Roger was dispatched from the area with a military boot on his seat – but that was better than being dispatched to Siberia. He had not been able to discover the calibre of the guns, but for the first time he had satisfied himself that it might be possible for a lone Englishman in a foreign country to be of service to the Empire.[5]

Back in Britain, preparations were going ahead for the 1897 Diamond Jubilee celebrations. The North-West Mounted Police were sending over a contingent and this was commanded by Roger's old Commanding Officer, Inspector A. Bowen Perry, now a Superintendent. Having returned home from his spell of globe-trotting, Roger went to Windsor to call on Perry and then travelled back to London with him on the special train that had been provided for the N.W.M.P. men and horses. Perry had noticed that his old trooper had put on quite a bit of weight and his beard was now most definitely an 'Imperial'. Perry whispered secret instructions to his men and invited Roger to dine at their temporary quarters at Chelsea Barracks. Roger accepted and was told he must travel in Perry's open coach, which had been provided for him as the senior representative of the N.W.M.P. The train arrived at Paddington Station and Roger climbed into the coach. He was somewhat puzzled by the way the troopers mounted their horses and formed up to ride by the coach. Then he found that Londoners were stopping what they were doing to crowd the streets and cheer. The troopers had formed themselves as a Sovereign's Escort. Roger took the practical joke in good heart and waved to the crowd as he made his regal way to Chelsea. Roger Pocock, the great egoist, wrote later: 'Could I help it if the Prince of Wales was always being mistaken for me ...'[6]

Having enjoyed the joke immensely, Roger rewarded some of those who had worked it by taking them to the theatre to see his sister in a play. The Review of the Fleet at Spithead was due. The N.W.M.P. were to be present on a chartered steamer and Roger was anxious to attend. As it happened, one of the troopers was taken ill the day before the Review, so Roger was smuggled into the Chelsea Barracks by some friendly troopers and the next day paraded in the sick man's uniform, trying desperately to disguise his limp. He was shuffled around the parade in an attempt to camouflage him and then, to his great pride, they marched off with Roger again back in the N.W.M.P. All was going well until the *Turbinia* made her sensational appearance while they were steaming up and down the lines. Roger completely forgot who he was supposed to be and went over to Bowen Perry and grabbed his sleeve to draw his attention to her. Very quickly, the sergeant-major reached out and dragged Roger back into the main body of the men. It is very likely that Perry knew all about Roger being there, as C.O.'s have ways of finding out such things. In any case nothing was said and the officers never referred to the incident in front of the men.[7]

His day or two of nostalgia had worked on Roger and he felt he must go back again to Canada and to the wide open spaces. His mind went back to the words of Rudyard Kipling. The joys of civilisation had palled and Roger went to see the editor of *Lloyds Weekly Newspaper* offering to go to Canada as special correspondent and, using his N.W.M.P. contacts, to ride the Thousand Mile Patrol, sending back a series of articles about life in the great Dominion of Canada. The fact that the Thousand Mile Patrol had not been ridden for some years did not deter Roger. He persuaded the editor to agree and so he went off to Canada to send back articles to be entitled 'Into the Great Dominion; blowing the trumpet for Canada'.[8] After 1885, when the Mounted Police felt it necessary to strengthen their hold on the country after the poor showing in the Riel Rebellion, a weekly patrol passed a letter westwards from outpost to outpost, district to district, until it had passed from Manitoba to the Rocky Mountains. The trail went along a ridge midway between the United States boundary and the Canadian Pacific Railway, and from its height a rider could scan the country both left and right to keep an eye on the wild lands below for wayward Indians, horse thieves, the start of prairie fires or even straying cattle. It was indeed an ideal route for policing with limited numbers, but unfortunately, due to manpower shortage, the regular patrol had been suspended. Roger went right to the top, to the Commissioner himself. First of all Roger was asked about the Diamond Jubilee celebrations. The Commissioner wanted to know how his men had acquitted themselves in front of the pride of the British Empire and what opinions were passed on the N.W.M.P., particularly by the old cavalry experts: 'Why, sir, the cavalry of the British Empire passed by their windows and what they wanted to know was "Who are those men who can ride?"'[9] The Commissioner was satisfied.

When Roger asked to ride the Thousand Mile Patrol, the Commissioner was not keen, but as Roger was a Police pensioner, he agreed and soon copy started arriving in London. He began the first article 'I helped build the Canadian Pacific Railway.'[10] Something of an exaggeration! The Patrol consisted of just one trooper, but if he had to sleep before he could reach a house on a normal day's ride, safety decreed that a second man should go along with either a wagon or a pack horse. This was very important, particularly in the winter in bitter cold and snow. In addition to drinking in the scenery and enjoying the friendship of the folk he met, he was studying further the skills of the tracker and speculating in his newspaper articles on the future of Canada. The newspaper was very satisfied with him and took more of his fiction writings, which were serialised in 1900 and 1901. Roger decided not to return home at once but to join the many seeking their fortune at the Klondyke Gold Rush. There was more copy in this as many hot-headed young British were planning to travel the long distance in the hope of making a fortune. Many came, but few made money, and *Lloyds Weekly Newspaper* published his advice to those intending to join the rush. Things to take included: pocket medicine case, needles, knives, fishing tackle, snow goggles and fur coat – but it was best to get winter clothes in Winnipeg. You would need a .45 rifle, but weapons were not to be carried actually in Klondyke. A mining outfit and a boatbuilding outfit were needed, also no man was allowed to enter the country without one year's supply of provisions. Roger costed it all out carefully for his readers and found that the total, including fares, would be £185, a large sum for those days.[11] Even already being in Canada, Roger could not afford to join the Rush, but was only able to do a little prospecting on the banks of the worked-out Fraser River with a partner called 'Weary', watching the packed trains and coffin-ships heading for the Klondyke. Having made barely enough to exist on, Roger gave up and returned to London.

Back in London, Roger was fretting deeply at not being able to take part in the Klondyke Gold Rush. Many members of the Legion of Frontiersmen had strange tales to tell, but the adventure that Roger Pocock was to embark on next was to have an effect, not only on him, but on the Legion he founded. The Legion of Frontiersmen has always had to battle against the suspicions of authority. The Legion had a named unit in the First War, but this was not allowed in 1939. It is also often asked why Roger Pocock was never honoured by his country. The strange answer is that it was suggested that Pocock was an unconvicted murderer. The case of the Vanishing Baronet could easily have come from a Victorian melodrama, or even the allegation from one of Roger Pocock's own works of fiction, although it was the one adventure that wounded him so deeply that he could not bring himself to adapt any part of it for one of his stories.

In London, Roger was sharing rooms in Great Ormond Street with Charles Mason, who had been in the Chinese Customs, had started meddling with revolution and only just escaped with his life, and also with Cutcliffe Hyne. Hyne had not yet become famous for his 'Captain Kettle' stories and was writing advice to girls in a nondescript magazine as 'Aunt Ermyntrude'. These three were regularly joined by other adventurers for a pipe and a yarn. From this group of similarly minded men grew the Filibusters Club, the seed bed from which the Legion of Frontiersmen sprang. There was no membership fee for this club and the only qualifications to join were a high percentage of time spent in far foreign parts. Pocock and Hyne were later to use the same illustrator, Stanley L. Wood, who made the picture of Captain Kettle famous throughout Edwardian England. It has often been remarked that there was a similarity between Wood's drawings of Captain Kettle and Roger Pocock, although Wood denied any intention.

Early in the winter of 1897, 'Experienced Western Traveller' advertised in *The Times* offering to lead a Klondyke expedition. Talk of the great Gold Rush was in all the papers and he had 63 replies. Pack horses were in great demand on the Klondyke to bring in the large quantity of goods needed by the ever growing numbers of fortune seekers and miners. The idea was to buy pack animals for £4 each at Ashcroft in British Columbia and run them the thousand miles up the old telegraph trail to the Skeena River, where he could renew acquaintance with old friends among the Gaetkshian Indians. He would then obtain guides to the Stickeen where the horses would fetch £40 each. Each man in the expedition would make a tidy profit or even, if some did not care to go off prospecting, earn 1s. 8d. per pound with the horses to carry cargo 'only another seven hundred and fifty miles'[12] to the Klondyke.

As Roger Pocock said, 'It looked very nice on paper.'[13] Unfortunately some ideas that look good on paper can have a nasty tendency to go wrong! From the 63 replies he picked eight, but were they the right eight? We hear little of seven of them after the expedition was over, but some of their comments lived on to help us piece together the story. From those eight he asked for £250 cash in advance (a considerable sum in those days). In return he offered a slight chance of riches, but certainty of hard work, short rations and getting drenched, frozen or fried. He worded it in such a way that hinted that they might just strike it rich, but would certainly find adventure. There were problems that should have been thought out. The Klondyke was a magnet attracting fortune hunters from all over the world. It was true that high prices were being asked for freight at Telegraph Creek, but not many were prepared to pay and the horses that arrived were worn to skeletons after what proved to be a terrible trail. Many a man bankrupted himself.

The member of the expedition who is the central figure of our story is Sir Arthur Colin Curtis, a baronet aged 40, married with a 12-year-old son and commissioned in the Royal Garrison Artillery. Why Curtis wished to go on such an unwise adventure must remain a mystery. A brother officer, Sir Robert Maziere Brady, took no part in the adventure but will have a bearing on the solution of the mystery. On 25 January 1898, the party assembled in Pocock's London rooms. It was agreed that Roger and one other should go ahead to buy horses, the others following behind. Two weeks later Roger Pocock and his companions were riding out of Ashcroft in British Columbia on to the Cariboo trail to the Cariboo mines – but 3,000 men with 7,000 horses had the same idea and the thousand-mile trail was churned into mud. Spring came late that year, leaving them little time to buy wild horses and get them broken in. The rest of the party arrived to hear the bad news. Every night still brought frost and very expensive hay had to be bought for the horses, so it was not until late May that they were ready to take to the trail.

The route was to Quesnel, through Blackwater country to Stuart Lake, past Nation and Germansen Lakes and then eastwards to the Skeena River where the Suskoot joins it. From there they were able to follow the telegraph trail to Telegraph Creek and the Stikine. This trail had been blazed in 1865-7 by the Collins Overland Telegraph, which was planning to get a line from New York to London via Siberia. (The project was abandoned when the Atlantic cable was laid.) By 1898 the trail was much overgrown, but was soon trampled into a narrow mud track, with complete wilderness each side, by thousands of human and animal feet. After 16 days they found an area of lush grass by the Fraser River and turned the horses loose – but a wild stallion turned up and captured all their mares! Struggling over the Fraser River they reached Quesnel and met up with many outfits who all had exactly the same idea. First of all, an all-British outfit was looked on with disdain as 'tenderfeet', but a good sense of discipline soon won them the respect of the Canadians. Norman Lee, who drove two hundred cattle on the same route a few days ahead of the Pocock party, reported crowds flocking north. 'Every half hour one or more pack trains would go up the trail.'[14] Each side of the blazed trail the undergrowth was so thick that no-one in their right mind would venture far. The track became like a busy but narrow highway running through a thick jungle. Relations between Roger Pocock and Curtis had been poor from the start. Curtis did not like Pocock's blunt manner. Bear in mind that in those class-conscious days Curtis was an officer and a gentleman, but Roger was an adventurer who had never been an officer, although he was leading the party. He thought that Curtis seemed only at home on water, which had a basis in truth. Curtis was the quiet Englishman, quite taciturn. I believe that he also had a lot on his mind regarding problems left at home. Matters between Curtis and Pocock finally came to a head when they were camped by the Mud River on 8 June. The bitter cold spring had suddenly given way to summer heat and they were plagued by black flies and mosquitoes. Ten horses had gone astray and had to be found, so the party was forced to spend the night in camp. Roger had been working hard since 3 a.m. and by nightfall at 9 p.m. there was still much to be done. 'Curtis had been thinking all day and when he offered to help me wash up after supper, I told him roughly to "go away and rest".'[15]

I am sure that Roger Pocock offered these words with all the sarcasm he could muster. What asides he had been making to the other members during the day while Curtis was 'thinking' we do not know, but the atmosphere must have been electric. Curtis had been bottling feelings inside him and I believe that by next morning he had come to a decision. Pocock was up very early next morning cooking and serving breakfast. He got the men away as soon as possible to search for the horses. Curtis would not come over and eat. He finished his personal chores and lit his pipe. He then walked over past Pocock at the fire. Roger was feeling that he had been too hasty and that his leadership was at fault. He called to Curtis in a friendly way, begging him to have some breakfast; 'Without noticing my presence, he went on and passed between two willow bushes out of sight.'[16] That was to be the last that was ever seen of Sir Arthur Colin Curtis and was the beginning of a mystery that was the subject of conversation around British Columbia for many years. For weeks afterwards it was the only subject of trail gossip. The story was always turning up in newspapers and has even done so within the latter half of the 20th century. It was to haunt Pocock to his dying day, the whispered suggestion that he had murdered Curtis following him through his life. After half an hour the missing horses had all been rounded up and were on their way back to camp. The recall signal of three revolver shots was fired and everyone was busy breaking camp for the rest of the morning. The next intended camping spot was 16 miles on, but Pocock was getting anxious. He was riding ahead of the main body and met a lone horseman. Had he seen Curtis? No, he had met no-one. Pocock rode back and, after a hasty conference with some of the rest, decided to ride back and leave food and a letter at the site of the last camp. Pocock changed his mind over the position of the night's camp and set it up on the shores of Bobtail Lake only about ten miles away. Night fell and they settled down. Next morning Pocock sent men back to the Mud River camp. They fired a few hopeful shots in the air and reported back by noon. Roger then decided not to go on any more and most of the party returned to organise a search. There is another puzzle. Although the rest of the party were comparative greenhorns, Pocock had a good knowledge of survival in that country. It is probable that his second-in-command also knew the correct procedures. Why, then, did they wait a day before organising a search? Probably it was partly because they were irritated with Curtis and thought he was just stringing them along. Also the massive problems of getting the horses through had taken over their lives to such an extent that Pocock made the inexcusable mistake of not ensuring the safety of his men before anything else.

With much of the evidence that virtually solves the mystery I was helped by the late Cecil Clark of Victoria.[17] Clark spent 35 years in the British Columbia Provincial Police. Even in his days, it was dangerous to wander off accepted trails, even a couple of miles from civilisation. The search for Curtis began in earnest. A Colonel Wright from Toronto was passing. The whole group started searching but with no results. At Wright's suggestion, Pocock sent a man to Stoney Creek to bring back five Indian trackers. Although several days had passed and rain had fallen, they found Curtis' trail and followed it westward for several miles. They decided that Curtis had spent the first night resting against a tree. A grizzly bear had crossed the trail but Curtis had not been harmed. Pocock's party had a conference. They had been searching now for ten days without success. They were on short rations by now and Pocock's leadership was obviously in question and very much at fault. He renounced his share in the expedition. His duty was to return to London and report to Lady Curtis. The remainder of the party did eventually arrive at Telegraph Creek after exceptional hardships, but with only 16 of their original 51 horses. By the time Pocock had reached London, he was very near a breakdown. He reported to Lady Curtis. She cabled the Hudson's Bay Manager at Quesnel, Alex McNabb, to hire more trackers to renew the search. The result was the same. There could be no doubt that Sir Arthur Curtis was dead.

I place considerable importance in the fact that, as soon as it was legally possible, Lady Curtis had her husband declared dead. Very shortly afterwards she married again – Curtis' brother officer mentioned earlier, Sir Robert Maziere Brady. Accusations flew around, mainly directed at Pocock that he had murdered Curtis for his money belt. The mud that was hurled in Pocock's direction and the stigma remained throughout his life. It was often whispered behind his back by those who did not approve of him that he was an unconvicted murderer and that, had there been sufficient evidence, he would have hanged. The rumour also harmed the Legion of Frontiersmen in the early days when Pocock was at the head. Clark's investigations produced sufficient evidence to prove that Pocock did not murder Curtis. There has to be strong circumstantial evidence that family problems drove Curtis to join an expedition for which he was totally unsuited, perhaps in the hope of starting a new life under a new identity in the days when divorce was not socially acceptable. Roger Pocock's description of Curtis's actions on the last day before disappearing describes a man clearly suffering from clinical depression. Curtis's decision to walk away into the wilderness fits entirely with the likely actions of a man in the grip of severe depression. His widow had him declared dead with the utmost haste and immediately married a brother officer. Lady Curtis speedily closed that chapter of her life, but the mystery had long-term repercussions both on Pocock and on the Legion of Frontiersmen.

After a short time back in London, finding he could not escape the rumours, Pocock decided to do something really notable or die in the attempt. He revived an idea that had been in his head for some years, a horseback ride from Canada to Mexico through the American deserts. He gained the backing of *Lloyds Weekly Newspaper*, which agreed to pay his expenses and a fee for a weekly report. Even today, that 3,600-mile ride on horseback would be an achievement, but although the Wild West had been mainly tamed, it was still not friendly country. The war in South Africa was making all the headlines so Pocock's Great Ride only gained a regular spot on page 14. Parts of the journey through Canada and on through Montana and Yellowstone National Park were reasonably safe, but Pocock could not resist visiting Jacksons Hole and also Brown's Park Ranche. Outlaws usually gave this unarmed eccentric Englishman the polite interviews he requested. Pocock, strangely, listed the religions of each of these men living at what he called 'just an ordinary ranche'.[18] According to Pocock, Captain M'Carty was in charge of what we know as the Wild Bunch with Mr Butch Cassidy his second-in-command. Roger Pocock names several other well-known outlaws.

In Pocock's *Horses* he wrote, 'The robbers were much the most truthful men I have met on the stock ranges.'[19] Through the heat of the Painted Desert he rode, and followed this with a visit to what was already a tourist spot, the Grand Canyon. On his route Pocock met many strange characters, such as Texas Bob who gave him a piece of human skull from an old white prospector that the Apaches had killed. Pocock apparently kept that piece of skull on his mantelpiece for the rest of his life – maybe an unusual conversation piece. Pocock eventually arrived in Mexico City suffering from dysentery from a brief spell in a Mexican jail. Pocock told readers back in Britain that 'Three good horses covered the whole distance, but, including pack animals, I used in all nine, at a total cost of £44 9s. 7d.'[20]

Roger Pocock then had to return home urgently. His sister, Daisy, was being pursued by her husband for a divorce. It had been a bad marriage and the worry had caused Lena Ashwell to seek some relief in drugs. When he had sorted out his sister's problems, Pocock made for the South African War where he joined one of the band of Irregular, mainly colonial, Scouts until the National Scouts were formed to regularise the Irregulars; Pocock saw some action with them, finishing as a corporal. From the end of the South African War until 1904, apart from a short visit to Greenland, Pocock concentrated on writing, bringing out his most successful fiction book *Curly* and his first volume of autobiography, *A Frontiersman* was published with some differences in America a year earlier as *Following the Frontier*.

Three

'LISTING THE LEGION

It was time for the 'listing of the Legion', to quote again from Roger Pocock's favourite Kipling poem. Headed such, a letter signed Roger Pocock appeared on Boxing Day 1904 in ten major newspapers saying:

> ... It is time to enlist the Legion, for good fellowship, mutual help, and possible service to the State in time of war. A few thousand men would form a sufficient army of observation, a unit for field intelligence in peace and war, its duties being those of scouting – to see run and tell – in case of any menace to the British peace.[1]

One can see some confluence with the thinking of Baden-Powell in this letter. The idea was a simple one and could have been brilliantly effective, but for some problems which neither Roger nor his Legion could hope to influence. For a start politicians had a mistrust of any type of 'Secret Service' and there was rivalry between Naval and Military Intelligence. There was also reliance on the gentleman amateur or the officer on leave bringing back information of use, such as the famous story of Baden-Powell the butterfly collector on the Dalmatian coast. Professor Christopher Andrew confirms this: 'Baden-Powell was a firm believer in the superiority of the gentleman amateur over the career professional. "The best spies", he declared, "are unpaid men who are doing it for the love of the thing." He insisted too on the great "sporting value" of amateur espionage.'[2] This was a principle firmly adopted by the early Legion of Frontiersmen.

The final incentive to persuade Roger Pocock to form the Legion of Frontiersmen came as a result of some success he enjoyed as an amateur spy in 1904. He had been sent to Russia by the weekly newspaper, the *Illustrated Mail*, and early December found him in St Petersburg. Russia was seething with discontent and trouble started there the following month. Roger's series of articles ran over three weeks from 14 January 1905. They were headlined 'Well known writer describes the visit to the country that is now at war with Japan', and continued,

> What is the true state of affairs in Russia? Will there be a revolution? These are the questions that everyone is asking. With a view to learning

what the people of the great Russian Empire think of the disastrous war, the *Illustrated Mail* sent Mr Roger Pocock to Russia, and his observations, gathered on the spot, will be read with special interest.

The choice of Mr Pocock for such a task was particularly appropriate. He is admitted to be one of the finest descriptive writers of the day. Not only is he a capable writer, but a great traveller who has seen and depicted life in all parts of the world.'[3]

It was not the journalistic effort that was so important, but the spare time espionage that Roger undertook totally on his own initiative. At his hotel, he made friends with a man, a British subject, although from one of the other countries of the Empire. This man was employed as an engineer in the building of the Naval Base at Libau. Roger suggested to him that a plan of the base would be of use to the British Government, if the man could draw one from memory.

'Easy,' said the man, 'Come to my room where I can draw it in private.'

'Oh, no,' said Roger, 'Far too suspicious.'

Although he was rather too inclined to see spies in every corner, in this case Roger was probably right as a waiter was taking great interest in the two men and this 'mad Englishman's' exploits at Sebastopol years earlier might just have been noted and Roger have been identified for surveillance. They sent for paper and pencils, which made the waiter very suspicious, but when he looked over their shoulders they were engaged in a game of noughts and crosses. The 'mad Englishman' was up to his usual antics. When the waiter was sent out again, this time for more beer, the rough squares were turned into canals, basins and buildings while the scores in the margins became soundings, bearings and ranges. When the waiter returned, Roger's pipe and tobacco hid the paper. Later on in his room Roger stowed the paper in the useful space in his right boot where the toes should have

5 *Roger Pocock in Frontiersmen uniform, 1905.*

6 *H.S.H. Prince Louis of Battenberg.*

been. He nearly ruined this exercise in amateur spying by absent-mindedly putting his boots outside the bedroom door that night to be cleaned! Fortunately, he woke up with a start at 3 a.m. to realise his error and rescued them in time. He left Russia by the last boat to get through the ice before the troubles started.[4]

Back in London, and before he could call in on the offices of the *Illustrated Mail*, he happened to meet Jack Brotherton, a friend who was also private secretary to Admiral Fisher. Roger gave him the plan and asked him to pass it on to the right quarters. Much to Roger's surprise, the next day a letter came from Prince Louis of Battenberg, then Director of Naval Intelligence. Prince Louis thanked him and asked if he had any more information. Roger had taken his camera with him to Russia to bring back photographs for the *Illustrated Mail*. Roger said that his camera 'always liked to sit in a porthole and blink'.[5]

So he sent Prince Louis some photographs; one of some small submarines loaded on flat cars for transport east to the Russo-Japanese War; one of the destroyer *Gromovoi* being towed by two tugs through the ice lane; one of a turret battleship of the *Sissoiveliki* type under major repair; one of the refacing with steel armour of the Kronstadt batteries. Prince Louis was obviously pleased.[6] How much of this information he already had is unknown, but it would in any case have been useful confirmation. During this period there was little cooperation and intense rivalry between Naval Intelligence and the Military Intelligence section of the army. Roger claimed that the War Office had a plan of Libau at the time, but the navy had not, and the army were not prepared to let Naval Intelligence see theirs or even admit they had one. Naval Intelligence treated Roger with much courtesy (remembering his father had been a naval officer) and early information that came through Legion sources was offered to Naval Intelligence first while Prince Louis was D.N.I. Prince Louis joined the Governing Council of the Legion and became one of many men of influence promoting the Legion. Mark Kerr, in his biography of Prince Louis of Battenberg, said:

> In the winter of 1904-5, Captain Roger Pocock, the principal organizer of the Legion of Frontiersmen, forwarded to Prince Louis some secret information with regard to Russia. This led to his taking an interest in the Legion of Frontiersmen, and joining the Council of the movement.

> The Legion is composed of men who have been in the services, whose commercial work takes them abroad, or who are in the Merchant Service, and who are veterans not available to the Forces in time of peace. Since the War [writing in 1934] the Legion has been extended considerably, and has Imperial branches overseas. All the members are in a position to give information about affairs all over the world to their headquarters, who can then send it to the Heads of the Public Services that would be interested. In August 1914 their strength was 17,500 men.
>
> At the time that Prince Louis took notice of the Legion and became a member of its Council, the body was not recognized by the Admiralty or War Office, and it was typical of his practical imagination to see how useful they were going to be in the near future, and to give them encouragement.[7]

Roger's visit to Russia, with a brief stop in Germany on the way back, had convinced him that war with Germany was inevitable and he claimed in later years that he believed that England had ten years to prepare. He reasoned that, had someone else returned to England with the information that Roger had brought, but without knowing the right channel to place it in, valuable information would be lost. What was needed was a channel acceptable to the authorities and an organisation to co-ordinate the watching eyes around the world. The organisation would be the 'eyes and ears of the Empire'. All round the world there were men similar to Roger in that they wandered the outposts of civilisation. They were men who would never take kindly to the current orthodox military discipline, but who held a deep and abiding loyalty to the Sovereign and the British Empire.

For his great project, Roger had £23 in the bank and £1,200 invested.[8] He rented an office at 6 Adam Street in the Adelphi in London. A steep narrow twisting staircase led up to the top-floor office and it would not have been too easy a climb for a man who had celebrated unwisely and over-well his return to England. Although Roger was a member of the Savage Club, in 1904 he was one of the many travellers who had formed the Filibusters Club, and it was around their globe-trotting members that the core of the Legion was formed. As well as the members of the Filibusters Club spreading the word, the Legion attracted a number of newspaper men. R.D. Blumenfeld, H.A. Gwynne and Edgar Wallace soon became members as did War Correspondents such as Edmund Chandler, Capt. Walter Kirton, F.A. MacKenzie and Frederick Moore. Roger enlisted friends among well-known authors and travellers such as Cutcliffe Hyne, Morley Roberts and Harry de Windt.

Politicians started to consider the Legion a good idea, but these were mainly Conservatives and some influential ones became members, such as E.G. Pretyman, who had served as Civil Lord of the Admiralty and maintained the Naval links. Sir Henry Seton-Kerr, Member of Parliament for St Helens, was better known as a big-game hunter. The number of Conservatives who supported the Legion may have worked against them because they soon had to talk to a new Liberal Government.

One puzzle, unresolved for some many years, was that Lord Haldane was listed in some Legion documents as one of the first 25 members of the Legion, although all the evidence points against him being enthusiastic about such an organisation. When I realised that the list was taken from one in the Founder's handwriting, it soon became apparent to one deciphering that hurried and urgent script that he referred not to Lord Haldane, but Lord Haldon, better known as the Palk family of Torquay.

As well as men of influence writing and talking about the Legion, the 15ft square room at the top of 6 Adam Street came to be constantly filled with a motley collection of seamen, soldiers of fortune, cowboys, explorers – many of these men with strange life stories and knowing the shadier sides of the law. Some of the stories of these early Frontiersmen are extraordinary. One of the oddest was a visitor to the office who was perspiring heavily on a bitterly cold winter's day. When he was asked why he was so hot, the man cursed the chain-mail vest he was wearing, or rather the chamois lining. He showed Roger a chain-mail vest of phosphor-bronze weighing about eight pounds. He complained that he had been followed from Brazil by a man who kept dodging round corners and stabbing him with a dagger – 'he's spoiled three of my suits already!'. Evidently the dealer who supplied the armour sold on average a couple of dozen a year to politicians and royalty.[9] These were the colourful characters with much frontier experience joining the Legion, but Roger's admiration of those among them who had a contempt for the law and sometimes publicly flouted it was not likely to encourage official acceptance of the Legion. Roger never explained how he balanced his friendship with, and sometimes admiration for, outlaws and desperadoes of all kinds with his proud ideals of British justice. The Legion of Frontiersmen gradually began to be considered as one of the groups of eccentrics who kept warning about the spy menace to Britain. No apparent action was taken against possible and potential spies and the War Office appears to have ignored anything that came in from the Legion. When Lt Col D.P. Driscoll came into power in the Legion the emphasis was changed to training members to act as guerrillas to work behind enemy lines. Between 1904 and 1914, the Legion of Frontiersmen was to be the nucleus of two ideas: the gathering of intelligence plus counter-intelligence in Britain, and the formation of an almost S.A.S.-type of unit many years before such a combat regiment was to be considered in official circles. In both ideas, the Legion was greatly ahead of its times.

A high percentage of those who joined the Legion of Frontiersmen had served in South Africa, and members from the outposts of the Empire had been, like Roger, irregular soldiers. They were men who could ride well and shoot straight. They were men who admired the fighting skills of the Boer and had learned from his way of warfare. Even the military men who joined, ex-officers from the regulars as opposed to the 'range' men from the Colonies, were often highly critical of the British conduct of the South African War and the blinkered attitude of many senior officers of the British Army.

However, another early member who was influential and highly respected was Major-General Hutton who had commanded Mounted Infantry in South Africa and who had returned from organising the military forces in Australia. The Legion has seldom had any firm upper-age limit, maintaining that a man of any age can serve his country in some way. Consequently, the Legion has always attracted retired officers and n.c.o.'s who have fretted at being laid aside when they still felt they could do something useful. Erskine Childers, who became an influential member of the Governing Council of the Legion of Frontiersmen before his obsession with Irish Home Rule and Irish affairs led him on a different path, bitterly criticised the British generals in his writings and emphasised the value of guerrilla warfare. Childers was one of those who helped guide the Legion to a change of emphasis around 1909. The biggest influence on the Legion's 'intelligence work' was Frontiersman William Le Queux, the author who produced books at a prodigious rate and who Roger had first come to know in the 1890s when both were writing for *Lloyds Weekly Newspaper* and other publications. It is a pity that Le Queux did have such an influence as he was a 'Walter Mitty' character who was always hinting at his spying activities abroad. Le Queux was loud in his warnings of the 'German menace'. His story, *The Invasion of* 1910, which he claimed was based on German plans he had learned from a contact close to the Kaiser, caused a sensation when it was serialised in the *Daily Mail* in 1906. Le Queux insisted that there was in England a 'civilian army' of German spies – waiters, clerks, bakers, house servants and the like, serving the Fatherland. He gained many disciples for his ideas, including the ageing Lord Roberts. Le Queux had a magnetic personality and Roger believed everything Le Queux said.[10] Many others who believed Le Queux implicitly were Frontiersmen. Northcliffe was delighted at the way *The Invasion of* 1910 aided his circulation. He had persuaded Le Queux to alter his story so that the Germans invaded through towns where the *Daily Mail* attracted a good readership. Christopher Andrew considered that Le Queux's position in society brought influence for his ideas: 'At least part of Le Queux's secret lay in his immense clubability. He moved effortlessly around clubland and society dinners, establishing a reputation as wit and raconteur.'[11]

In October 1906, General Ewart appointed Lt Col James Edmonds, a great friend of Le Queux, as head of MO5, and it was Edmonds who recommended the appointment of Capt. Vernon Kell to be head of what we know as MI5:

> One of my friends, F.T. Jane (founder of the 'Naval Annual') who was on the lookout for spies, kidnapped a Portsmouth German in his car and deposited him in the Duke of Bedford's animal park at Woburn. He naturally got into trouble and publicity. Another friend, William Le Queux, the popular writer of thrillers, produced out of his imagination a volume called 'Spies of the Kaiser'. In both cases, the outcome had been that the kidnapper and the author received dozens of letters telling them of the suspicious behaviour of Germans.[12]

Even Baden-Powell was convinced of the German menace and began warning about it and, according to his biographer:

> When the German invasion scare was at its height in Britain between 1906 and 1910, Baden-Powell was sold a bogus invasion plan by an enterprising group of German-American forgers who had set up a 'spy-Bureau' in Belgium. They contrived to sell similar material to Major-General J.S. Ewart, the Director of Military Operations, and to William Le Queux, the espionage writer.[13]

There was considerable co-operation between the Legion and the Boy Scout movement before the First War. Many Frontiersmen were also Scoutmasters.

> ... the Legion undoubtedly made a considerable impact upon Baden-Powell. The emphasis which he would soon place upon 'frontiersmen' as role models and heroes to the boys is plainly due to the Legion ...
>
> When Baden-Powell launched the Boy Scouts, many members of the Legion became Scoutmasters and named their troops 'Legion of Frontiers' Boy Scouts'. Roger Pocock would be a contributor to the very first edition of the Boy Scouts' newspaper *The Scout*, in which Baden-Powell's boys were described as 'The Legion of Boy Scouts'. The fact that this name was ever seriously considered is another indication of the extent to which Baden-Powell had been influenced by Pocock's creation.[14]

A colourful and enthusiastic Frontiersman, 'Jungle Jim' Biddulph-Pinchard, who died in the early 1980s at an advanced age, was a friend of Baden-Powell and told me that Baden-Powell and Pocock had been in discussion about the relationship between the Legion and the Boy Scouts. There had been ideas for a much closer link between the two organisations, but the eccentric behaviour of Roger Pocock and some of the Frontiersmen dissuaded Baden-Powell from an official relationship. A sub-committee of the Committee of Imperial Defence reported that: 'The evidence which was produced left no doubt in the minds of the sub-committee that an extensive system of German espionage exists in this country, and that we have no organisation for keeping in touch with that espionage and for accurately determining its extent or objectives.'[15] and Christopher Andrew concluded: 'That naive conclusion, which owed as much to the imaginary spies of William Le Queux as to the real machination of German Intelligence, led directly to the foundation of the modern British Secret Service.'[16] In his book, Professor Andrew is quite scathing about William Le Queux and his stories of spies, but, even if many of his stories were pure fiction, the above statement by Britain's most noted historian of Intelligence means that Le Queux and the Legion of Frontiersmen were most important to Britain's history. The problem was that the truth on its own was insufficiently exciting, so Le Queux, being a good storyteller, embroidered on simple truths, on suspicions, on imaginations, and then believed the whole lot himself. However, he was far from being the only Frontiersman who could be described as a romantic or even an eccentric.

Doctor Bodkin told his story that, as a doctor at Port Natal, he was asked by some Bantu whom he had healed to go with them to their country 'Makualand' in Portuguese East Africa. He found the heads of all previous Portuguese visitors impaled on poles, but Bodkin was not killed; he became Court Physician and later Grand Visier, a post he held for over twenty years. He married without favouritism the sisters, daughters and aunts of all the leading citizens, eventually finishing with quite a large harem. Roger asked Mrs Bodkin how she liked that. Her reply was that it was really the only way to keep her husband out of mischief. At the formation of the Legion, Bodkin had fallen on hard times and Roger allowed him to sleep on the hearthrug as it was more comfortable than the embankment. Roger was a generous man to any lame duck he met, particularly one with such an outlandish tale to tell, and he was always ready to give away money to anyone he considered poor and deserving. Roger had eventually managed to find Bodkin a job as guide to a film-making expedition to Africa but Bodkin died suddenly. His story is not one that can be easily checked but, like Le Queux's, it was a good story.[17] This was the type of man attracted to the Legion of Frontiersmen. All great patriots, but very much individuals and not the type of man to accept the discipline that the Army would expect if the Legion was to be recognised and taken under its wing. This sort of man was likely at any time to go off and search for adventure on his own. Another insurmountable problem was that the Legion ignored the class structure of the day and from very early times insisted on electing its own officers and leaders in a democratic manner. There is no doubt that the idea of the Legion attracted many influential and well-known men who thought its objectives valuable and laudable right up until the Second World War. The first President of the Legion was Lord Lonsdale, known as the 'Yellow Earl' due to his liking for that colour and praised as 'the greatest white hunter of his time'. He did a lot of work behind the scenes, trying to raise support in high circles. Although his family was still involved with the Legion as late as 1929, he stepped back early on just as soon as he realised that the leader, Roger Pocock, did not have the personality to stamp his mark on the movement.

Roger was a dreamer, a visionary and at times even a Don Quixote. The Boy Scout movement was to start with the great 'Hero of Mafeking' at its head. The Legion of Frontiersmen was started by a pleasant but little-known fellow who had his fair share of human failings. He came from a good enough family but had never been commissioned in the Armed Forces. He was just an ex-corporal from a most irregular band of South African War Scouts. Many of the men with military experience objected to having to take orders from this man just because he was the Founder, and thought they were better fitted to take charge of the Legion than Roger was. From the start, discipline on a Frontiersmen parade was very tough and probably stricter than any army unit, but off parade all ranks were equal – something we hear of today in the

S.A.S. to a certain extent and think of as recent. In Edwardian times it was revolutionary for the lord and the estate worker to socialise together after parade. When the Legion was formed into the 25th Fusiliers (Frontiersmen) to serve in East Africa in the First War an exceptional number of the officers were rankers who had joined as ordinary soldiers and were commissioned in the field. We will find how officers transferred from other units later in the War were not treated as part of the 'family' of the Legion. Throughout its history many a man, however senior his rank in the armed forces, refused to take rank in the Legion saying that to serve as a Frontiersman was honour enough. The later example of this was Jan Smuts who joined the Legion in 1922. The Prime Minister of South Africa gained a high opinion of the 25th Fusiliers (Frontiersmen) in the First War. Smuts would take no other rank than Frontiersman, and his statement that 'to be a Frontiersman was honour enough'[18] was taken as an example by many Frontiersman officers.

The lack of toes on his right foot meant that the Founder could not march as smartly as even the least experienced Frontiersman. He was short-sighted but would never wear spectacles in uniform or allow himself to be photographed wearing them. Another factor working against Roger was his sister who was prominent in her support of, and publicity for, the Legion. She was well known as an excellent actress and an actor-manager and was on the fringes of the Royal circle, but being an actress in Edwardian London with its strict class boundaries, particularly an actress who specialised in playing 'fallen women', did not make her the most socially acceptable cheer-leader for the Legion. Added to this, she was a divorcee and one around whom occasional scandals were whispered. Where Roger Pocock scored was in dealing with the rougher, tougher Colonials who rapidly set up units of the Legion all over the Empire, often well away from any centre of western-style civilisation. He delighted in receiving and replying to letters from these men from all over the world, and it was Roger who always considered the Colonies equally important to Britain and not just London as the only centre worth considering. It was not until Lt Col D.P. Driscoll became a really major power in the Legion after Roger's expulsion in 1909 that the movement began to pull as one, but by then most of the damage had been done and some very uncomplimentary opinions about the Legion had been put into the heads of the men of power at the War Office.

Driscoll was one of the heroes of the South African War. He had served in the 3rd Burma War, but made his name in South Africa, where he eventually formed his own Corps – Driscoll's Scouts. Driscoll's biographer tells us that: 'It was with this unit that he made his name, dashing and completely fearless he was awarded a D.S.O. for his services at Wepener and Mentioned is Despatches twice. He ended the war as a Lieut. Colonel in charge of a column. The subject of numerous articles, he became a hero figure for magazines such as 'Boys of our Empire'. A.G. Hales wrote a novel about him and later he was painted by Abe Turner, a well known portrait artist.'[19] A commercial venture after the war failed when he was cheated by a partner and he arrived in

London around 1906 armed with a letter of introduction to Roger Pocock. 'There can be no argument about Pocock's offer of paid employment, it saved Driscoll and in return he worked unstintingly, travelling the length and breadth of the Kingdom promoting the cause of the Legion.'[20] Driscoll's influence on events steadily increased as the years progressed.

Roger Pocock thought long and hard about a rank for himself. As the Legion was organised on basically military lines, everyone had to have a rank. He took for himself the title of Commissioner, which he said meant nothing as a rank to anyone and would stop people accusing him of taking false rank. This it did not do, as anyone who knew anything of Canada – and many Frontiersmen did – knew it was a senior rank in the North-West Mounted Police, the equivalent of Colonel. The Legion wrote letters to all the great British leaders, Generals and Admirals. The replies they received were far from encouraging with the exception of Prince Louis. Lord Roberts is believed to have considered that they were quite unpractical although he did offer some support by word and by letter.[21] He was in any case President of, and totally occupied with, the National Service League and he considered that the only answer to the German threat was conscription into the armed forces. Lord Kitchener replied blandly to a request for support: 'Lord Kitchener hopes you will tell those who were his comrades in service in South Africa how glad he is to learn that they are still serving the Empire in the Legion of Frontiersmen, and thanks all for the message you have sent him.'[22] The Legion did gain strong support from newspapers, with many newspapermen belonging to the Legion. Thomas Marlowe, then editor of the *Daily Mail* which championed Le Queux and his spy tales, became a member of the Governing Council of the Legion in the 1920s. He wrote a somewhat puzzling letter which Roger quoted in his autobiography *Chorus to Adventurers*: 'Dear Roger, I have read your scheme, studied your plans, and given a great deal of thought to your warnings, and now I am going to bed resolved to sell my life dearly.'[23]

Although Lord Lonsdale was stirring up support from his noble friends, the War Office was most unhappy about the Legion and making noises about a 'private army'. In May 1906 the Legion received a letter from the Treasury Solicitor in response to an enquiry, which pointed out to the Legion that in Britain it was illegal to raise a private army.[24] The nobility, such as Lord Lonsdale, were accustomed to fit out their Yeomanry Cavalry as he did the Westmorland and Cumberland Yeomanry Cavalry in the 1890s his own design of uniform similar to the 10th Hussars and at his own expense. The line between what was allowed to the nobility and to organisations was somewhat hazy. Dawson's biography of Lord Lonsdale says that: 'The photographs of an escort of Westmorland and Cumberland Yeomanry Cavalry on special occasions show nothing to distinguish them in turn-out from the regulars; and they were probably better mounted. It is unnecessary to remark that particular attention was paid to horsemanship, care of saddlery, feed, etc.'[25]

The Legion was inaugurated at a dinner hosted by Lord Lonsdale on 10 April 1905. A detailed document was circulated to the senior military and naval officers present. Committees were elected and plans of action were devised. Roger's diary reports that he went to Lowther Castle on Saturday 6 and Monday 8 May: 'Rode in Legion dress as Lord Lonsdale's orderly – mistaken by yeomanry for Major Burnham [the famous South African scout, Major F.R. Burnham, who also became a member of the Legion in later life]… Lunched at officers' mess.'[26] Lonsdale had already sent the Legion one hundred pounds in March.

Many at the War Office were unhappy with Roger being in such a high profile position. The rumours were still circulating that he had murdered Sir Arthur Curtis on the Canadian expedition. These rumours were to come to a head at the end of October in 1908 when the papers brought up the story of Curtis' disappearance again and, according to Roger, the *Daily News* actually libelled him.[27] By this time Roger was fighting a rearguard action against the many who thought him the wrong man for the job. At the beginning of September 1905, Roger was on holiday in the Wye Valley and received a letter to say that the King had asked for particulars of the Legion. The King would have heard about the Legion through friends of Lena Ashwell in the Royal theatre set, and he was always well aware of what was going on in the country. However, Roger reported in *Chorus to Adventurers* that a certain Colonel had told the King that Roger Pocock was a notorious murderer who had escaped justice through lack of evidence – he was the man who had killed Sir Arthur Curtis. The King was shocked and came very close to getting orders issued that the Legion should 'cease to exist', as its Founder was a most unsuitable person. Fortunately Lord Lonsdale asked a lady who 'had got the King's ear' to speak up when the subject should arise. It was raised at a subsequent dinner. She reminded the King of the kind of motives that would underlie a backbiting attack of this nature against a man who had been, and still was, of such outstanding service to Empire interests, by one who might possibly covet his position in the Legion. King Edward thought deeply for a while, and then the matter was dropped.[28]

The early enthusiasm for the Legion waned, as often happens with new organisations and the pressure began to tell on Roger. His health started to suffer, and also his bank balance. His pocket diaries give an idea of the problems and also of those of influence in Society working for the Legion: 'June 22nd, 1905: Cheque dishonoured, wired Lord Lonsdale to assist … December 27th 1905: Message from Lady de la Warr that Lyttelton says, "Don't worry. I'll look after the Frontiersmen."… December 29th, 1905: £ 123 of my capital left. Took over payment of staff and office.'[29] In one year Roger had spent well over a thousand pounds (a very considerable sum in those days) of his own money on the Legion. In its formative years, the brunt of everything fell on him. The Legion took his time, his money and his health. In December 1905 the Legion of Frontiersmen forwarded to the War Office a statement showing the aims and objects of the Legion with a request for the 'tacit approval of the Crown and Imperial Military Authorities'.[30] Roger Pocock, with a deputation from the Legion, was ordered to wait on the Army

Council. 'What', asked Sir Neville Lyttelton, 'do you propose to do in the event of war with Germany?' It is worth mentioning that Lord Lonsdale was friendly with the German Kaiser and a slightly curious choice for President of a Legion whose founder predicted, and insisted on preparation for, war with Germany by 1914. The answer to Lyttelton's question seemed obvious to Roger: 'Blow up the Kiel Canal Sir'. Of course I had examined the ground, consulted experts, drawn up plans, and was ready when needed to cut the German Fleet in halves.[31] This would contain the German Navy but would require a guerrilla action to do it. These men who had served in South Africa were convinced of the value of guerrilla actions and Driscoll was to propose similar activities to the War Office at the outbreak of war in 1914. The Army Council thanked Roger and told him that they would give the proposals their consideration.

On 15 February 1906 the Secretary of State for War in the new Liberal Government sent his answer to the Legion. The letter was carefully worded so as not to express War Office backing and yet not to slap down completely an organisation which had a number of influential backers. The reply was not worded carefully enough and produced a reaction which caused the War Office considerable problems. Even now, nearly one hundred years after the letter was sent, the inaccurate claim is made that the Legion is 'officially recognised'. Haldane expressed his

> ... sympathy with the aims and objects of the Legion, noting that the Association was to be self-governing and self-supporting in times of peace. He ... recognised it as a purely private organisation, in no way connected with any Department of State, but one which, should a suitable occasion arise, he might be able to utilise.[32]

Roger and the Legion pounced on the word 'recognised' with great delight and took it completely out of its context. From then until the present day, the Legion have rather too regularly announced in publications and the Press that they were 'officially recognised' on 15 February 1906. As with many early records which were destroyed in the bombing of London, the Legion no longer have this letter, but a record does exist in War Office files and a contemporary copy is now in the Legion of Frontiersmen archives.[33] The War Office were to regret deeply the use of this one word and from then on were at pains to deny the recognition and insist that the words 'take cognisance of' should be used in correspondence and never the word 'recognition', although the difference in meaning is a slender one.

Pocock was kept very busy: 'An endless stream of visitors began once more to fill the office hours, and the press work of Legion propaganda ... kept me from any idleness at night.'[34] Many of the names mean little to us today, but others, such as Basil Lubbock, are still remembered due to their writings. Lubbock's *Round the Horn before the Mast* was re-printed many times and is still known today. A giant of a man for those days at 6ft 6ins, Old Etonian Lubbock had already seen many adventures when he strode into the

7 Early Legion of Frontiersmen badges.

Legion office in Adam Street to enlist. He had been to the Klondyke Gold Rush without success and from this unsuccessful adventure he had signed on before the mast on the four-masted *Royalshire* for the journey around the Horn, which formed the basis of his most famous book. When he arrived back, he found that war was already being fought in South Africa. He immediately headed there. When he later walked into the Frontiersmen office to join the Legion, Roger Pocock asked him about his South African War service – and had he ever had suckling pig for Christmas dinner when there? It seems that when Lubbock was serving in South Africa some scoundrel from a group of irregular Scouts had managed to creep unseen into the canteen of Lubbock's unit and steal their Christmas dinner of suckling pig. It turned out that the rogue was none other than Pocock who had used the Native Canadian lore learned in his Canada days to creep in unseen and acquire an excellent pre-cooked Christmas dinner for his comrades. This was the first time that the two adventurers had met officially, so this time it was Pocock's turn to buy the new recruit a meal.[35]

The War Office were to be additionally upset by the appointment of the London Commandant of the Legion, Manoel Herreira de Hora, a self-confessed pirate. de Hora told a tall story about being involved in a minor South American revolution in 1876 which involved a British ship, H.M.S. *Shah*. de Hora also claimed that, when he was in South Africa during the Boer War, he gathered a group of men together when the Boers retreated from Johannesburg to keep order, and then handed over to Lord Roberts.[36] Roger said that it was later found out that de Hora had been a Boer spy for four years.

Whatever the truth of de Hora's tales, this great bulldog of a man was at first immensely popular with the early Frontiersmen and was unanimously elected their London Commandant. The War Office was horrified with the choice and many and loud were the noises made to Roger to get rid of him, but Roger was not the sort of man for that precipitate and strong action, particularly as de Hora was rather handy with his fists and had been

8 *Pocock and Driscoll at the formation of a new unit, 1907.*

democratically elected. The matter was not resolved until de Hora infuriated the Frontiersmen by having the Legion Bandmaster, Willard, flogged on parade at the end of February 1907!³⁷ He was then removed by general consent, but even afterwards caused problems by writing to the War Office requesting arms, ammunition and saddlery. The early files of MI5 in 1909 state that: 'the first commandant of the London Command of the Legion of Frontiersmen was almost certainly in the secret service of Germany and therefore had to be got rid of.'³⁸ There is a note in the border 'Who is this?' If de Hora was indeed a German spy, it makes an important point that the Germans were taking the Legion more seriously than the British. London Commandant was probably one of the most influential positions in the Legion, as Driscoll proved when he took over that position and gave access to much of the information that came in.

The Frontiersmen held a meeting to decide on uniform. Each man was asked to attend in whatever he considered to be the ideal dress for frontier activities. By far the greatest majority attended dressed almost identically in slouch hat, silk neckerchief, shirt, breeches, high boots or boots and leggings, spurs, cartridge belt and revolver. The only real difference was in the weight of cloth. Men used to hot climates were wearing lighter cloth. And so the uniform was decided quite easily, an amalgam of the uniforms of various forces; blue tunic like the South African Police and breeches as worn in South Africa; the stetson hat and Strathcona boots of the Canadian North-West Police; the British Sam Browne belt, and shoulder chains as a token to history and the gallantry of the days of knights and swords. They took their motto 'God Guard Thee' from the inscription on General Gordon's ring.³⁹ A Frontiersman today will still end a letter with this blessing. One can see in this uniform a distinct similarity to that adopted by early scoutmasters, which was to raise the cry of 'militarism' among pacifists. Quite a few early Frontiersmen ran Scout troops as well.

As a result of the 'recognition' letter, the Legion was able to press for publicity and increased membership. *The Times* was regularly printing news of the Legion and more and more men joined. On 27 April 1906 *The Times* said, 'We are informed by the Secretary of the Legion of Frontiersmen that the formation of the Corps has been officially approved by the War Office, and six thousand men have applied for membership.'[40] The Yorkshire Command was to be in the hands of Capt. Lionel Palmer, son of Sir Charles Palmer, M.P., a friend of Le Queux. The Northumberland and Durham Command had H.S. Orde, who was one of Roger's greatest supporters in the troubles to come and reputed to be the Legion's strongest man. Hants and Wilts were under the command of F.H. Grinlington, C.M.G. On 4 September 1906 *The Times* also reported that the Bradford Command had been founded under C.J. Cutcliffe Hyne, author of the 'Captain Kettle' books. '... an admirable auxiliary to the existing forces providing Scouts, Pioneers and other material which could not be subjected to ordinary military discipline ... The King had expressed his approval of the idea.'[41] This powerful statement received no official challenge. The Executive Council began to read like a mixture from *Burke's Peerage* and *Who's Who*. Pocock was delighted:

> Surely the nations of the Empire would realize that here was a totally new principle of service, a powerful bond of fellowship in peace, a greater security in time of war, a loyalty to the Crown made active instead of passive. The Corps gave no offence to any interest, and even at full strength would not trespass upon the recruiting area of the fighting forces, because we were all past military age, weather-beaten veterans beyond toleration by any medical officer.[42]

The one man that many disapproved of was their Founder.

In spite of Roger Pocock's protestations, there was no way that such an organisation which declared itself independent of all official control, which elected its leaders by democratic ballot, and which had the totally unacceptable Founder at its head would be granted the status it wished. As Christopher Andrew wrote, the constant bombardment of letters and 'information' from the Legion with the pressure of the popular press had to have an effect: 'The assorted naval, invasion and spy scares of late Edwardian England threw into sharp relief the deficiencies of Britain's intelligence system.'[43] The government appointed a subcommittee of the Committee of Imperial Defence, which had been set up in 1902 after the South African War. Major-General Ewart, the D.M.O., appointed Major Edmonds as head of MO5. As we have seen, Edmonds was a friend of Le Queux and some of the Legion 'intelligence stories' started to make Edmonds think. Once Captain Vernon Kell became head of the new Secret Service Bureau in August 1909, the Legion stories were looked at far more analytically.

In October 1908, the Foreign Office passed on to the War Office a letter they had received from Sir E. Serjeant of the Legion of Frontiersmen (Serjeant was to succeed Roger as Commissioner a year later) offering the services of the Legion to assist in the prevention of gun-running in Morocco or elsewhere. Serjeant said he was 'in the habit of furnishing information obtained from members of the Legion to the India Office'.⁴⁴ The War Office had a standard reply to enquiries about the Legion and gave this to the Foreign Office. They pointed out that the Legion of Frontiersmen was a civilian organisation and not recognised. The passing of information to Naval Intelligence, India Office, Foreign Office and War Office meant that government departments who enjoyed considerable rivalry all felt that the Legion was out of control and were unsure how much trust to place in what they received.

Even had the Legion been co-operating with the War Office, the Army must certainly have been upset with some of the Legion's 'exercises'. The Legion had offered the use of their scouts on manoeuvres, but in spite of the experience on offer, this had been refused. There had been little co-operation with the military. The Birmingham *Gazette and Express* of 8 April 1907 reported the results of a one hundred-mile ride staged across country over two days. The two teams were composed of officers and men of the Birmingham Command of the Legion of Frontiersmen and officers of the 1st Warwickshire Volunteer Artillery. When it came to military exercises, the Army was not prepared to let the Legion take part, but Orde's Northern Command learned of one to be carried out in his area. A 'Pretender to the Throne' had landed and was making his way inland and sections of the Territorials were sent out to capture him. The Legion decided to take unofficial part and their training skills, and the experience of many members as Scouts in South Africa, made them ideal for this type of anti-insurgency action. They decided that 'pretenders' would be certain to be thirsty, so they stationed men at all strategic public houses. They actually found the 'pretender' and dragged him off, justifiably protesting vigorously, to local Legion headquarters much to the fury of the local Army Commander. They increased the Army's anger by interfering in another exercise and finding the headquarters camp before the searching Territorials, dismantling the tents and carrying off some apoplectic Staff Officers. At that time the Northern Commandant of the Territorial Army was Lt Gen. Robert Baden-Powell. His opinion of the antics of the Legion of Frontiersmen is not recorded.⁴⁵

February 1908 brought success and defeat. Success came when Pocock went to Ipswich on the 8th and E.G. Pretyman, who had been Civil Lord of the Admiralty in the earlier Conservative Government when he had worked well with Prince Louis when D.N.I., agreed to become Area Commandant.⁴⁶ Problems came from Sir Henry Seton Kerr, who had worked at recruiting a Sharpshooters Corps of the Imperial Yeomanry for South Africa. He was used to dealing with officers and gentlemen and we are given the strongest impression that he disapproved of ex-Corporal Pocock leading the Legion and the sooner he was replaced the better. Seton-Kerr had his way to a certain extent when, on 13 February, Roger's resignation was accepted at an Executive Meeting, but he was appointed with the same rank for purely promotional work and recruiting. This was probably a sensible move by the Executive Council as at first sight the new Chief Executive Officer, Major Patrick Forbes, was a good choice. In fact Roger and Forbes soon became friends, and Forbes was well known in the right circles. The Annual Report of that year gave the Legion strength at around three thousand five hundred, and even the War Office file on the Legion commented that the Legion quoted many very well-known names as members. The War Office would not 'recognise' the Legion, but after much consideration regarding the influence of the Legion's supporters, decided to write to all their Commands and ask their opinions of the Legion of Frontiersmen. This they eventually did in 1910. By then, many senior officers had been involved in a brush or two with the Legion and its individual ideas. Reactions were in most cases unfavourable. The Adjutant-General wrote that he considered the Legion 'a harmful and essentially unmilitary organisation'.[47] As a result of the War Office enquiries, a new paragraph, 449A, was inserted into King's Regulations in June 1910. Anyone on active service was forbidden to take cognisance of any private organisation of a military character. All Commands were informed by letter that this paragraph was aimed at the Legion of Frontiersmen in particular. Paragraph 449A was continued as 518 in King's Regulations, 1926. It seems that even 'taking cognisance' was to be considered as unsuitable and the War Office were moving even further away from the recognition the Legion so desired. Even so, the War Office continued to take a deep interest in the Legion and its activities and kept a substantial file of them, and in spite of everything, was pleased to take the Frontiersmen as a named unit of the Army at the beginning of the First War.

Let us return to 1908 and the intriguing case of Major Patrick Forbes. According to Roger, he was the 'conqueror of Rhodesia' who became a magistrate in Salisbury (now Harare). Writing in the *Canadian Frontiersman* magazine in 1941 a few months before his death, Roger said, 'A report reached Forbes that a Portuguese Military Mission was in British territory, busy swearing in the native chiefs as subjects of Portugal. Forbes took nineteen troopers and rode hard for Messakessie, where he found the kraal held by five hundred infantry. He charged through them, caught Colonel Andrada swearing in the Chiefs, arrested him and his Staff Officers and sent them down as prisoners to Capetown'. This led to an international unpleasantness.

> Long years afterwards when Forbes was Chief Executive of the Legion (1908), a dirty scrap of paper came in by post, with news from Lisbon. A hired murderer had been engaged at the Palace of the Necessidades as valet to His Majesty Dom Manoel II. 'I think', said I, 'that this might interest the Portuguese Minister.' 'Go to the Marquis de Soveral,' said Forbes, and off I went in a blinding fog to the Portuguese Legation, where the Minister granted me an audience. 'I'd better report, Sir,' said I, 'that I am sent here as representing Major Patrick Forbes.' 'Go back,' answered de Soveral, ' and tell the good Major that we bear no malice.'
>
> De Soveral was an intimate friend of King Edward VII to whom he reported this action of the Legion of Frontiersmen in preventing the assassination of the reigning sovereign. King Edward told the War Office

> to grant us a gift of three hundred pounds, and put Lord Esher in charge of Legion affairs.[48]

Roger told the story in print more than once without apparent contradiction, although he wrote in 1941 without first consulting his old diaries where he had recorded the gift as £500 a year. His part of the story can be accepted as truth, but the subsidy was almost certainly withdrawn in the light of subsequent events. He was slightly adrift with his year also, because his pocket diary records him calling on de Soveral on 27 January 1909: Big fog.'[49] In fact Lord Esher in his diary also comments on the thick fog on that day.[50] Major Forbes is one of three men who played a part in the history of the old Rhodesia whose stories are repeated with pride by the Frontiersmen. The other two are F.C. Selous, who comes into the story of the Legion with the 25th Fusiliers (Frontiersmen) in the First War, and F.R. Burnham.[51] Although Roger and the Frontiersmen referred to Major Patrick Forbes as the 'Conqueror of Rhodesia', they did not mention Forbes' part in the 1893 war against Lobengula, King of the Ndebele. Forbes led a joint column from Salisbury and Victoria which, after two battles, entered Bulawayo in triumph. On 14 November the famous (or infamous, depending on your opinion) Dr Jameson sent Forbes with a mounted force to capture Lobengula. Forbes with 160 men arrived wet and exhausted on the banks of the Shangani River, only a day's march away from Lobengula. Forbes sent out a patrol of 15 men under Major Allan Wilson before dusk on a scouting mission, but, thinking he could capture the King himself, Wilson disobeyed orders and sent back for reinforcements. Instead of recalling him because it was now dark, Forbes sent Wilson a further 21 men under Captain Borrow. This only served to encourage Wilson in his recklessness. During the night the river rose and next morning Forbes' men heard heavy firing, but the river had become impossible to cross. Forbes was short of food and had to retreat towards Bulawayo. It was not until some two months later that the story was pieced together with the help of a captured Ndebele warrior. Wilson and his men had fought to their last cartridge and it was said that, when their ammunition ran out, they sang the National Anthem as they waited for death. The legend of the Shangani Patrol lived on in white Rhodesian history and many a painting depicted the heroic last stand. The bodies of the Patrol were eventually recovered and interred in the Matapos close to the graves of Rhodes and Jameson themselves. Forbes took the blame for the massacre and was banished to be a Deputy Administrator in the far North East of Northern Rhodesia. Modern thinking blames Jameson for sending Forbes, but as the man on the spot Forbes must be seen as a major culprit. The Shangani Patrol had not been forgotten 14 years on, even in England, and the discredited Major Patrick Forbes was not a person to be looked on by the War Office with any sort of favour as Commandant-General (the far more splendid title which began to take over from Commissioner as soon as Roger had to relinquish it) of the Legion of Frontiersmen.[52]

Had the Legion's records not been lost in the bombing of London, we might have found more about the £300 gift. The War Office only records their constant battles with this thorn in their flesh, and, had the money been actually paid, it would have come from a secret account. Roger stated categorically that he tried to return one cheque for £100 personally to Lord Esher in 1909 after Roger had been expelled from the Legion.[53] Lord Esher was Chairman of the Esher Committee, which re-modelled the Army and set up the Territorial Army. He was a friend of de Soveral and very close to the King. He became deeply involved with trying to sort out the Legion in 1909 when the in-fighting became intense. The result, which was Roger Pocock's expulsion, was in hindsight good for the Legion in the long run. However, 1909 and its traumas left Driscoll with a massive rebuilding which he completed with honour. The Legion had its own 'Intelligence Department' and one could be forgiven for feeling that it had taken Le Queux's *Invasion of 1910* as its gospel. It was not only the *Daily Mail* that warned of the German menace. The Frontiersman influence on writers and journalists was seen in many popular newspapers – Marlowe at the *Mail* and R.D. Blumenfeld, another keen Frontiersman, editor of the *Daily Express*. Another journalist and possibly a member of the Legion in its early days, Hamilton Fyfe, gave his opinion: 'Blumenfeld, who gave German spy stories prominence in the *Express* … He complained that whenever he called attention to the system of espionage which was openly carried on, he was "assailed by the Radicals and called a mischief-maker".'[54] Blumenfeld himself referred to another Frontiersman and journalist H.A. Gwynne 'the Editor of the Diehard *Morning Post*, a man who rises in the morning dreaming of knights in armour, barons, landlords and masters, …'.[55] The Intelligence Department claimed many counter-espionage successes, although vivid imaginations must have played their part. They claimed to have captured a German spy on a hill overlooking Leeds. Frontiersmen had great fun at restaurants pretending to talk military secrets and collecting 'quite a buzz of attendance'. A Frontiersman who spoke German would order a 'waiter-spy' to name his reporting station and 'with a click of the heels they would respond'. They found and reported to the War Office a nest of machine-guns, five thousand rifles and some ammunition in City Road, London E.C.1 'which may have belonged to Russian revolutionists'. They also found another cache under a hotel in Bournemouth; elsewhere a supply of brassards ready and waiting for the German spies to put on when the German army attacked.[56] By the time Captain Vernon Kell had begun the work of MI5 on Monday, 23 August 1909, the Legion reports of 'spies' to the War Office had become a flood, sent in by the many enthusiastic amateurs of the Legion of Frontiersmen. Another chronicler of the Secret Service, John Bulloch wrote:

> After four months, Kell had so much to do that he asked to be provided with a clerk to assist him … It was then known as MO5 in the War Office. Later, when its work had to be mentioned in the courts or in Parliament, it

was called the 'security service', and later still, it achieved an air of glamour and mystery as MI5. But in December 1909 it was strictly a one-man affair which had produced no tangible results.[57]

Kell's notes in MI5 files make a number of references to the Legion of Frontiersmen.

> June 6th 1910. Met M & L at Temple offices 10.30. Told L I would like him to join the Legion of Frontiersmen. M had a talk with me about suspicious Germans. Went to see Major Jarvis of the London Territorial Force, Craigs Court, who is in touch with the horse contractor at whose school so many Germans learn to ride. He said he would find out where all these foreigners come from. This is a matter that Lord Esher asked us to investigate. [Roger reported meetings with Jarvis on 13th and 14th January, 1909]
>
> General Ewart the DMO also asked me to see what use the Legion of Frontiersmen along the coast might be in time of war. I told him that I had got L to join and should instruct him to find out and make a list of suitable men.
>
> July 5th. Met L at the office and explained to him that I wanted to keep the expenses [travelling] down to a minimum ... He is going to visit Brighton, Ipswich and Yarmouth and get in touch with the Legion of Frontiersmen there.
>
> July 22nd. I saw L at the officers [club] on his return from the East Coast where he had been trying to get in touch with some of the Legion of Frontiersmen in those parts. He submitted a report which I attach, 1, 2, 3, 12 & 14 might be worth noting. I will enter them among my likely agents.
>
> July 28th. Saw DMO in afternoon gave them L's opinion of the Legion of Frontiersmen.
>
> July 29th. New DMO General Wilson. Copy of L's report was attached but not here.[58]

What was to become MI6 as we know it was begun on 1 October 1909 under Naval officer Mansfield Cumming.

> ... the two men were quite different ... Kell was quieter, more studied and tactful, perhaps more bureaucratically wily ... Kell was never formally senior to Cumming but there is little doubt that, in War Office eyes, his part in the SSB was the more important, and this is reflected in Cumming's diary ... The fact that Kell was already embedded in the War Office intelligence machinery doubtless made a difference; Cumming, despite coming under War Office direction, seems to have been seen as a sea-boot in the door on the part of the old rival.[59]

The Legion had decided that most intelligence reports that came in from overseas should be sent to the Foreign Office, and it is possible that departmental rivalry would have prevented many of these getting to Cumming. In any case, we can see that the Legion managed to upset Supt. Quinn, of Special Branch, who worked closely with Kell. One of the letters sent to the Foreign Office by Roger Pocock in March 1909 claimed that Ellerman Liners sailing to Egypt were taking war materials marked as 'gas piping'. In a footnote to a letter telling the story, Supt. Quinn wrote: 'There is a good deal of fantastical matter in this letter and very few facts. Reckless charges are made against the Police without any show of proof to substantiate them. This kind of information might be suitable for newspaper copy but for practical police work it is valueless.'[60] A Legion leaflet from the 1920s made many claims about the Legion's intelligence gathering:

> During the pre-war period they discovered and reported a new secret base in the Caroline Islands. They reported German attempts to establish a base in North-East Africa to cut our communications with India. They surveyed the Kiel Canal with a view to blowing it up in the event of war; reported systems of gun-running which supplied the Pathans in Afghanistan for the purpose of war with India and the Young Egyptian party for revolt; suppressed a number of illegal expeditions mainly directed against South and Central America; discovered an artful attempt to cheat the British Government out of an African Province where gold had just been found; charted the Elbe defences and mine fields.[61]

This volume of information of extremely variable quality and value was something that no Government department or service knew how to deal with. What the Legion had done was to reflect a changing world and show what could be done, although an independent and self-governing body of amateurs was not the right way of going about matters. The Legion had showed 'the road for the rest' (Kipling) and the infant organisations being set up by Kell and Cumming gradually placed the Intelligence and Counter-Intelligence services on a sensible footing. Kell and Cumming's departments also placed these duties firmly under the control of the British Government.

The Legion claimed that its greatest feat of intelligence was the responsibility of Hugh Pollard, the First War story of the 'phantom Russian Army', although we would consider this and other Pollard stories to be propaganda rather than intelligence. Pollard was one of Roger's friends, another Frontiersman journalist of their 'Intelligence Department'. He was the epitome of a Frontiersman although much of his life remains a mystery. 'Pollard looked, and occasionally behaved, like a German Crown Prince and had the habit of letting off revolvers in any office which he happened to visit. When I asked him once if he had ever killed anybody, he replied, "never accidentally".'[62] In 1937, Douglas Jerrold was to involve Pollard in the bringing back of Franco from the Canaries to Morocco. Jerrold passionately believed that the Communists had been responsible for many appalling atrocities and that Jerrold's action had been correct, but this was to cause both him and Pollard much pain over the following years. Pollard's cousin, Ivor Montagu, wrote about Pollard in his autobiography:

> His slightly cynical air and knowing smile, his constant traveller's tales, made him the hero of his younger kinsmen. What adventures he had had! What places he had been to, and what events he had seen! He had been with bandits in Mexico, reported rebellions in Algeria. He handled, and showed us, pistols; even gave father a book he had written about them. In the First War he was with Intelligence ... How we laughed at his cleverness when he told us how his department had launched the account of the German corpse factories and of how the Hun was using the myriads of trench war casualties for making soap and margarine. He explained he had originally thought up the idea himself to discredit the enemy among the population of Oriental countries ... To the surprise of the authorities it had caught on, and they were now making propaganda out of it everywhere.[63]

In a very brief history of the Legion of Frontiersmen that Roger wrote for the *Canadian Frontiersmen* in 1941, Roger told the tale of how the Phantom Army story was started. This story is often quoted, and the origins have puzzled many researchers. Having served in Intelligence, Hugh Pollard was a very secretive man and would have told this tale to very few people, so he has apparently never been publicly named as the originator:

> In the early days of the last war, three Frontiersmen were having tea at the Cottage Tea Rooms in the Strand. Hugh Pollard and Alan Osler were friends of mine, but I forget the third. They thought it would be a jolly good thing if a Russian Army of, say, three thousand men were to be embarked at Archangel and brought through our island to cut in behind Von Kluck's army as it invaded France. All three were journalists, and they got the story into the newspapers as having actually happened. [Both were working for the *Daily Express* at the time]. The War Office adopted the 'Phantom Army' and provided a hundred trains with whitewashed windows on each of four trunk lines. [The War Office were assisted by Colonel Roustam Beg, a Russian Kurd.] An embarkation staff of actual Russian officers was equipped by the theatrical costumiers, and a [barrister] friend of mine who owned a Rolls-Royce car was their chauffeur between Bristol and Avonmouth. Three hundred bearded Newfoundlanders were marched from King's Cross Station to London Bridge, again and again all night for four whole nights, coming back by Underground. But the greatest feat of lying was Hugh Pollard's special invention of the charwoman who knew it was them 'Roosians' because she had swept the snow out of their carriages. There were at the time 43 German wireless transmitters in London, which sent on the news to Germany. That was why Von Kluck's army was deflected on Paris, away from the channel ports. That saved the

channel for the movement of our army. The 'Phantom Army' was the greatest feat of Legion Intelligence.[64]

The additions in brackets are from some of Roger's other writings on the story. The exact claim of 'forty-three German wireless transmitters' immediately makes us wonder how much embroidery had been added over the years to what was a basically true story. The 'Phantom Army' certainly caused much excitement, as such good propaganda should, and fed on itself, being added to by people all over the country. The newspapers were divided as to whether they encouraged the rumour or denied it. An eventual official denial did not convince everyone because governments are expected to lie in time of war.

PRO file HD3/139 in The National Archives records a number of letters sent to the Foreign Office by Roger Pocock. On 13 November 1908, he forwarded a letter from J.B. Tighe, Butte, Montana asking for mercenaries (for where is not mentioned) and thanking for information on de Hora, who we must assume was now abroad somewhere in search of adventure.

27 January 1909 Marquis Ivrea – an obscure continental title not recognised in Britain, but an advantage to yet another journalist – applied for 500 Frontiersmen to serve as filibusters in Portugal. There was no way that the British Government wanted armed mercenaries in that friendly country, so Ivrea was dropped from the list of membership of the Legion. He turns up again in the First War serving as a Major in the army. Information on gunrunning was supplied by Edward Else of Forest Gate. He reported a gunrunning syndicate to revolutionaries in Columbia and also to the North-West Frontier. He claimed a leakage of Scotland Yard information through an Inspector Froest or a friend of his. This was another claim that would have annoyed Supt. Quinn: 22 May 1909: 'Enclosed is a letter from R. Bate our O.C. Newchwang & is guarded in expression because letters are tampered with on the Trans-Siberian railway. It may be intelligible to the Chinese dept. of your office.'[65]

Four
THE SECRET GOVERNMENT SUBSIDY

The Legion was usually very short of money. Not many of its wealthy members seemed to care to put their hands deep into their pockets. On 19 March 1909 Roger wrote to the Foreign Office, 'The Legion has not many weeks to live, unless we can get help'.[1] He also referred them to an article in the *Telegraph* reporting on the capture of gunrunners. On 10 May 1909 the distinguished and highly regarded Military Correspondent of *The Times*, Colonel Repington, wrote an article on Territorial Forces. The writer came out in support of the Legion. He wrote 'It is not in principle a sound thing to disseminate effort by creating semi-military bodies outside the accepted military organisation of the Country, but some latitude may be allowed where such bodies were created before our present organisation took shape.'[2] He suggested that the Legion could work in with Rifle Clubs and Boy Scouts to provide a National Army of Second Line in Britain – in other words what we had in the Second War, a Home Guard. He also suggested that the Legion of Frontiersmen should have a Government subsidy of £1,000 a year as it was short of money. Three days later, Roger sent a letter to the Foreign Office to back up this request. It could be that Colonel Repington had friends in the Legion, but this article was a Godsend to Roger. It was time for help from his sister, who wrote a letter to *The Times*.[3] As well as being very well known as Lena Ashwell the actress, she had by now married Mr Henry Simson, a surgeon well regarded in the highest society. He had operated on her and, in absolute storybook fashion, she had fallen in love with her doctor. Although she was an actress and divorced, he fell deeply in love with her and the marriage was apparently a happy one. He was later to become appointed to the then Duchess of York and helped bring our present Queen and later Princess Margaret into the world. He received a knighthood. Lena Ashwell had ventured into management backed by American money, taking over the Kingsway Theatre, where she opened with *Irene Wycherly* to a blaze of publicity. With true artistic temperament, she was later to fall out with her backers and lose the theatre. The Kingsway had originally been the Great Queen Street Theatre. She had some notable successes at the Kingsway. Lord Esher wrote in his journal on 14 February 1908, 'Saw Miss Ashwell in a very original fresh kind of play, about the young work-girls of London'.[4]

9 *Frontiersman William D. Kemp.*

This was *Diana of Dobsons* by Cecily Hamilton. Lena Ashwell had come to the Legion's aid before. She had organised a Garden Fete in the grounds of the Botanical Gardens, Regents Park on the night of 10 July 1906 and had attracted some well-known performers, including Albert Chevalier.[5] An example of the extraordinary influence exerted by the Legion occurs in the Empire Day entertainment organised by the Legion on 24 May 1907 in front of an audience of 2000 people in Regents Park which was reported in the

Northern Command magazine: 'Fifty of the leading swordsmen in England, under the direction of the greatest of English swordsmen, Captain Alfred Hutton, gave a display of combat in all ages. Two of our London Command men Captain Graham Hope, R.A. and Mr R.A. Smith, fought in suits of plate armour, weighing over 70lbs. The whole spectacle was one of great interest and beauty.'[6] One is left to wonder whether another voluntary and independent organisation since then has been able to organise a fund-raising event in Regents Park with '85 regiments being represented' and also 'the famous band of the Coldstream Guards' attending?[7]

Lena Ashwell was just the person to start an appeal and in response to that article in *The Times* her letter appeared on 13 May 1906, saying that the Legion needed £700 a year. She offered £50 of that if others would subscribe. She asked that the money be sent to her at the Kingsway Theatre. *The Times* would soon learn that the Legion always made the most of any opportunity, and on 15 May an article appeared headed 'Legion of Frontiersmen':

> We have learnt with some surprise that the following appeal has been somewhat widely circulated:
>
> 'May 12th, 1909, Private and Urgent.
>
> A patriotic fund is to be opened under the auspices of *The Times* to finance the Legion of Frontiersmen. Support is being organised on a large scale, but in the meantime interest must be sustained. Mr Roger Pocock appeals to his personal friends and asks anybody who cares for the welfare of the Legion to get sums of money from one shilling upwards with letters in support addressed to Miss Lena Ashwell, Kingsway Theatre.'
>
> The statement 'a patriotic fund under the auspices of *The Times*' is entirely unfounded and Mr Pocock has expressed his sincere regret for circulating it. All *The Times* has done is to publish Miss Ashwell's letter which it will be seen, Sir Henry Seton-Karr supports.[8]

There followed a letter of support from the Chairman of the Executive Council of the Legion, Sir Henry Seton-Karr of 47 Chester Square. He said there were 3,000 members, 2,500 of whom had seen active service. If required, 75 per cent of them could ride and shoot. They were guides, linguists, scouts, pioneers etc. Seton-Karr said there were two main objections raised to the Legion. The first was that they would interfere with recruiting for the regular or territorial forces. He answered this by saying that they did not seek young men with no frontier experience at all. All the Legion publicity, even in later years, encouraged such men to join the regulars or territorials. The second objection was that such an organisation was unnecessary as in time of war all such men would flock to the standard. Seton-Karr considered that it was far better to organise first. He had seen too much haphazard recruiting in the South African War. His final paragraph was that 'While military authorities and the War Office look kindly on us, the Government have refused to assist us.'[9] He was very much wrong there, and in any case, every time they wrote to the War Office, the Legion insisted that they were 'self-governing and self-supporting' and always made a point that they were not asking for money. The publicity seems to have had its desired effect and sufficient money was raised by public subscription to keep them going for a while.

Still the moves went on behind the scenes to oust Roger Pocock, even though losing him would mean losing also the powerful and public support of Lena Ashwell. His departure from the helm did, in fact, bring an increase in numbers and from 3,500 in 1909 the Legion membership world-wide had risen to an estimated 14,500 by the start of the First War, thanks in a large measure to Driscoll. Why were some members so keen to force Pocock out of the Legion he had formed? We know his personality was at fault and he was not a strong enough character nor ruthless enough to stamp out any opposition. Roger Pocock was prepared to agree that, although Driscoll was a great leader, he accentuated the differences between the range men and the military men:

> In the autumn of 1907, Lt Col D.P. Driscoll joined the Legion and never was a man so welcome ... I knew Colonel Driscoll as an honourable man, unselfish, with a gift of leadership which I solely lacked. Yet perhaps, in those days, I had more actual experience of Legion work, and of the deadly need of caution in recruiting. A body of ex-soldiers has been trained, through discipline, for fighting. A body of range men has been trained, through necessity, for field intelligence. The recruiting of a force of ex-soldiers in London offended the range men and checked the growth. Driscoll was a military man, and favoured ex-soldiers as recruits. Personally I favoured the range type, and men of the frontier. Men whose success depended on their intelligence of conditions. At least, so far, the Legion's work had been mainly Intelligence work for the War Department.[10]

Here we have a recipe for some more problems. Driscoll was busy recruiting ex-soldiers in London and starting to change the emphasis in the Legion from Intelligence to guerrilla training, whereas out in the Empire the recruits were all range men, adventurers like Roger who made their living in the outposts of the world. Roger always claimed that, if it had not been for these range Frontiersmen, the First War would have started earlier. According to Roger, the delay was due to their vigilance as vedettes watching the frontiers and reporting back any impending crisis that could have escalated into war. He wrote that the ten years from 1904 to 1914 were exceptional in the general peace on the frontiers, the quietest ten years for a very long time. 'We had set the whole of the wolf pack to guard the sheep.'[11] As we have seen, Roger Pocock was often inclined to exaggeration, but the Legion of Frontiersmen was the first real peacetime attempt to organise and band together the adventurers who abounded in the Victorian and Edwardian times.

Still seeing spies in every quarter, Roger was convinced that the military men who were so opposed to that bounder Pocock included German spies or pro-Germans.

> I received a message from the War Office, forbidding me to quote authority, but naming two prominent members as German spies who were financing the London Command in a campaign for my overthrow. Concerning one of these men I think the War Office was mistaken, but concerning the other I found evidence that the Authorities were right. 'Get rid of them at once', said the War Office, but they gave me no authority or the slightest aid.
>
> Driscoll believed in all his men, was loyal to them, as they were loyal to him. I couldn't convince him of the danger that existed. Personally they were quite friendly to 'Old Pocock', but politically resolved to drive me out of office. They were defeated at the Annual Meeting of 1908, but were sure of success at the Meeting of 1909. To Driscoll I might have yielded, but not to men controlled by German spies ...[12]

Sir Henry Seton-Karr was the ringleader of those trying to expel Roger, although to suggest that this barrister and highly patriotic Conservative Member of Parliament had anything to do with German spies was totally ridiculous. The battle went on and on, with Roger fighting an increasingly desperate and losing action against a domineering man used to getting his own way, certainly in the case of a man of a lower social class. The trouble with lawyers was that their opinions were usually opposed to what Roger wanted to do, or thought was morally right. He commented about the soldiers who now composed a large proportion of the London Command:

> ... it was Counsel's opinion, and supposedly Common Law, that this body of excellent ex-soldiers, being able to vote at an annual meeting, had the full right and power to expel the Executive, and take possession of Legion Headquarters. The Provincial and Overseas Command, unable to attend an Annual Meeting in force, had no rights whatever, in fact were totally disenfranchised. My plea for a postal ballot was ridiculed by the lawyers whose brains had been extracted in infancy.[13]

He never wrote the name, but was referring to Seton-Karr as closely as he could. Roger infuriated the Council even more when a minor magazine *Modern Man* published an article attacking the Legion in February 1909. Instead of ignoring it, as it would be seen by very few, Roger replied and got into a ridiculous argument with the writer which culminated in the suggestion of a duel with swords on the Belgian coast, where duelling was still legal. A General Purposes Committee meeting of the Legion on 11 March attacked Roger for his stupidity and *Modern Man* got all the mileage it could from the affair. Roger tried to persuade General Sir Henry Hildyard, who had been G.O.C. South Africa from 1905-1908, to become Commandant-General, but he wisely declined. The rift in the Legion got deeper. Roger went to see Lord Esher, who he maintained was in charge of the £300 a year grant to the Legion, personally authorised by the King, and set to watch over it. Lord Esher gave him a long lecture on how to control the Legion, and then told Roger to give all the details of the troubles to a friend of Esher's. That friend had a German sounding name and a German sounding accent. By now a distressed Roger was becoming almost paranoid.[14]

Roger Pocock's pocket diary tells the story of his final actions as the prime mover of the Legion. 'Friday 11th June, 1909. 11 a.m. Esher's secretary told me to call at 3. At 3 p.m. Esher said that subject to abolition of Council and appointment of his nominee as Commandant-General, he would grant £500 a year for 1 year trial. I to have £300 a year. Wired Forbes. Wrote S-K [Seton-Karr] demanding dissolution of Council'[15]

Only five days earlier, Esher had written in reply to Lord Roberts, who was advocating compulsory national service.

> After all, the naval and military professions, the profession of arms, at the root of which lies the obligation to die for your country, are the most honorable of all – and that they should be based upon the willingness of a man to come forward, rather than upon compelling him, is an ideal worth contending for, and not be submerged without reluctance.[16]

The notion of voluntary service, as practised by the Legion of Frontiersmen, meets therefore with the approval of Lord Esher, even if the way it was run left a lot to be desired. What is surprising are the sums of money being granted to the Legion, particularly when compared with the apparent shoestring budgets of Kell and Cumming when they started their new organisations. It also shows the access that the King and Lord Esher and his committees had to secret funds. The immediacy of notes written on the day in a pocket diary show the truth of the story and parts of it were confirmed later by Roger in his writings without contradiction.

His diary continues:

> Saturday 12th June, 1909. Wrote to various of the Council. Tamed Driscoll completely. 5.50 to Cookham to find Col. Ricardo, Esher's nominee. All my wolves are smiling now because I gave them the Council to eat instead of me – bless 'em. Called on Col. Ricardo at Cookham, first impression bad appointment.

> Sunday 13th June. 10 a.m. Submitted Legion scheme to Col. Ricardo for one hour. Considering. Loafed all day at Cookham.[17]

On 17 June, Roger wrote to the Foreign Office with further information from Newchwang and added:

> There can be no harm in my telling you privately that under Lord Esher's powerful guidance and with his very generous help, I have made arrangements which next Thursday will dissolve the Council of the Legion in favour of a retired soldier as Commandant-General. Subject to these conditions an income of £500 a year will be provided – one year's test, so that we are no longer in financial trouble.[18]

One can feel that there was indeed every harm in Roger telling the Foreign Office about this subsidy to a purely private and self-governing organisation, even with considerable strings attached. It was supposed to be a secret subsidy and one can imagine the opinion of the Foreign Office when they received this letter. 'Friday 9th July, 1909. As instructed by Esher per Quick. Went to Cookham lunched with Ricardo arranged for his meeting the Council on Friday next; got Todd to write notice & office to issue it. Esher orders me to meet Sir Francis Frittell at Bath Club. I advocate salary for Driscoll.'[19] Esher began to work further behind the scenes: 'Tuesday 14th July, ... 4 Chief Constables came to call. Wednesday 14th July ... Called Esher, sent to Sir Evelyn Wood at War Office, asked him to nominate.'[20] Col Ricardo refused the position on that day, and who could blame him? In any case, recent researches have suggested that Ricardo was the man whom Kenneth Grahame used as the model for Toad of Toad Hall.[21] While many Frontiersmen were eccentrics, Ricardo's eccentricities would not have given him suitable authority to command this diverse body of men. 'Friday 16th July ... Morning interview Driscoll & Smith, Senior Chief Constable Warde.'[22] This was Lt Col Henry Warde, Chief Constable of Kent from 1895-1921. It must have been Esher's influence which caused a number of Chief Constables to call at the Legion Headquarters in Adam Street. File MEPO 2 1193 in The National Archives reports the Legion writing to Scotland Yard to say they had a request from a police constable for permission to join. The reply was that there were 'substantial objections – difficulty in adjusting duties – impossible to spare more than a limited number of men in time of war. ... it is a purely private organisation and, that being so, it is perhaps undesirable to recognise it by granting permission.'[23] A casual observer could feel that the same comments could be made about the Freemasons, but there has never apparently been any objection to a policeman joining them.

A fortnight later, Esher appointed Commander Hamilton Currey as Commandant-General – perhaps in desperation? Currey was from the North-East and it was doubtful how much support he would have in London. In any case, other than as an author, he was not really a well-known figure nationally, although he was one of the earliest members of the Legion. 'Wednesday 28th July, Esher appointed Currey in charge of L.F. and handed over £500 a year.'[24] Probably the most important of Esher's two actions that day was the handing over of the £500 which gave financial stability for a while. We are left to wonder how close did Britain come to employing the enthusiastic amateurs of the Legion of Frontiersmen, rather than the professionals who became MI5 and MI6. The Legion held an Annual General Meeting at the end of August. The War Office was watching the internal politics of the Legion with a horrified fascination and their files in The National Archives report that the meeting was 'a scene of wild disorder'.[25] Roger got up and announced that, as no invitation had been given to the Northern Command or to the various overseas commands, the meeting was unlawful. He invited all present to the annual meeting of the Northern Command at Scarborough the next day and, followed by his friends Orde, the Northern Commandant, and Harry Fife Scott, walked out. The strain must have been telling on them all, because on the train north, Orde appeared to suffer a mild heart attack.[26] Nevertheless, they were able to hold their Northern meeting under canvas. The Legion sorted out the various niceties of their rules and convened a second 'Annual General Meeting of 1909' in September at Chandos Hall. Roger spent much of the intervening weeks camped out in Wembley Park. He wanted to avoid the risk of bumping into any of the members and was also using his preferred medicine for all ills, life in the open air. On 20 September, orders came from Esher to do nothing until 1 November, but the meeting was finally held on 15 October. Roger attended the meeting in civilian dress, saying he was afraid that what was to come would disgrace the uniform he prided, but probably because he knew the result was inevitable. The Council had made sure there would be no repeat of the August events and Roger Pocock was expelled from the Legion and replaced by Sir William E. Serjeant. With a beautiful piece of logic, the Officer Commanding Dublin Command proposed that no-one else should be offered the position of 'Founder of the Legion'.[27] So Roger Pocock remained on Legion headed paper as Founder. Lord Esher was probably relieved at the change, but the upheavals were sufficient to put an end to further subsidies. Roger's sisters went in the deep of night to Legion Headquarters and removed all the papers they thought were of relevance. They did not seem to think they were acting unlawfully. To them, and particularly to Lena Ashwell, Roger Pocock *was* the Legion of Frontiersmen.

In addition to the departure of Roger Pocock, the Legion also parted company with Seton-Karr. The new Commandant-General, Col Sir William Eldon Serjeant, also a barrister, set out with Driscoll to revitalise the Legion. A South African War veteran, Serjeant had commanded the 5th Battalion The Rifle Brigade, and they apparently made a good team. The Executive Council still included influential names such as The Rt Hon. Lord Elphinstone, the Earl of Meath, Viscount Mountmorres and Sir Francis Vane, and the General Council added Sir Eric Barrington, Prince Louis of Battenberg, the Earl of Onslow, General Sir Leslie Rundle, Sir Claude Champion de Crespigny, as well as men such as Rider Haggard and Cutcliffe Hyne. Sir Eric Barrington was a man of considerable influence. He was a long-time friend of Roger Pocock and his sister. He had entered the Foreign Office in 1867 and had been Private Secretary to, amongst others, Lord Salisbury and the Marquis of Lansdowne. He had retired from the Foreign Office in 1907 where he had ended his career as Assistant Under Secretary of State for Foreign Affairs. Here was a man with great knowledge of the Foreign Office and its ways and who would have been able to promote the interests of the Legion of Frontiersmen in very high circles. Sir Francis Vane is most interesting, as the February 1910 *Frontiersman* magazine reports that he was in command of the Legion's Cadet Yeomanry. Vane was a strange character who Baden-Powell had appointed London Commissioner of the Boy Scouts.

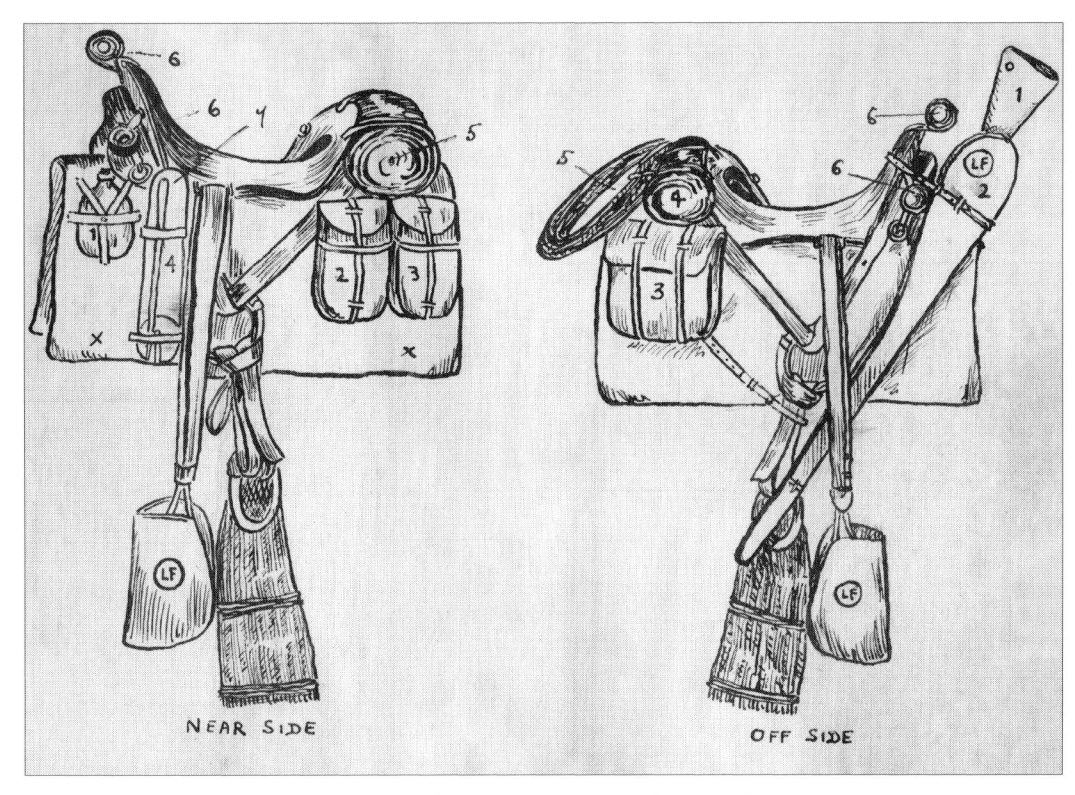

10 *Drawing of one-man outfit for a Frontiersmen by an unknown artist.*

Yet Vane, as Baden-Powell would discover, was a disconcerting man. As a serving officer in South Africa he had written a book criticising his own countrymen for their treatment of Boer civilians ... From the beginning Vane wanted to give his local councils the power to run their own affairs and to elect their officials rather than be dictated to by Elles (Sir Edmond Elles, Baden-Powell's Chief Commissioner). Because Sir Edmond was a member of the pro-conscription National Service League, Vane mistrusted him from their first meeting.[28]

Obviously Vane shared the democratic ideals of the Legion. In February 1910 Vane had just been dismissed from the Boy Scout movement after a very messy dispute. Vane accepted an invitation to be President of the British Boy Scouts, a breakaway organisation which during 1910 apparently had about 50,000 boys as members. 'The Vane revolt convinced Baden-Powell that if the Boy Scouts were ever to become a democratic organization he would always be in danger of being voted into a position of powerlessness akin to a constitutional monarch's ... '[29] No doubt also, Baden-Powell had seen what had happened to Roger Pocock in the democratic Legion of Frontiersmen.

While the Boy Scouts had *Scouting for Boys*, the Legion had produced *The Frontiersman's Pocket Book*, which was one of the books that was recommended reading in some editions of *Scouting for Boys*. *The Frontiersman's Pocket Book* was as much the vital handbook for the Legion as *Scouting for Boys* was for the Boy Scouts. It is quite a startling book, a virtual guerrilla warfare manual for Edwardian times. Roger had worked very hard in editing it. The first edition came out in 1909. It was re-printed in 1911 and is supposed to have received a third printing in 1914. It gives a good insight into Frontiersmen thinking, and is now rather rare. The book contains instructions on everything a man might need if he were alone or in a small group behind enemy lines. The publishers, John Murray, gave thought in the 1980s to republishing it as a curiosity, but the section on demolitions was far too explicit. It told how to blow up bridges, buildings, guns, railways, telegraph lines; how to manufacture various explosives and the amounts needed for different demolitions with the best spot to place them for optimum effect. Other sections showed identification of warships – French, German and British with silhouettes. It covers how to survive in extremes of heat and cold (apparently the most important thing seemed to be to keep the bowels open). With regard to cold, the book considered that warmth is not in clothing or housing, but in diet, as an adult needs 23 ounces of fat and sugar in each day's rations for carbon fuel in the body. The reader was advised to warm the blood and keep away from fire, but don't sweat out of doors and keep the pores of the skin open by cleanliness. The book is full of such useful tips as 'a good medicine for scurvy is the warm blood of a newly killed animal' or 'a piece of tape thirty inches long rubbed with mercurial ointment and hung round the neck is good for a month, when it should be renewed. It will keep lice off.'[30] If you do get troubled with lice, you should take off your clothes and lay them on an ant heap. Unfortunately, the book does not tell you how to get rid of the ants! Failing soap, one should rub or beat clothes in snow, although that would be of little help in the tropics. The book informs you how to find water and how to purify it, how to get food, how to trap animals, even the best way to kill a sheep with simple butchering. When you have killed your animal, you are told how to dress the skins and which of the sinews are best to use as threads for sewing. Weapons are discussed, as is self-defence; sailing is not left out, with an item by Erskine Childers on the sailing of small boats. The Legion was certainly forward thinking. Lord Montagu of Beaulieu wrote on the value of motor boats and S.F. Edge on motor cars and the possibility of their use as armoured cars and ambulances. Near the head of the alphabetical list of contributors to *The Frontiersman's Pocket Book* comes the name of Lt General R.S.S. Baden-Powell. This does not prove the deep involvement with the Legion that Roger and many other of the members would have liked. All that the Legion got from B-P was a small paragraph in the section on horses.

> Lt. General R.S.S. Baden-Powell has furnished us with the following corrective note, 'Letting a man sit side-saddle on a tired horse is the easiest way of giving it a sore back. At a walking gait it is far better for the rider

to dismount and walk ... frequent cantering and walking ... sugar and molasses in water are better than gruel for a tired horse.'[31]

There was one curious article by a lady, Elizabeth Robins, wrote on women and the frontier. She was an American and a noted beauty. She came to England at about the same time as Lena Ashwell returned, and made her name on the stage specialising in Ibsen roles. In Edwardian times she was concentrating on writing books. She was a friend of Henry James and also of the famous and nearly famous. She was already a widow when she arrived in England, although she was only a year or two older than Roger. She was probably one of Lena Ashwell's circle of friends. Elizabeth Robins wrote on the great problem of ladies clothes on the frontier (abjure the corset!) and what to do with long hair. Petticoats only get tangled in the undergrowth so it is better to wear 'knickerbockers' under the skirt. It would be of great advantage if they could be the same colour as the skirt.

In all, about seventy people were involved in the book as contributors. Barrister E.R. Bartley Denniss told all that would be needed about Marriage, Wills, Baptism, Death and Burial on the frontier and at sea, with the correct prayers for every occasion from the former Bishop of Tasmania. Bishop Montgomery had a more famous son. There would be no need to be bored in any spare time; 'how to make a fiddle' comes under the heading of amusements. All the Executive Council contributed and two further well-known names appear; Ernest Thompson Seton the naturalist, friend of Baden-Powell and founder of the 'Birch Bark Roll', the American boys' association of Scouting, and also F.C. Selous. In a letter written just before Selous joined the 25th Fusiliers (Frontiersmen) in 1915 and quoted in Millais' biography of him, Selous is reported to have said 'I know absolutely nothing about the Legion of Frontiersmen as far as service is concerned'.[32] Yet he was a contributor to the *Pocket Book*, and Roger Pocock reports dining with him and Driscoll at least once in 1911.

The preface to the *Pocket Book* says,

> The Legion of Frontiersmen is a civilian self-supporting and self-governing association, officially recognized [!] in the United Kingdom, Canada, Australia, South and East Africa and Bombay, as a means of securing for the State men of good character who have been trained in wild countries at sea or in war. The Council registers such men in view of their individual usefulness to a field force as guides, scouts, craftsmen and irregular mounted rifles ... For a man on the frontier in time of need, the conditions are: that he is broke and beyond reach of shops while he wants water, food, guidance, fire, shelter, clothing and equipment. Only a tenderfoot takes pride in dirt and disorder which he calls 'roughing it'. A real traveller is known by his cleanliness, method, health, speed and freedom from accident. He concentrates large efficiency into scant supplies and will not burden the army transport with his luggage on active service.[33]

In February 1910 there came a request to the War Office from the Legion of Frontiersmen, China, that they should have first call on any stored arms in any time of trouble (the Legion claims that the China Commands had their members in the fields rescuing Europeans during the Boxer Risings). The War Office pointed out that the Legion was, by its own admission, a civilian organisation and made some discreet further enquiries. It transpired later, according to their information, that the 'Far Eastern Command' consisted of only 32 men who were not prepared to take part in any officially organised scheme of local defence. On the other hand, a proposal in November 1911 that a separate unit of the Volunteer Reserve in East Africa should be known as the Legion of Frontiersmen unit – an idea that would hardly have caused any harm as long as the Frontiersmen were prepared to submit to standard discipline – was firmly nipped in the bud with a letter to the Colonial Office advising them to reconsider because of the 'unsatisfactory character of the Legion's organization and method.'[34] Driscoll had another shot at getting official recognition in March 1912, sending Colonel Seely at the War Office a mass of 'Intelligence Reports' (in inverted commas in War Office records). Needless to say, the request was refused. There is no doubting the keenness of the Frontiersmen.

The Legion had a clubhouse where Frontiersmen, including those who were visiting London, could try to replicate life on the frontier and forget the cares of London. It was situated in the Middlesex town of Shepperton and Roger Pocock used to visit there as often as he could. The Sunbury and Shepperton Local History Society published an article with my assistance in 1983 on what were, and still are, known as the 'Shepperton Cowboys'. If you have several postcards of old Shepperton there is a good chance one will depict the 'Cowboy Wedding' – a series of views of bride, groom and guests arriving and leaving Church Square were published of this event in 1908. Old residents recall that one of a group of 'cowboys' living in Green Lane married a local girl, and examination of the church register showed them to be Cecil Morgan and Emily Skelly (widow), married by the Rev. Gidney, Rector, on 8 December 1908; beyond this little seemed to be known about who the cowboys were, where they had come from, or where they went.

> A phone call and subsequent letters from Mr Geoffrey Pocock have added considerably to our knowledge ... I was able to tell him a little about the two log cabins which stood on the site of Duppa's Close ... The Green Lane settlement was 'The Imperial School of Colonial Instruction.'[35]

The principals were Captain Morgan and Evelyn ffrench who offered courses in '... All types of colonial craft ...'. Morgan was also the inventor of the 'Morgan Packsaddle cum boat'. The *Illustrated London News* for 25 April 1908 showed a drawing by W. Koekkoek of a demonstration of this extraordinary invention with a number of Frontiersmen demonstrating the various uses of it.

> Besides becoming a centre for the Legion of Frontiersmen, the Imperial School is believed to have been the home of 'El Desperadoes', a club of adventurous western minded men.
>
> Mounted cowboys became a common sight around Shepperton; after the wedding there was a mounted procession to a marquee for lunch. It was headed by Sir Henry Seton-Karr, a former big game hunter and M.P. … he was not in uniform but wore a light coloured cape and Homberg hat, making him noticeable in many photographs.[36]

Both Morgan and ffrench had served in South Africa, but it was Roger who introduced them and they set up the Shepperton ranch. Morgan eventually returned to Canada, while ffrench, who had toured the Halls of Europe as 'Jeffrey Silant, Stockwhip Artist', was killed as an Air Force pilot three days after the Armistice in 1918. Roger told of making a film *The Texas Elopement* at Shepperton in July 1908, with ffrench as the hero, Morgan the villain and Roger the foreman of the ranch. When the heroine fled from the villain, of course she crossed the 'wild Texan river' in a Morgan patent boat. The scene had to be re-shot a number of times when swans and passing craft intruded. The film evidently received at least a local showing.[37]

When a 'Buffalo Bill's Wild West Circus' visited England, it recruited a number of Frontiersmen to ride with it. At the end of 1913 Trooper Roberts, as he was known to the Frontiersmen, arrived on his ship in Australia. While the ship was in dry dock, Roberts went to work with horses, and at the Boundary Riders Remount Department at Alice Springs he was introduced to the Australian Frontiersmen, who taught him to ride and found him a natural. Roberts joined the Legion and was pleased to arrive back at his home in Manchester in Frontiersman uniform. By the summer of 1914 he was one of 12 Frontiersmen riding with this 'Buffalo Bill Cody's Circus', as Earls Court had requested the Frontiersmen's help. There is a flaw in Roberts' memory when he dictated his memoirs as the elderly and ailing Cody was not in Britain at this time and had not been for some years. It can only be assumed that this was one of the copies of the Buffalo Bill Circus that were travelling around.[38]

'It was good riding and a fine show. Bill Cody asked us to stay over the weekend and we did, also to let him have more men for 20th July, they paid us better than if we were working at our own jobs.'[39] Roberts was one of the men of the Manchester Troop who were the first British troops in action in Belgium at the start of the First War, before Britain was officially at war.

By 1914, the Legion was strong in all the major centres of the Empire, but these were men of action not words. As this was an unofficial body, they considered records less important than deeds. Canada and New Zealand have reasonably good records, in some cases spread around the units, but far less is known about the various Commands in Africa and in the furthest flung outposts of the world, in spite of the fact that Roger wrote of a 'huge Command in Burma'.[40] We can see that the Legion had units even in remote places such as Alice Springs in Australia, although the Headquarters records were lost. Roger Pocock reported Major-General Sir Sam Steele, one of the heroes of early Canada and of the North-West Mounted Police, as accepting the position of O.C. Legion in Canada and using his substantial influence for the Legion. The Legion built up great respect in Canada, culminating in September 1936 when the Legion was granted official affiliation to the Royal Canadian Mounted Police, as the N.W.M.P. had become. Both Sam Steele and his son Harwood were good friends of Roger. Steele was also a friend of Baden-Powell as reported by his biographer Robert Stewart.

> Baden-Powell came back from England at the end of 1901. He and Steele worked together on plans to convert the South African Constabulary from a military to a police and peace-keeping organisation. Steele set out to train the officers and recruits along the lines of the N.W.M.P. ... In a short time he [Steele] had a body of men under his command who could well have been North-West Mounted Police in their broad-brimmed Stetson hats ... When Baden-Powell formed the Boy Scouts a few years later, he modelled the uniform on that of the S.A.C. ...[41]

When Steele completed his term in South Africa in 1906, he did not return immediately to Canada. 'The Steele family spent the next eight months in England while he worked as acting adjutant general to the Inspector General of cavalry for the British Army, his friend Robert Baden-Powell.'[42] It was while he was in England that Steele had meetings with Roger, who persuaded him to command the Canadian Division of the Legion, although Steele seems to have passed the running of the Legion in Canada to others.[43]

Although New Zealand Command records in its History that 'Early in 1911, actual recruiting for the Legion commenced in New Zealand',[44] *The Frontiersman* magazine of February 1910 reported that Commandant John Cook of Christchurch was doing good work there. He was also taking responsibility for New South Wales until a man was appointed there as there had been much interest following an article in the *Sunday Times* of New South Wales. New Zealand history tells us that,

> During the following year, recruiting was extended to the North Island and, at a meeting held in Auckland, it was decided to form a branch. Among those attracted to the movement was E. D'Esterre, of the *Auckland Weekly News*, who applied for membership and was duly accepted. Some time later his badge, addressed to him direct from London, arrived along with a lengthy personal letter from Colonel Driscoll, who knew all about the applicant's prospecting and exploring work ... Membership increased rapidly, and in a short period of time as fine a body of picked men as could be found anywhere in the world had been attracted to the Legion, which was in a well organised state on the outbreak of war in 1914 ... On 3 August 1914, prior to the rupture between Britain and Germany, an offer was made to the New Zealand Government to have two squadrons of

11 *Frontiersmen acting as Mounted Police Reserves, London, during the First World War.*

> the Legion, fully equipped, available at 24 hours' notice. A further offer of some hundreds of Legionnaires with reserves, fully equipped, horsed and saddled, was forwarded to the Government, which was to supply arms, ammunition and a ship to transport the troops, the Legion to provide the ship's crew, from captain to greasers. While the offer was appreciated by the authorities, it did not coincide with Defence Department procedure, and a request was made that all Legionnaires wishing to enlist should do so individually ... The fact that as many as 40 members entered camp in one group gives an indication of the response of the Legion ...[45]

Throughout the British Empire this story was repeated, with Frontiersmen volunteering and wishing to serve as a unit with comrades whom they trusted with their lives. Nowhere would the authorities accept them as they wished, until Driscoll's persistence in Britain brought eventual results. New Zealand's *History* gives the picture:

> If the careers of all the members of the Legion who passed through the Expeditionary Force Camps could be written up, they would form a book telling thrilling stories of deeds of daring and heroism. Represented there were the Canadian North-West Mounted Police, Cape and Rhodesian and Australian Mounted Police, Imperial Light Horse, Kitchener's Scouts, Strathcona's Guides, Driscoll's Scouts, New Zealand and Australian Contingents, the Foreign Legion, and many famous regiments of the Britiah Army. Omdurman, Dargai, Somaliland, Matabeleland, Zululand, Jameson Raid, Transvaal, Relief of the Legation at Peking, and many

other actions were household words amongst the members of the Legion assembled there.

The record of the Legion in this war is a proud one, enhanced by the fact that of the seven V.C.'s awarded to New Zealanders, five were won by its members.'[46]

One of the strong Squadrons was 'C' Squadron of Gisborne under Capt. Frank Twistleton. They made their point by riding into Trentham Camp on their own horses as a disciplined body of about a hundred men, of whom 92 were killed and are buried in foreign lands. Twistleton won the Military Cross and was posted to Palestine where he was killed in July 1918. He remains a New Zealand hero. Born in 1867, the eldest son of Thomas Twistleton of Settle, Yorkshire, he went to New Zealand first in 1895 and worked in various parts of North Island. For a short while in 1899 he went to Queensland, Australia, but soon returned to New Zealand. In 1900 he enlisted with the 2nd New Zealand Contingent in South Africa where he served with distinction under Colonel Craddock for 18 months. On his return to New Zealand he began farming in the Poverty Bay district and in 1911 joined the Legion of Frontiersmen, founding and commanding 'C' Squadron, Gisborne, Poverty Bay. Contemporary photographs show numbers of Frontiersmen at camp and on exercise at his farm. In December 1914, Capt. Twistleton led his Squadron mounted and in uniform from Poverty Bay to Trentham to volunteer as a unit. The military authorities were amazed by the ability and bearing of these men and immediately asked them to form camp guard on visiting day. Much as they pressed the point, they were not allowed to be a named unit, but the military authorities did grant them permission to wear their lapel badge on their uniform. Twistleton was gazetted Lieutenant in the Otago Mounted Rifles and was sent to Egypt and then on to Gallipoli, serving throughout that campaign, where he was awarded the Military Cross for conspicuous bravery. Promoted to Captain, Twistleton was then transferred to France in the New Zealand Pioneer Battalion. Many of the New Zealanders who had survived Gallipoli were transferred to Palestine, where the Frontiersmen among them endeavoured to serve together where possible and called themselves the Mounted Rifles Active Service Troop of New Zealand Command, meeting regularly. Morale among them was raised when Twistleton was posted to the Brigade. Sadly, he was only to serve with them for a very short time, being fatally wounded during a heavy engagement where his command was greatly outnumbered. He had been an able, organised and a charismatic and born leader of men.[47] He was survived by a wife and two daughters, who were able to visit Col Driscoll in London in April 1918. Driscoll wrote that year of the New Zealanders who visited Legion headquarters in London after the War that, 'they all speak of poor Twistleton in the highest terms of praise'.[48] In his early life, Twistleton had little time for the Maoris, but changed his mind completely after having Maoris under his command in France. He wrote in his diary that 'given sufficient Maoris he would attempt any obstacle'.[49]

Throughout Canada, members of the Legion were keen to enlist. The Legion of Frontiersmen has always claimed that around 600 men joined Princess Patricia's Canadian L.I. and the 210th (Frontiersmen) Battalion was formed. Back in the United Kingdom, Driscoll had been busy building the Legion into a formidable organisation. Roger Pocock had been kept out of the way, as Lord Salisbury had engaged him to take his grandson, Randle Cecil, on expedition across Canada and down into America as a kind of toughening-up exercise. Whether someone of influence had suggested Roger to Lord Salisbury as a way of getting him out of the country to stop him trying to interfere, we do not know, but the Legion was a more efficient body without him. When war came, Driscoll came up with a revolutionary idea – too revolutionary for the War Office. He wrote to the War Office, stating the Legion membership as 10,500 throughout the world – it is likely they never actually knew the correct membership. He offered to land with a thousand of his men on the French coast to work behind German lines 'to clear the country of all detached bodies of the enemy'.[50] That is not quite such a crazy idea as seems at first sight. The German lines of supply in the first months of war were very stretched and they were in a hostile country. Guerrilla warfare was possibly an idea and, although it would have cost the lives of many Frontiersmen, no more would have perished than actually did when they went to East Africa as the 25th Fusiliers (Frontiersmen). There was no way that the War Office of those days would agree to Driscoll pursuing his own brand of independent guerrilla warfare behind German lines. We have seen how the Frontiersmen had been trained for this for four years on the basis of the *Frontiersman's Pocket Book*. The War Office did go so far as to ask Driscoll to parade his men, and he did so on 8 September 1914 in front of General Bethune, whose report was quite favourable. He said that Driscoll had a good hold on his men who were typical 'toughs' who would do most excellent work as irregulars. Sadly the Legion was told at first that the War Office had no use for its services, and many men then enlisted into other units. The War Office changed its mind in January 1915 and accepted the Legion for service in East Africa as the 25th Fusiliers (Frontiersmen). Driscoll had until April to make arrangements.

The Legion of Frontiersmen could already claim to be the first British troops in action in the First War. The East Cheshire Troop, based in Salford, could not wait for the War Office to give the Frontiersmen its own named unit, so they crossed the Channel, horses and all, at their own expense. Newspaper photographs showed them landing on 2 August, when Britain did not declare war until the 4th. Their horses were good working horses, which looked similar to Clydesdales. They attracted newspaper headlines such as 'These men paid to get in the firing line'.[51] The Frontiersmen were prepared to go into battle with no pay and to make their own arrangements for rations, supplies and fodder. The French would not be willing to accept them, but the Belgians offered to take them as a troop of their crack 3rd Belgian Lancers.

12 Manchester Frontiersmen with 3rd Belgian Lancers.

When they were old men, some of the Frontiersmen who served with the 3rd Belgian Lancers told of their reminiscences. Because of the confusion of the early days of the War and the memory of old men, it is not possible to write down a totally accurate record of their adventures – also many men considered that they had done their duty and nothing needed to be recorded. Belgium had always taken the guarantee of their neutrality seriously and had neglected its army. It had six divisions of infantry plus a cavalry division to face the 34 divisions that Germany had scheduled to go through Belgium to attack France. Following a visit to the Kaiser in 1913, King Albert realised the seriousness of the situation. He called for a progress report on mobilisation plans and found that no progress had been made. Trooper Roberts maintained that London Headquarters of the Legion of Frontiersmen had received a request from Belgium for volunteers to help in the event of an invasion. Roberts, as we saw, was riding with a 'Buffalo Bill Cody's Circus' with a number of other Frontiersmen. He said that King Albert visited the circus at Earls Court, London, on 24 July and asked for volunteers himself, as the Belgian Army would need scouts with the ability of the Frontiersmen. Roberts went to see the Belgian Consul in London who signed the Frontiersmen on 'in case of trouble'.[52] In August 1914, Dr Percy McDougall was 43 and he offered himself to the army but was told he was too old. He joined the Manchester Troop of the Legion. His family were away on holiday so he put up several members of the troop at his house and picketed their horses in his garden. He and Dick Reading (one time editor of the newspaper *The Sporting Chronicle*) went to try to see Kitchener and persuade the great man to take the Frontiersmen into the British army. He said that

13 Manchester Frontiersmen with 3rd Belgian Lancers near Dixmude, 1914.

he heard through the door Kitchener saying, 'Oh, give them passes to the Belgian Army'.[53] Perhaps this explains how British citizens gained permission to serve in a foreign army? So the men from Manchester and East Cheshire embarked at Folkestone for Ostende wearing Frontiersmen uniform and with their horses. Things there were understandably confused. At two minutes past 8 a.m. on the morning of 4 August the Germans attacked. Ostende came under heavy bombardment and Roberts said that they set to and helped with the wounded. He reported that, following instructions from the King, they were told to make their way to exchange their horses for trained ones at his stables at De Haan. Dr McDougall and Reading told how they went to help with dog teams drawing light guns from Antwerp to Ostende. They managed to 'liberate' (a British army soldier's term) some British motor cycles which were loaded on a boat, and put them to use. Later on Reading was badly wounded and had both legs shattered. He died in Australia after the War, but his widow's plight was brought to the attention of King Albert who granted her a pension. By 5 p.m. on the 4th, Roberts heard that some Germans had broken through, so barricades were built and the Frontiersmen fired from behind them. Although historians state that, having declared war on Germany on 4 August, Britain had no troops on the continent, in fact the Legion of Frontiersmen were in action as the first British troops, and fighting in defence of Belgium. The history of the 3rd Lancers says that the Frontiersmen were accepted on 16 October, ten days after they had disembarked at Ostende, but Roberts reported it as being in August. No doubt it was not officially recorded until October in the confusion. At De Haan they got their horses and equipment and were enrolled in the 3rd Lancers

14 *Manchester Frontiersmen with 3rd Belgian Lancers attack a farmhouse.*

as the 'British Colonial Horse'. Roberts reported that more Frontiersmen from London joined them at the depot. There are many stories about the exploits of these men. Roger Pocock wrote about one, Pat Cowan, who preferred German rifles, so he had to capture prisoners in order to keep himself supplied with the proper ammunition. In one pursuit on foot he lost his rifle, but chased his victim into an estaminet, disarmed him, bought the man a drink, and then marched him into captivity.[54] Some of the stories about these Frontiersmen seem far-fetched, but many have been proved to be true! There would have been many more had Driscoll been allowed to take his men over for guerrilla work. Roberts told of the scouting activities of their men. His story is the somewhat confusing one of an old man, but he did describe the battle at the Yser Canal and the 3rd Lancers holding the Yser Bridge. He referred to a fight with six German Uhlans.

> We got mixed up and I made for one, and one of them made for me with his sabre behind me, but our chaps caught the one in front and took him off me, but the one behind caught my sabre and came down to the hand breaking my sabre off and cutting through the guard. I rode for two days with it on my hand until the Doctor found a blacksmith who cut off the guard. My hand was only cut a little and the Doctor bandaged it up and put a few stitches in it and it soon healed up.[55]

Just before Christmas 1914, King Albert made contact with the Frontiersmen serving with the 3rd Belgian Lancers. Charles Thompson, Regimental Quartermaster, recalled that King Albert, after tasting their rations and pronouncing them good, spoke to the men in perfect English. He told them that he was much touched that a troop of gallant English sportsmen should have rushed overseas to join his army and so he had made a point of coming to talk to them. Dr McDougall found himself working as a despatch rider, but was called on to do emergency treatment on a general who promptly got him transferred to the Army Medical Corps – he was no longer too old! At the end of January 1915, an order came through (probably originating from the British War Office) to disband the detachment. They were transferred back into the British Army, but they were awarded the honour of being permitted to wear the ribbon of the Belgian colours on their uniform.[56]

Throughout the British Empire and the World, Frontiersmen were joining the colours for the war against Germany that the Legion had been convinced was coming, and for which they had been preparing. Many made the ultimate sacrifice and most of those who returned bore the scars of their sacrifices. The Legion of Frontiersmen had made their mark on the ten years before 1914; they were about to make as important a mark on the years of the Great War. What to do with the Frontiersmen was a problem for the War Office. For the past ten years they had been sometimes a help, but more often a thorn in the side of authority. They still had the support and influence of men of power. Even if the War Office had agreed with Driscoll's revolutionary idea, by the time they had deliberated the War in Europe had begun to be what it remained, a more or less static trench war. These were not the sort of men to fit into that sort of campaign. Many of the Frontiersmen were much older men and a considerable number had served in the Boer War.

A campaign was beginning in East Africa which was going to be a mobile and fluid one. There they would be part of the force against Colonel Von Lettow Vorbeck, later to be a general. Von Lettow Vorbeck was to prove himself one of the finest and cleverest senior officers of the German Army who aided the German cause by tying down and frustrating ever greater numbers of Allied troops. These problems were unexpected at the start. The War Office considered the Frontiersmen ideal to send out. They paid them the extraordinary compliment of permitting Driscoll to form his unit and dispatch it without any basic training in Britain. Cherry Kearton, already famous as a wild-life photographer, had been rejected by the army and the Flying Corps, and had been in Belgium as a War Correspondent.[57] Driscoll snapped him up as an Intelligence Officer and Kearton was impressed. 'There was certainly one unit, however, in which experts were employed in their proper place, and that was the 25th Battalion Royal Fusiliers, in the campaign in German East Africa.'[58] Driscoll's battles with the War Office were not finished. 'He undertook to have a battalion ready for service by the end of January and was told to get ahead. Within a fortnight he received a War Office letter cancelling those instructions and at the end of January a further letter asking if the battalion could be ready to sail by February 10th.'[58] It is a tribute to Driscoll that he had a battalion of 1,166 men fully ready to sail on the *Neuralia* early in April 1915. Many of his Frontiersmen had already signed up with other regiments, but Driscoll's authority was such throughout the Empire that Frontiersmen came from all corners. Angus Buchanan had been in the Canadian wilderness on behalf of the Provincial Government of Saskatchewan studying the rarer flora and fauna in the far north-west of Hudson's Bay. For nearly a year he had been out of touch with civilisation, but when he heard at the end of October about the war, he immediately struck south and eventually, like many another Frontiersman from far-flung outposts, reached London. The first stop was always the headquarters of the Legion at 6 Adam Street. As Buchanan said, these Frontiersmen were 'Men who had come to fight for their native land from Honolulu, Hong Kong, China, Ceylon, Malay States, India, New Zealand, Australia, South and East Africa, Egypt, South America, Mexico, United States of America, and Canada. Men from the very outer edges of the world.'[59] With modern communications, we would find it difficult to bring together men from all over the world. This was before all that, and when communication was primitive. The brotherhood that had been nurtured for ten years was proving its worth. Even then, some could not reach London, and only joined the 25th after great difficulties. Parker Sutton-Page, whose family home was at Andover in Hampshire, was working as a journalist in Egypt.

> With a number of other aspiring recruits, he attempted to board a French ship at Port Said to take him on his way back to England. However, the ship was full and they were advised they could not be accepted as passengers. Determined to enlist, the aspiring recruits refused to leave the ship and when it sailed they were still on board. At Marseilles, however, the ship was boarded by French troops who arrested all the troublemakers – and sent them to the Foreign Legion. All in all, the 25th Royal Fusiliers must have been one of the most interesting collections of men brought together in any campaign.[60]

How Sutton-Page and his companions got away from the Foreign Legion to join the 25th is not clear.

Driscoll wanted men with him whom he had known from the Boer War, although some were a little old for active service and had often suffered in earlier campaigns without fully recovering. His first choice for second-in-command was Major E.B.B. Williams, ex-British South Africa Police, who had served in the South African War and had been at the Relief of Mafeking. He had been commissioned in the field in 1903 and then a J.P. for Southern Rhodesia, but had been retired since 1911. However, when he sailed on the *Neuralia* a medical board was held and he was invalided out with 'Varicose veins, varicose eczema and a left patella liable to displacement in sudden exertion'.[61] He left the ship at Gibraltar. The next choice for second-in-command was much fitter, Major H.H.R. White, who had served with distinction in the KRRC and came from a wealthy military family who owned Lough Eske Castle in County Donegal. Driscoll, himself, was Irish. White was a strict by-the-book officer and extremely brave and efficient. There are reports of his frustration with the sometimes independent and cavalier behaviour of some of the Frontiersmen, but he was the ideal man for the job.[62] Driscoll asked for Martin Ryan, a well-respected hunter from Rhodesia, who had been a Trooper in King Edward's Horse and, as seemed usual, the War Office acceded to his request for Ryan to be commissioned. He also got a commission for George Outram, who had served in the Boer War and had been a hunter in East Africa ever since. In addition to Cherry Kearton as Intelligence Officer, Driscoll asked for F.C. Selous. The War Office strongly objected to the employment of a man then 64 years of age, but the already famous Selous had been in Africa as a hunter more or less continuously since 1871 and knew more about Africa than probably any living Englishman. Driscoll prevailed, as he apparently did with all the officers he required. Some of his officers, such as Elverie Haggas and Charles Hollis, had apparently no previous military service. Haggas had been a 2/Lt. in the Legion of Frontiersmen and there is a note in his W.O. file that special permission was granted for him to be commissioned without first attending an Officer Cadet Unit.[63] Others, such as John Handel Bowles, had good records as n.c.o.'s in South Africa.[64] Again, permission was given for them to be commissioned without attending an Officer Cadet Unit. Questions can be asked about the fitness of many of Driscoll's men, often far from the first flush of youth. This was an extraordinary unit, more like a family returning for a reunion from all over the world. The Legion has always had the view that any man, whatever his age or physical fitness, can be of service to his country and fellow man. Some of the men had already been rejected by other units. The (almost literally) larger than life A. Harold (Baby) Reed had enjoyed an adventurous life. He had served in the 1898 Greco/Turkish War, in the South African War, and from 1910-1912 with the Mexican forces. In 1912-1914 he had been a Colonel in the Honduras Army. Returning to Britain he immediately volunteered and was commissioned into the Shropshire Light Infantry. This was a remarkable unit to send him to as he was known as 'Baby' Reed as an example of military humour due to the fact that he weighed some 300lb! The Colonel of the Shropshire Light Infantry took one look at this man mountain and immediately had him gazetted out 'appearance unfavourable'. This left poor Reed in an embarrassing situation as he had spent what little money he had on purchasing a new uniform which he could not now use. The War Office received a letter from Mulberry Farm Dairy to say that Reed owed four months' milk bill. The War Office had to reply that there was nothing they could do as he 'no longer holds a commission'.[65] Fortunately for Reed, Driscoll considered his size no problem and his commission was restored into the 25th Fusiliers, where his expertise was welcomed in command of the Stokes Mortar Battery. His explosive experiments were to cause interest and some alarm in East Africa.

Richard Meinertzhagen's embroidered and error-strewn references to the weird and wonderful trades of the members of the 25th in his *Army Diary* have been regularly quoted (and misquoted) by historians since the publication of the book and Meinertzhagen's veracity has only in recent years begun to be slightly questioned. Embroidery of the truth is a hindrance to the historian. For example, nowhere have I been able to trace 'circus clowns of ten years standing'. However, I think his exaggeration could have been about John Pyman, who after serving in the Scots Guards 1894-5 became a Music Hall Artist, perhaps the 'professional strong man' referred to in Capt. Dolbey's *Sketches of the East Africa Campaign*.[66] By the end of 1915 he was the R.S.M. and was commissioned in June 1917. Driscoll always wanted to commission within the 'family' and disapproved of outsiders being posted in. This six-foot tattooed ex-Guardsman would have been looked on with askance in most Regimental Officers' messes of the day – but the Frontiersmen were different in their outlook.[67]

Many of the 'family', when they were invalided back home, found it difficult to serve in more ordinary units. Capt. Welstead had a distinguished military career stretching back to service with the Cape Mounted Rifles from 1893. He was a fluent linguist in Swahili and Arabic, and yet, when he was invalided to England, he was posted to France – to command a Chinese Labour Company. In spite of a glowing testimonial from Driscoll, he was a fish out of water and in France his Colonel of the old school sent him back as 'unsuitable'.[68]

Five

THE WAR IN EAST AFRICA

Driscoll had a contempt for red tape. As we have seen, this did not always endear him to the War Office. He was desperately keen to have Major John Leitch, a Canadian, in the 25th. Leitch had served in the Cuban campaign with the American forces and in the Boer War with the 1st Canadian Contingent and the Scottish Horse. Leitch held the substantive rank of Major in the 3rd Scottish Horse, but Driscoll had his full complement of majors, so he persuaded Leitch to drop down to Captain with the promise of the first available promotion to Major. Driscoll never troubled to do anything about this officially, and Leitch kept his Major's rank badges and was always treated as a Major. In 1916 he was seconded on special extra-regimental duties to the Arab Rifles under Major Wavell in action against a much superior German force. Wavell and 30 of his force of about 80 were killed and Leitch was seriously wounded in the lungs, shoulder, chest and back. On recovery he was given a job as D.A.A.G., still treated as a Major. The problem only surfaced when he claimed his pension. It is pleasing to learn that the War Office treated this very brave man with sympathy and awarded him his promotion back to Major with the pension of that rank.[1]

On 27 February 1915, Driscoll wrote from 6 Adam Street to the War Office that Lt Hargreaves had reported for duty and made one final request.

> William N. McMillan. The last name to complete the list. This gentleman is willing to place all his resources at our disposal in East Africa as he is a very wealthy and important person in that country. He can command the services of large numbers of materials. He is also willing to present us with two or more machine guns. I would like to have him as Lieut.[2]

Here was another problem for the War Office. Northrup Macmillan was an American citizen and friend of President Teddy Roosevelt and his son, but he was immensely wealthy and held great influence in East Africa. The War Office granted the commission and after the War he was knighted for his services. I have been unable to find evidence of him leading a company into action. If 'Baby' Reed was big, Macmillan was a veritable giant. His sword belt had to be made to go round his 64-inch waist. He would have made a slow and ponderous target for German snipers. What he did do was put his houses

15   *War Illustrated.*

and farms at the service of the troops and many a soldier reported of these fine convalescent homes where Mrs Macmillan helped with the nursing.³

On 23 March 1915, Driscoll could write and request clothing allowances for his final group of officers, Jenkin, Grenfell, Jones, Banning and Macmillan. The official *History of the War in East Africa* recorded of the new 25th Battalion of the Royal Fusiliers that 'Their average standard of experience and intelligence was so high that it was decided the battalion should carry out its military training in East Africa, and it sailed from Plymouth on 10th April 1915.'⁴

16 *Frontiersmen working with remounts, Shirehampton near Avonmouth, 1914.*

Many of those who sailed were not to return, and those who did so bore both the scars of battle and of the climate and conditions under which they served. The fighting claimed the lives of Wilbur Dartnell the Australian hero, who was awarded a posthumous Victoria Cross, and Selous who was killed at the age of 66 – as well as many with less famous names. Others, such as Captain Arthur Wynell Lloyd, for years Punch's political cartoonist,[5] brought back wounds which, half an inch to one side, would have killed them. Lloyd also brought back a well-deserved Military Cross.[6]

* * *

The ordinary Frontiersmen had been torn between wanting to get into action and their desire to serve under Driscoll, their charismatic leader. Driscoll managed to keep the older Frontiersmen busy – those whom other units rejected as too old – by employing them in Remount Depots. Early in the War it seems that the Frontiersmen apparently had the only men capable of breaking the large numbers of horses that were coming from Canada and America. They were apparently authorised to virtually run some Remount Depots until early 1915, particularly at Avonmouth and at Eastleigh near Southampton. Duties were performed in full Frontiersmen uniform.[7] As soon as Driscoll was authorised to form the 25th Fusiliers, in addition to advertising in papers, he

> **LEGION OF FRONTIERSMEN.**
>
> **25th (Service) Battalion Royal Fusiliers (Frontiersmen).**
>
> On receipt of this card, if you desire to join you should proceed to the nearest Recruiting Depot without delay and get attested, as we close as soon as our numbers are complete.
>
> On being attested, you come on the pay list. You should then return home, and make all your preparations for joining me in London, when you can get away for good, but with no delay Report to me if you pass or fail.
>
> Our service abroad will be in a wide beautiful country abounding with Big Game, it will be a healthy life. Several big Game Hunters have joined as guides and scouts. You should make it your duty to get at least one or two men to join.
>
> Duration of Service to end of war. Age 25 to 45.
>
> We sail as soon as we are ready. Produce this card at the Recruiting Office and keep it by you always. When ready to leave, the Recruiting Officer will give you a Railway Warrant to proceed to London.
>
> Battalion consisting of the best stamp of men is approaching full strength, so make haste and join.
>
> 6 Adam Street.
>   Strand,
>   London.   D. P. DRISCOLL, LT.-COL.
> Feb, 15th 1915.   O.C.

17 *The card sent out by Driscoll to all Frontiersmen.*

had a postcard printed and posted to all Frontiersmen: 'Our service abroad will be in a wide beautiful country abounding with Big Game, it will be a healthy life. Several big Game Hunters have joined as guides and scouts. You should make it your duty to get at least one or two men to join.'[8] The Frontiersmen did recruit friends with enthusiasm, but those few who did return, and with their health badly damaged, could have been excused a rueful smile on their return home if they had read again, '… it will be a healthy life'.

One of the clearest descriptions of the other ranks who joined up in the 25th comes from Charles Stoneham, a footloose adventurer who was on holiday in England in 1914 following a spell in Canada. As an ex-public schoolboy who hade been in the O.T.C. he tried unsuccessfully to obtain a commission, but eventually enlisted as a private in a tough Battalion of the East Surreys. An un-named friend who had been commissioned in the 25th followed Driscoll's request to enlist others and engineered a transfer for Stoneham. Because he was intelligent and, according to him, was also a smart parade-ground soldier, he was promoted sergeant.[9] My own researches make me prefer the accuracy of Stoneham's description of the motley crew that formed the 25th Fusiliers to Meinertzhagen's constantly quoted (and misquoted) version:

> They were the oddest crew; from music-hall comedians to border gunmen, with some university professors thrown in. There were Moroccan bandits

and Chinese generals, all British, but imbued with the exotic customs of their adopted lands. In common, they had knowledge of the remote parts of the Empire, and the will to fight. But their discipline was deplorable and to the last they considered themselves guerrillas rather than regular troops ... We had two ex-members of Parliament, cowboys, prize-fighters, ex-regular officers, a one-time submarine commander – all in my company alone. Distributed elsewhere were painters, singers, acrobats, comedians, and, I should imagine, burglars. We could put on a concert composed entirely of well-known stage professionals and hold a boxing tournament in which famous glove-fighters contended. Professional composers wrote our marching songs, idols of the footlights sang them.[10]

Certainly, these men had considerable contempt for organised authority; their loyalty was to the 'family' of the Legion of Frontiersmen. Private Clifford Hall said about them in his reminiscences: 'They were men's men. You could stand back to back with them and know they would never let you down.'[11] A six-foot tall, 15-stone sportsman, Hall joined with two friends, both well-known rugby players, Ingleby an Oxford Blue and Eager a Rugby League forward.[12] The loyalty of these men to the Legion was such that they were prepared to desert other units as soon as they received Driscoll's card so that they could sign up with their charismatic leader – sometimes under assumed names. According to Stoneham, the police sought them desultorily, having more important tasks to occupy them. Stoneham gives the example of a typical Frontiersman under his command where he was billeted:

> One night I was berating a reveller who had returned very late. He was a young man who in private life was a member of the Six Brothers Luck, a famous vaudeville team. He stood sternly, though a little unsteadily, to attention, saying, 'Yes, Sergeant; no Sergeant,' like a ventriloquist's dummy. After a reprimand I dismissed him to bed. In the hall he suddenly turned upside-down and climbed the stairs on his hands with considerable ease. I thought in that no other unit would one see a man go to bed in that fashion.[13]

Frontiersmen loose in London waiting for embarkation were a handful. Some other ranks would be in East End pubs, while others would dine in Mayfair or visit the theatre.[14] When the time came for embarkation they marched off to Waterloo. Cherry Kearton was apparently photographing in some sort of official capacity and a motion picture film of them marching off was taken, although it seems to have disappeared. Part of Kearton's films in East Africa still survive in the Imperial War Museum film archives. On the train at Waterloo, the police appeared to search for deserters from other units. Sgt Major Bottomley, who was one of the early fatalities of the War, went down the train to issue a warning and numbers of Frontiersmen climbed out of the far side of the carriages to hide until the police had gone. At Plymouth, the 25th embarked on the *Neuralia* for Africa. Stoneham was disgusted that in typical army fashion they were given plenty of drills and fatigues which he considered infuriating and useless. Angus Buchanan, then a private, quoted an old soldier, Robson, who told them all, 'Before you again see England you, who are "green hands" will have seen and experienced what "roughing it" really is, and you will be the stronger men for it; you who live through.'[15] Those, like Cherry Kearton, who were eminently suitable for the continent for which they were heading, were not necessarily parade ground soldiers – Kearton admitted as much – but were dead shots with rifle and revolver. This did not stop all officers, including Kearton, George Outram and Selous, being detailed for instruction by Guards Sergeant Pyman who was attached to the 25th as an instructor. Pyman stayed with the 25th and Driscoll got him commissioned towards the end of the campaign.[16] They were given medical checks and Major E.B.B. Williams, as we have seen, only got as far as Gibraltar before he was invalided home.

18 *William Reginald Wilson prior to leaving for campaign in East Africa.*

Originally, the War Office considered East Africa merely a side-show, and when asked for reinforcements it turned to India. Apart from the one British unit, the 2nd Loyal North Lancashire Regiment, the quality of the troops sent was at the very least questionable. The War Office considered the European Front of the greatest importance where the finest troops should be stationed. Von Lettow Vorbeck considered his task was to aid German efforts in Europe by tying down as many Allied troops as possible. In this he succeeded. A complete military disaster when troops under Brigadier-General Aitken attacked Tanga, but then retired with ignominy, forced the War Office to send reinforcements.[17] The toughs of the 25th Fusiliers with their experienced leader and officers were considered ideal. It was also a chance to get the irritating Legion of Frontiersmen off the backs of the War Office and out of the way. Driscoll was supremely confident that his Frontiersmen would storm into the Colony, round up Von Lettow Vorbeck and his Germans, and bring their commander back to London in chains. The actual story was to prove less of a boys' adventure novel, but still a tale of valour.

The War in East Africa

19 Nyanza *as she is today, still operative.*

One of those who joined up was Frederick T. Elliott, 44 years of age, who claimed to be 38, and suffering from a hernia. He had already been discharged from the Territorials as unfit, but, as with many Frontiersmen, this did not stop him. His personal record of his experiences tells us: 'At Malta the French warships in the harbour saluted us with God Save the King and cheers from the French sailors. Our little band responded with the Marseillaise.' Through the Suez Canal and the Red Sea they sailed to arrive off Mombasa, which appeared to Turner like a city from the Arabian Nights. 'When we entered Kilindini Harbour, cheers from the Europeans, Indians and natives sent a thrill through every one of us ... Our orders were to proceed to Kajaido at once by the Uganda Railway ... a marvellous piece of engineering.'[18] It had been realised on the journey that not all of the 25th were ready for immediate action, so a number were sent to Nairobi for further training. Cherry Kearton was not happy with the camp at Kajaido:

> I do not know who selected the site for our camp, but it must have been some staff officer who was used to the amenities of Salisbury Plain. He found a most suitable looking piece of ground – so suitable that it had recently been used by Indian troops, and before that by the natives who built the railway – but he didn't know that in Africa a camping ground must on no account be used again, or it will become the scene of a bad outbreak of dysentery. That camping ground began our casualty list.[19]

Certainly, dysentery and malaria were to plague the 25th from the very start. Constant vigilance had to be maintained as the enemy regularly attacked the railway. After the debacle of Tanga, the War Office had decreed that a defensive attitude should be maintained. Von Lettow Vorbeck was already a master at guerrilla warfare and, according to the introduction to the Battery Press reprint of his *My reminiscences of East Africa*, was used by the Russians as a training manual; also military schools worldwide used the book 'to study not only insurgency warfare but also leadership techniques'.[20]

General Tighe persuaded the War Office that an assault should be made on Bukoba on the western shore of Lake Victoria to destroy the German wireless station there, which was the only reliable contact they had with Berlin.

General Stewart was placed in charge and as well as the 25th, units of the KAR, the Loyal North Lancs and the 29th Punjabis were assembled and on 21 June sailed on some old steamers – the *Usoga, Winifred, Nyanza, Kavirondo* and *Percy Anderson* – from Kisumu. It was intended to be a surprise attack, but Stewart was afraid of his ships colliding so they were not blacked out and the Germans were aware of the attack. Angus Buchanan with a couple of others were due to go ahead and attempt to kill the sentry. Stewart changed plans to attack in daylight and set the 25th Fusiliers and the North Lancs to land at the base of a 300 ft. cliff. The Germans did not believe it could be scaled so did not defend it. Laden with rifles, kit and machine guns, the determined Frontiersmen still scaled the cliff. Meinertzhagen reckoned that the rapidity with which the Frontiersmen scaled the heights and the initial success was a major factor in the capture of Bukoba.[21] Moving south towards Bukoba, resistance was met in the banana plantations and resistance became serious when they arrived about two miles from the town. The enemy were using old rifles with black powder and the tell-tale puffs of smoke showed where they were concealed. Selous said that a number of German civilian sharpshooters were using sporting rifles with soft-nosed bullets.[22] The mountain battery guns soon dealt with the one German piece of artillery, but the machine guns were more of a problem. A final charge in late afternoon captured the main enemy defensive positions, but darkness fell and the Frontiersmen camped for the night. No arrangement had been made for supplies so they spent it cold, wet and hungry. Driscoll had been keen to go ahead and storm the town at night, but the cautious Stewart insisted on waiting until the next day.

Next morning a thunderstorm broke but, little by little, they achieved their goal and captured the town, where they blew up the wireless station, the fort, all ammunition and the stores. Sgt Major Bottomley was one of those killed. He died instantly with a bullet through the head while lying next to Selous and Selous' gun-bearer and friend Ramazani.[23] The Germans had burned the grass on the approach to the town and the Frontiersmen immediately adopted a camouflage for their sun-bleached uniforms of rolling in the burnt grass to blacken them. This acquisition of protective shading appealed to the naturalist in Kearton.[24] The Germans had retreated from the town and with virtually their last shot killed Pte Mucklow.[25] The wireless station was a very large structure, some 200 ft high. Instructions were given to destroy the town and make it uninhabitable for any returning Germans. Possibly the instructions given to the Frontiersmen were insufficiently clear, but many of these men had served in the Boer War where they were expected to live off the land and also to conduct a scorched earth type of policy. They were unlikely to have much respect for the property of those who had only recently been trying to kill them. Meinertzhagen's comments in his *Army Diary*, 'All semblance of discipline had gone, drunkenness was rife and women were being violated',[26] have always been treated with greater weight than those of the Frontiersmen. Selous said, 'I saw no drunkenness amongst our men'[27] and Cherry Kearton told how Col Driscoll had become tee-total and wrote, '…he was continually

20 *Lieutenant F.C. Selous (with felt hat), and his Platoon of 25th Battalion R.F., at Kajiado, in East Africa, c.1915.*

filled with anxiety lest the men in his charge should suffer from drunkenness … his first orders to me were to go into every bungalow and smash every bottle of alcohol. It proved a long job …'[28] Kearton also took it upon himself to prohibit looting. The Frontiersmen got the blame for any excesses, but officers from other units were far from blameless. He found an officer aimlessly cutting piano wires and a Colonel (who Kearton thought should certainly have known better) carrying off the door plate of the Governor's house. 'It is one of our national hypocrisies that the British soldier never falls to the instinct for looting and that that crime is only committed by the people who happen at the moment to be our enemies.'[29] Whilst Meinertzhagen placed the blame for events entirely on the Frontiersmen, the *Official History* told a different version '… the force re-embarked, leaving Bukoba empty and a prey to the surrounding tribes, who joyfully complete what was sometimes called the "Sack of Bukoba"'.[30] Perhaps the truth lay in between, and the accounts of other ranks are nearer the truth. Frontiersman D. Pedersen, one of five New Zealanders in the 25th, wrote: 'Unfortunately looting broke out among the native troops and I am sorry to say some of own men.'[31] Frederick Elliott was clearer in his accusations, saying that some of the men got out of hand: 'On their arrival they were surprised to see our officers waiting for them with drawn swords, threatening to have every man shot if they did not leave the loot and embark on the steamship at once.'[32] Lt Dartnell, who was photographed hauling down the German Eagle, was recommended for the D.S.O. and one of his men the D.C.M. but General Tighe refused to authorise the awards. Pedersen wrote,

> After landing at Mgadi from Bukoba, there was a general inspection of the Legion (the 25th were still known even in official circles as the Legion of Frontiersmen) and the G.O.C. of operations in East Africa,

> General Tighe of the Indian Service, gave us an address consisting of the usual bullshit and a pat on the back. As a counterblast, we were then told how disgusted he was over the looting of Bukoba and that certain recommendations for decorations would not now go through for approval – and that was that.[33]

The Frontiersmen returned to camp with their regular round of patrols both local and distant. Their resident inventor, 'Baby' Reed, gained permission from Tighe to use the Uganda Railway workshops to construct a 'giant' gun, which he then demonstrated to various senior officers. Meinertzhagen was his normal contemptuous, deprecating and exaggerating self in his writings, calling Reed a 'Sergeant', saying that the dynamite bomb this glorified mortar was designed to project had exploded in the barrel. In fact a film of the event that survives in the Imperial War Museum Archives shows the wheeled weapon to be reasonably easily transported by several men. It did project its bomb, but nowhere near the distance intended, and the barrel exploded in a follow-up firing. Reed was not permitted to continue his experiments.[34] The Frontiersmen returned to their patrol duties and two companies were sent to Maktau to relieve an Indian Battalion.[35] The Germans were constantly attacking the railway, which was vital for supplies. Frederick Elliott had a number of narrow escapes. Small groups of men under an n.c.o. were sent out at nightfall to guard against night attack. One night there was a most violent tropical storm.

> Not expecting anything to happen on a night like this one we started to go back to camp in the morning along the railway track like a lot of drowned rats. We had not gone many yards when there was a terrific explosion just behind. The Germans had mined the tracks during the night in spite of the storm, but had mis-timed it by two or three seconds. This is only one of the many narrow escapes I had when stationed at Maktau.[36]

Australian Lt Wilbur Dartnell had impressed Col Driscoll at Bukoba and had been unlucky not to get the D.S.O. On 3 September 1915, leading a body of mounted Infantry, Dartnell found them ambushed by a greatly superior force. Frederick Elliott wrote:

> Picked men who had seen service in bush fighting were formed into a mounted section. These men were mounted on mules, although they were of uncertain temper and hard to handle, they were more sure over rough ground than horses ... When they had travelled about three miles through the bush they were seen by the enemy from a lookout high in a baobab tree ... After scouting for another mile towards the German position ... [they] were ambushed by a strong force of German Askaris under the command of two German officers.[37]

They fell back and, according to Private Darling, 'I think they accounted for a pretty good number of the enemy'.[38] Lt Stanley Traill, a tea planter who had served in the 2nd Dragoon Guards in the Boer War and who had only been commissioned a month earlier, wrote in a letter home,

> Poor Billy Dartnell is dead. He was out with the Mounted Infantry ... when they were surprised by the Germans out on a bush patrol. His first wound was just above the ankle, which broke the bone. He, however, refused to go to the rear, and kept urging on his men to the attack, with the result that he got two more wounds, one in the hip and one in the chest, which finished him.[39]

Elliott's account continues,

> Although Sgt Phillips was killed and a few others either killed or wounded when a volley was fired from the concealed enemy, our men, undaunted, put up a good fight, but the odds were too great. Lt Dartnell then gave orders to all his men that were able to 'ride like hell back to Maktau and tell them to send back stretchers.' Wishing his men the best of luck he said 'I am staying to look after the wounded.'[40]

Dartnell's citation for the Victoria Cross said that

> ... Lt Dartnell, who was being carried away wounded in the leg, seeing the situation and knowing that the enemy's black troops murdered the wounded, insisted on being left behind in the hope of saving the lives of the other wounded men. He gave his life in a gallant attempt to save others.[41]

Elliott was off duty and was watching at the gates for the return of some of his pals who were with the group.

> When I saw the first man come galloping on his mule, out of the bush in the distance with blood streaming down his face, I knew that there had been a fight. I rushed to our tent and shouted, 'Get ready, lads, we shall soon be wanted'. After the report of this fight had been handed into headquarters, a strong force with stretchers left Maktau hoping to come to grips with the Germans and bring wounded comrades back. When we had arrived at the place where this action took place we found that the Germans had retired, but had left a horrible sight behind them. Our men that were killed, also the wounded and Lt Dartnell who stayed to look after them, were left naked and mutilated beyond description, even beyond recognition. When we saw this sight we swore revenge and no quarter in the future. Being late in the day it was impossible to follow up the enemy.[42]

Angus Buchanan reported that the Frontiersmen did get their revenge ten days later, completely routing the enemy and 'leaving thirty dead Askaris and one German officer on the battleground.'[43] None of the Frontiersmen on the stretcher parties were able to bring themselves to enlarge on the dreadful mutilations carried out by the German Askaris (presumably with the knowledge of their German officers) until C.S.M. Eddy Reed years later was able to let it be known that Dartnell's genitals had been cut off and stuffed into his mouth.[44] This was a campaign where sometimes old-fashioned chivalry was seen, and sometimes savage butchery. The Frontiersmen never forgot the atrocities of that September day. Col Driscoll had an answer to the mystery, which he gave in a newspaper interview to leading newspaper man Max Pemberton. Driscoll maintained that many of the Askaris were not the real natives of German East Africa.

> They are the old Arab slave raiders ... the men who had slave camps right across the African Continent. In the old days their butcheries were appalling ... The Germans knew what fighters they were, and armed them long before 1914. They made fine soldiers of them while they were building their railways ... The real native was no good to them. He was a meek fellow... that is why when war broke out, the native helped our men so readily.[45]

The death of Dartnell gave Col Driscoll a problem with the War Office. Dartnell had left a 'testamentary document' leaving his possessions to his fiancée, Miss Mabel Evans of Durban. Following usual procedure, Dartnell's few possessions were auctioned off. Although they were worth little, thanks to a certain extent to the generosity of Northrup Macmillan, over £50 was raised and sent to his fiancée in Durban. What no-one knew was that Dartnell had a wife and family in Australia and it took the War Office a long time to sort out the mess. They even suggested to Driscoll that he was responsible for the money which should have gone to his wife under the terms of his will lodged with the War Office. Driscoll pointed out that the possessions were worth no more than ten shillings, that he was unaware of the will, and that he was a soldier not a lawyer. In the end the War Office decided to letter matters lie, and that Mabel Evans should receive the money and no more. This did not prevent her visiting London after the War to ask for Dartnell's V.C. Dartnell remains to this day one of Australia's great heroes. He was not alone among the Frontiersmen in being a 'ladies man'. It was said that Driscoll himself could never leave anywhere without a number of admiring ladies wishing to bid him a fond farewell.[46]

The Frontiersmen continued with a variety of local patrols until March 1916 when they were detailed to join General Stewart's column, which was to move round one side of Kilimanjaro to meet up with Van Deventer's column at Moschi. Many of the Frontiersmen had fallen sick. Elliott had been forced to go to Nairobi for an operation on his hernia and was fortunate to be sent to the convalescent home run by Macmillan's wife at a property of theirs outside Nairobi, where the convalescents enjoyed a life of comparative luxury.[47] So many men had fallen sick on the advance to Moschi that orders were sent to Nairobi for all fit Frontiersmen to return to the unit. Some had been on staff jobs but all were keen to return and about thirty men under a sergeant made the trip.[48] The engineers worked hard behind the advancing troops and the railway line now extended almost to Moschi. The officers had proved less than satisfactory and General Smuts had been sent from South Africa to take charge. Stewart was relieved of the command of the column and replaced by Brigadier Sheppard. Driscoll made an impression on Smuts who already knew of his reputation from the Boer War. Smuts wanted to promote him but he refused. In a letter written in August 1934 by Robert A. Smith, one of the founder members of the Legion of Frontiersmen, he said about Driscoll, 'The loyalty he inspires in his men is merely an echo of his own loyalty to them. You probably know he was offered a higher command in the War, which he refused because it would have entailed his leaving the men he had raised and taken out.'[49] Private Jenkins of Leeds told the *Yorkshire Evening News* that Driscoll 'would go anywhere. The men, who come from Australia, Canada, and all over, idolise him. They call him "Jerry".'[50] Driscoll was admired by Smuts and also by many others, but he had the Frontiersman's attitude to 'Authority', unless orders were issued with sound judgment behind them. Lord Cranworth in his *Kenya Chronicles* gave a good picture of the man.

> Colonel Driscoll was a man of greatest gallantry, shown in a hundred fights, but he had no especial love for authority in general or the staff in particular. Unless there was fighting to do in that capacity he particularly disliked the duties of rearguard and the dust that was thereby entailed. On this particular occasion he was thus employed, and at a halt he marched his men to a flank and rested them in the shade of some convenient trees. The G.O.C. sent off a staff officer to order him to resume his position, who shortly cantered back with a flea in his ear and carrying a blunt refusal. The G.O.C. was somewhat nonplussed. I had heard the reply and ventured to suggest that I thought I could move the Colonel. 'Well go and have a try. The last thing I want is to have to put him under arrest.' So I rode off and came up to the Colonel seated smoking on the ground, and saluted. He greeted me, as I had hoped, with, 'Well, and what bloody push might you belong to?' I replied, 'Driscoll's Scouts, sir'. 'What the hell do you mean?' 'Well, sir, I served with you in South Africa.' And gave him my name. 'By God, so you are. You're the young blighter who tried to steal my horse. I'm delighted to see you.' And he wrung my hand. I then put to him colloquially what the G.O.C. wanted. 'Of course, my boy, and tell the General if he'd sent you before instead of that brass-hatted young swab, I'd have done it at once.' So the march discipline of the column was resumed. In justice to myself I should say that the accusation about the horse was grossly exaggerated. I had, anyway, no idea that it belonged to him.[51]

After three days' rest at Moschi, the battalion moved off towards Kahe and brisk action occurred. The rainy season had started, increasing the discomfort of the troops. All the time the Germans were retreating, fighting a guerrilla campaign as they did so. On 25 March, the Frontiersmen were returned to Moschi, where they remained for a month and a half while it rained unceasingly. Then they were off again to Buiko, the Pangani River and eventually on 17 June to Ssangeni. Transport of stores had become a nightmare so the exhausting march went ahead at nigh-impossible speed

21 *F.C. Selous on active service with 25th Fusiliers.*

in the conditions with very little food. Smuts was desperate to cut off the enemy so on 22 June they marched again and on 24th; after a virtually continuous march of more than 24 hours without proper food, they went into battle at Kwa Direma on the Lukigura. Angus Buchanan wrote that 'I have never seen men more utterly tired and woebegone than our men at the time of their approach on Lukigura River … and yet when they went into battle all fatigue was forgotten … they fought as madmen – and as heroes.'[52] The enemy held a strong position in a native village on top of a hill. The Frontiersmen were in a maize field under the hill under German machine guns. The Kashmir Rifles were also nearby, pondering what to do. Charles Stoneham was sent back by Driscoll to bring up Capt. Jones with the machine guns. He found confusion back along the path and said that the General was 'afraid his guns would be captured and ordered them to retire until the nature of the ambush could be ascertained.'[53] Unable to find the Captain, Sgt Stoneham returned back through what he considered was obvious panic by other units to report to Driscoll who was unimpressed by what was going on behind him. Capt. Jones had anticipated orders and come round the flanks on his own responsibility forcing the Germans to retire from the field to the village. Driscoll was under a tree talking to Major White, his 2 i/c. The firing had dwindled but Stoneham thought that the enemy were ready and waiting for them.

> The Colonel said in his loud hearty voice, "All right, go forward then, and as soon as you see them get into them with the bayonet and drive them off this hill." My heart took a dive into my boots. The Major answered, "Very good, sir" and came striding past us. "Go on – go on!" said the Colonel, waving at us impatiently. We got up and followed the Major.[54]

A hundred yards of open ground had to be covered to reach the village and the enemy opened up with machine guns and rifles. Many who fought in the 25th said that the Askaris tended to fire high and Stoneham also felt that

The War in East Africa

22 *Mail arriving at camp, East Africa.*

their aim was erratic when being shot at. Most of the Frontiersmen were good shots, even under fire themselves and Stoneham commented, 'We did some execution'.[55] Major White's whistle sounded and the Frontiersmen charged with fixed bayonets – although charge is not the word as these exhausted men rather shambled forward. They were outnumbered, possibly not by the six to one claimed by Stoneham, but the sight of these grim and tattered figures attacking put fear into the enemy and after a short but violent fight in the trenches, the enemy took flight. The Kashmiris had raised a cheer and followed alongside them. The natives had been told by the Germans on pain of death to stay in their huts, but this was too much for them and some came running out and were sadly mixed up with the Askaris to be the recipients of bayonet thrusts. Finally, after fierce hand-to-hand fighting, the enemy took flight into the bush. Major White ordered the men to re-load and volleys were fired into the cover, accounting for more of the enemy. It seems that the attack by the Frontiersmen had taken the Germans 'completely by surprise when our attack pounced on them from the west, and inflicted complete defeat and heavy loss',[56] according to Buchanan. The main column was able to carry the bridge-head over the Lukigura River with more punishment on the enemy and the fugitives from the battle had run into a battalion of the Baluchis on the road and been annihilated. The ever-calm Major White organised attention to the wounded. Three men had been killed and 15 wounded. After such an action, the Frontiersmen had one thought – time for lunch. Major White had a sandwich in one hand and a big pistol in the other. Suddenly an old native woman, whose experiences that day had obviously unbalanced her, rushed forward, grabbed the Major's sandwich and proceeded to wolf it down sat at his feet. 'Well I'm damned' said the Major.[57] They had captured the German officers' kit and food boxes. The Frontiersmen were disgusted to find that, whilst they had been on short rations, the Germans had tins of vegetables, fruit, sausages, and even champagne. A supply ship had run the Naval blockade. Throughout the campaign, blockade-running was a constant source of irritation between the Army and the British Navy. Major White was later awarded the D.S.O., and C.S.M. Poole and L/Cpl Stevens the D.C.M. Darkness brought a return of the heavy rain, but the Frontiersmen were not allowed by the M.O. to take shelter in the native huts, which he advised were full of the ticks that cause spirilium fever. In forty hours they had marched 57 miles, fought a battle, and this was an extraordinary climax, especially as the enemy started shelling them, although most shells passed overhead.

The next few days were spent in camp at the Lukigura. They were waiting for supplies and had no full rations since arriving. On 7 July they had moved to Makindu. By this time the 25th were down to less than 200 of the original 1,166 who had sailed. These were the toughest of the toughs, and only nine original officers remained including Driscoll, Major White and the M.O.[58] Selous had been suffering badly from haemorrhoids, and was sent back to England for an operation. Malaria and dysentery were taking steady toll, and supplies from Medical Headquarters at Nairobi were not arriving. Francis Brett Young, in his novel *Jim Redlake*, was able to put words into his characters' mouths that he could not use in his factual account *Marching on Tanga*:

> ... Medical Headquarters is up in Nairobi, in a snug little office five hundred miles from the front, playing bridge or billiards in the club at this very moment! Why? Because those complacent blighters evidently don't realize that in the last three weeks we've moved over three hundred miles into the blue ... The campaign's been going on for nearly two years, but Medical Headquarters in Nairobi don't know that it's begun. It's a month, to the day, since we started this new invasion. At the moment there isn't a field-hospital within three hundred and fifty miles of the front. And such miles![59]

And so the remnants of the Frontiersmen laboured on through impossible country until they reached Morogoro at the end of August. Buchanan wrote, 'Our object was, first, to follow the enemy, and, secondly, to clear all the country north of the Rufiji River of enemy. To reach the Rufiji River from Morogoro was a trek in all of some 130 miles, the first 55 miles of which was through mountainous country.'[60] It rained incessantly.

At Kissaki on 16 December, spirits were raised to an extraordinary level, and the delight is clear in Buchanan's writing, when Capt. Selous marched into camp with 150 fresh men as reinforcements. Incredibly, at the age of 66, and after what was in those days a serious operation, he had volunteered to return. 'Selous looked hale and hearty, and a grand old man he was. How fine an example of loyalty he gave, in thus, at his great age, returning again to the front to fight his country's battles!'[61] All the men had the same opinion. Private Jenkins of Leeds told the *Yorkshire Evening News*, 'The men thought the world of him. He was like a father to us.'[62] Sadly, his stay with the Frontiersmen was to prove all too short. On 4 January they moved out towards Beho-Beho. Later they learned that this harboured a large German camp and lively action soon developed. Private Clifford Hall, who served in Selous' company, told his younger brother that many raids were planned and led by Selous whose experience of the bush was of vital importance. Hall also told of the respect and affection the men had for Selous, whose jungle knowledge was a great asset in their struggle to survive in those conditions.

> Selous favoured about four o'clock in the morning for his attacks, the time when nocturnal activities ceased and the daytime life of the jungle commenced ... He showed them how to remove the burrowing insects [jiggers] from their feet by using thorns ... in action Selous was very cool, always picking a line of approach that was unlikely to be defended such as through a swamp, encouraging the men to crawl to their objective using cover and launching themselves at the enemy at close-quarters.[63]

Hall reckoned that, thanks to Selous, they had more supplies from the Germans than from their own supply lines. 'If the Frontiersmen got word that the Germans were having a party they would organise a raid while the enemy were occupied with their black women.'[64] The death of Selous had a great effect on the Frontiersmen. It was almost not Selous, but another great Scout, Major Pretorius, who was killed, as Smuts had originally detailed Pretorius to lead the expedition, but changed his orders and sent Selous, while ordering Pretorius on another expedition with the Camel Corps.[65] They were fighting spread out around a track to Beho-Beho. Accounts of the action vary, as is to be expected in such an engagement. Probably the most reliable is that of Cpl Davis who wrote to *The Times* to say that it was he who carried Selous out of action when he was mortally wounded at about 11 a.m. on 4 January 1917.

> I can give a graphic description of his death. He was not killed instantaneously, as I fought over him for fully ten minutes. He was shot in the head, but this wound was not the cause of his death; this wound was caused by a splinter some half an hour previous to the action fought on the hills outside the village of Beho-Beho, and when Capt. Selous was asked if he was wounded he stated that it was nothing very much and insisted on going on. He went over the ridges at Beho-Beho and was kneeling near a small tree, and was seen after the action had been in progress about 15 minutes to drop his rifle. I immediately went over to him and stayed with him for fully ten minutes before he received his fatal wound, and then I carried or dragged him to the rear of a small hill and there he died. His boy, Ramazani, who had been with him some considerable years, cried when he saw Captain Selous dead, and stood upright on top of the ridge in face of terrible German machine gun fire and brought out of a tree the black sniper who wounded Captain Selous.[66]

23 *Programme: rest camp for 25th Fusiliers in South Africa.*

In his *Battle for the Bundu* Miller says that 'Ramazani went berserk and charged the German lines killing several officers and askaris, as well as the sniper who had shot his master'.[67] The word that their great hero had been killed soon spread round the Frontiersmen and they were so maddened that they managed to take the strong German positions and drive the enemy back. Lt Dutch took over from Selous but he soon received a number of wounds, but still directed the attack. He was carried back but he also died of his wounds two days later.[68] Selous and the other men who died were buried in a clearing. Some years later the others were exhumed and re-buried, but Selous' grave remains in what is now the Selous Game Reserve. As news of the hero's death spread back home tributes poured in, and even Von Lettow Vorbeck paid tribute. Legion Lieut House, who had served in Selous' company, wrote in 1920 '… there was no-one who would have hesitated to sacrifice his life for that of their beloved officer … on the march he always kept ahead, carrying his equipment as they carried theirs.'[69]

Beho-Beho was taken. The battalion was relieved by native regiments and marched back to Morogoro, from where they went to the Cape for three months' much-needed rest and recuperation. On 12 May 1917 the battalion left Cape Town for Lindi. They were now to be part of the Lindi column which was to operate near the Portuguese border, part of the strategy of converging columns which had been applied throughout Smuts' time in command. According to Buchanan the rest had been glorious and joyful, 'months which had been filled with the joy and appreciation of men who had come out of scenes that had borne something of nightmare into the full light of life ...'.[70] Smuts had been replaced by British General Hoskins, who in turn was replaced by the Boer Van Deventer. Driscoll himself would have been far from happy, and the conditions had affected even his tough constitution. So many of his Frontiersmen had either been left in graves on their travels or had found their health destroyed by the climate. Many of his trusted officers were gone. Although he had replaced them from his ranks, he had not enough men of officer calibre left to him to commission. One or two of those he commissioned proved unsatisfactory, such as Percy Langham. He was one of those who had deserted another unit to join the Frontiersmen. He had a record of drunkenness and 'using obscene language to an officer'. He was a tough Frontiersman, good in a scrap, but not officer material. He lost his commission and was dismissed the service at the end of 1917 for a string of offences.[71] The biggest loss to Driscoll was his 2 i/c, Major White, a constant rock at his side. Major White already had a serious wound when in 1904 he had been shot through the chest at Jidball, in Somaliland, serving with the 60th Rifles.[72] Malaria and the effect of the climate on his chest had forced him to leave the 25th for less taxing duties. 'Baby' Reed had been invalided out in October 1916. According to the medical report he was 'extremely adipose' (i.e. fat) and had chest problems.[73] Major Hazzledine, who had been a capable adjutant, suffered measles on top of malaria;[74] Capt. Welstead had not recovered from being wounded at Beho-Beho.[75] Major Leitch had been seriously wounded on secondment to the Arab Rifles,[76] and many more could not carry on. Driscoll had lost more than half of his trusted officers and many of his faithful men. He was given some reinforcements, but these were not his Frontiersmen with their extraordinary loyalty to the brotherhood, which was almost similar to a family. The experienced officers he was given were not of the same thinking.

At the end of May they reached Lindi Bay by sea, looking across at the East African bush which had taken the health and the lives of so many of their comrades. Lindi was a low-lying and unhealthy town, as was the swamp of the Lukuledi River nearby. On 10 June it was decided to attack the enemy who were holding a nine-mile front inland to the west. Two columns moved out, one to the north, and the other with the 25th and the K.A.R. operating south. Early morning on 11th, the artillery started up, supported by guns from two Royal Navy ships in the bay. The German artillery responded. The 25th were ordered to dig in on Ziwani ridge and at 2 p.m. the enemy launched

24 *Breaking camp, East Africa.*

a strong attack on their left flank. Once again, the Frontiersmen suffered casualties, three rank-and-file killed and 11 wounded. Capt. Sutton-Page, once of the Foreign Legion, and Captain Martin Ryan were wounded, Sutton-Page in both legs. Lt Robinson was killed. Cherry Kearton, who had spent some time seconded to the Air Forces to command an airstrip, was back with the battalion. On a visit to Bradford in 1927 to lecture in connection with his travel films, Cherry Kearton was welcomed by the local Frontiersmen and he described to them how Robinson met his death. The Frontiersmen were always very strong in Yorkshire and Robinson had been their organising officer before the War. Many Yorkshiremen had joined the 25th. The *Bradford Argus and Telegraph* reported that Kearton had been with Robinson, who had less experience of bush fighting than the others, at the time. Robinson was in charge of supplies during the battle.

> At one period during the fighting, his caution forsook him and he stood up on his feet. A sniper shot him through the spine and death was instantaneous. His comrades kept a look out for the sniper and Mr Kearton finally located him in a tree. He fired two shots at him, and the second one got him in the stomach. The sniped sniper fell from the branches of the tree and crawled fifty yards, his dead body being found the next morning.[77]

According to Buchanan, '... one lost all reckoning of time, all reckoning of everything'.[78] They finally routed the foe at the point of the bayonet, not without 'one final trial to this grim encounter' as hives of bees had been shot down and inflicted terrible stings on the men. Once again, the German Askaris' machine-gun fire was too high. Had it not been, many more hastily-entrenched Frontiersmen would have been killed. The northern column finally reached its destination, but by now the Germans had yet again retreated.

The Frontiersmen returned to Lindi, but this was the most unhealthy place to stay. Between 16 and 25 June, the *Army Diary* of the 25th reported that the sick parade was increasing, averaging from 40 to 60 daily. Almost half the strength was in hospital. On the 26th they were inspected by the Senior Medical Officer, who examined all of those able to parade – a mere 155 men. In his opinion, only 36 men were fit to go on column. On 2 July, one soldier, Pte Cutts, died in hospital from heart failure caused by malaria. Major Hazzledine was now unfit and Lt Haggas had gone to Dar-es-Salaam. Three new officers were posted to the 25th, Capt Ellison, Capt. Bull, who took over the duties of adjutant, and Major Danby. The impression received from Driscoll's writings and those of Capt. A.W. Lloyd is that Danby did not fit in and his attitude and actions were unpopular. On 3 August, the battalion (according to Lloyd minus Major Danby) together with a K.A.R. battalion were in an engagement on Tandamuti Hill. They had been engaged on a flanking movement on the enemy, but the Germans sent out their own flanking movement, which almost isolated the British force. The 25th lost two sergeants and another five other ranks killed and Capt. Kemsley was wounded. The K.A.R. had abandoned their ammunition and Driscoll was concerned that it could fall into enemy hands. A Staff officer said that the K.A.R. should make an attempt to recover it and wanted a man to show them where it was. Driscoll wrote,

> I asked Capt. Lloyd for a man; he replied that he would go himself as the men were dead beat and fast asleep on the grounds. He walked back the four miles through the bush alone in the darkness and reported to the O.C. 1st /2nd/K.A.R. as guide but the latter decided not to make the attempt.[79]

It is easy to see the bottled up anger and contempt for his opposite number for his lack of action in response to Lloyd's effort. On 18 August at another engagement overlooking Narunyu the 25th together with the 1st /2nd K.A.R. found themselves attacked from all sides. There they followed the old, but in this case highly successful, policy of forming a square. Buchanan said that they could have asked for no better troops than the native African troops of the K.A.R. to fight alongside. No doubt, Driscoll was less enthusiastic about their officers. Casualties in the 25th were surprisingly light in comparison with the enemy. There was one man killed, Pte Carter, and the Padre and three other ranks were wounded. After five days with virtually no water and rations, orders came to withdraw under cover of darkness. Buchanan wrote, 'The withdrawal was quietly accomplished… and then we had what in the past few days we had come to dream of – tea, tea, tea.'[80] This was the last action that Capt. Angus Buchanan, M.C. was to see. For a few days he struggled on, proudly still caring for his treasured machine guns, but by 9 September he had not even the strength to walk and was taken to hospital. He had been through the whole campaign, missing just one, the final action of the 25th Fusiliers (Legion of Frontiersmen), where the tattered remnants were virtually cut to pieces.

Even Col Driscoll was to miss this one engagement as his health had finally failed, and he was forced to leave his men under the command of Major Danby, who apparently did not take part in the final engagement. There the 25th were in the capable hands of Capt. Ryan and Capt. Arthur Lloyd. In his *Battle for the Bundu*, Miller says that Mahiwa was the final showdown of the East African campaign, 'It is also confused beyond belief; many accounts have been written about Mahiwa, but none seems to describe the same action. Even the name is wrong; by rights it should be called the battle of Nyangao since most of the fighting took place there …'[81] As far as the 25th were concerned, it was the battle of Nyangao in their records. Miller again: '… it was simply a toe-to-toe slugfest … in which acts of heroism became all but commonplace.'[82] Von Lettow called it 'a splendid victory' but it had all but destroyed his army, and the British with superior numbers could suffer the losses. The Frontiersmen could not, as it spelled the end of the battalion. Although not present, Driscoll filed the report of the engagement as given to him:

> An attack was being delivered by several battalions against the enemy holding a lone line. No impression could be made. The Fusiliers, now sadly reduced after long service, consisting about 40 rifles, with Lewis

25 *Officer's badge and other ranks' badge, 25th Service Bn. Royal Fusiliers (Frontiersmen).*

and Machine Guns, total strength about 106, were sent forward. They got into the enemy positions but were not supported; it would appear that the others retired. The Fusiliers isolated, held their own and fought with their usual courage for several hours being attacked in front and flank. After sustaining some 70 casualties, they were relieved by the Nigerians. All the officers, including Capt. Ryan (killed), who was in command, were either killed or wounded, Capt. Lloyd being shot through the head. After this engagement the Fusiliers were sent home. Every man present in this engagement fought like a hero. Unfortunately, I was sent back by the Doctors some time before.[83]

So, from the 1,166 enthusiastic Frontiersmen who had sailed on the *Neuralia*, only a handful were able to see through the whole campaign of the battalion. Martin Ryan only fell at the last engagement. Arthur Lloyd, lost the hearing in one ear; but had the bullet been a fraction to one side, he would have been killed. Driscoll returned to London and tried to get another appointment, but no other unit would take this brilliant and unique soldier and fighter, but one who did not suffer fools gladly. He was offered to Cairo and to South Africa but was not wanted by either. He was removed from the Active List in March 1918, and wrote to the War Office that this was 'heartbreaking and humiliating'.[84] He fought to get a deserved Military Cross for Lloyd, disgusted that Major Danby, who had not been in the action 'having recently arrived from England and been placed on Staff Duty' was 'Mentioned in Despatches'. Major Danby had put forward no recommendations for decorations for others for all the bravery shown in the Lindi campaign.[85] Anyone reading the account of this final action in the War Office file on Capt. Lloyd might well feel that Lloyd probably deserved an even higher gallantry award than the Military Cross.

Six
The World Flight Expedition

Driscoll then concentrated his efforts on re-invigorating the mainly dormant Legion of Frontiersmen. Many of the men of services age had paid the supreme sacrifice. Others had seen their fill of uniform and wished only for civilian life and peace. He contacted units around the world. A correspondence began with his friend Ernest D'Esterre in New Zealand which tells us a lot. Driscoll was most unhappy with what had been happening in his absence. Although Burchardt-Ashton had apparently been Treasurer, his time had been occupied with the Remounts and also with the City of London Mounted Police Reserve, which was composed of Frontiersmen who served in Frontiersmen uniform; a relationship with the City of London Police which was to continue for many years.[1] The office had been left in the hands of a man called Longstaff as organising officer and 'a few old men … who had been requested by me not to attempt any serious changes until all our men were back again'.[2] Driscoll lost no time in calling a meeting of the General Council to have Longstaff's appointment cancelled.

In Driscoll's letters to D'Esterre we find the first official recognition of women being welcomed into the Legion with their own badges as the Circle Cross League. In later years the Women's Auxiliary Legion of Frontiersmen (WALF) was to make its mark.[3]

There had been few subscriptions coming in, due to the fact that most Frontiersmen were in the services. Driscoll was most gratified that New Zealand Frontiersmen in the services coming into the office when passing through London always asked 'What do I owe?'[4] Driscoll had the greatest affection for New Zealand and the New Zealanders. He was told by his doctor that the climate in Britain, and particularly London, was not doing his health any good after years spent in the tropics. He would have loved to move to New Zealand, but was existing purely on his pension and this was out of the question. A settlement scheme came up in East Africa and he was offered 1,000 acres of land there, so he reluctantly decided that this was the only way forward for him. He sailed at the end of 1919. Sadly, when he arrived, he wrote gloomily from Nairobi to tell his friend D'Esterre that the land

> … on which I built so much hope and dreamed so much about, has turned from a business point of view to be a failure … It is too high for

26 *The 'Vanduara' at Birkenhead, newly re-named S.Y.* Frontiersman.

> coffee ... it is too small for stock, and it is too far from the railway for wheat and such things, being 90 miles from the railway.[5]

Driscoll was to spend the rest of his life fighting to make a living. He was still the charismatic leader that Frontiersmen referred to and told yarns about, but he was too far away for his exemplary leadership to have much effect. From the day he left, the Legion of Frontiersmen has never been able to find a leader of a fraction of his ability. He left the Legion with funds of around £900 – a goodly sum for those days – but by 1922 it was back to its usual state, almost penniless and looking for financial support from more wealthy members. He was succeeded by a retired officer, Col H.T.Tamplin, who served for about five years and whose one success was to persuade Major-General Lord Loch to become President. In a period when the Establishment were worrying that red revolution might reach Britain from Russia, the patriotic and royalist Frontiersmen might prove an asset. At the end of 1921, Tamplin wrote to Burchardt-Ashton that Lord Loch would be attending a Council meeting:

> He is full of practical suggestions, and has a lot of influential people with him who realize the actual value as an asset on the side of law and order of the Legion of Frontiersmen. Loch thinks we *shall* be able to do without subscriptions altogether, means being forthcoming otherwise.[6]

Once again, with slight echoes of 1909, there is talk of the Frontiersmen being funded as an unofficial arm of conservatism rather than of government.

THE WORLD FLIGHT EXPEDITION

Certainly in London the Frontiersmen had experience as Special Constables and continued those duties through the General Strike.[7] Lord Loch was another of considerable influence who moved in the old-style corridors of power. He had been a Lord-in-Waiting to King George V from 1913 to 1914. He was a decorated soldier, 'Mentioned in Despatches' a number of times and in 1924 became Captain of the Yeomen of the Guard. Lord Loch was able eventually to attract other men of influence, such as Leo Amery, M.P., and Viscount Burnham and others to serve on the Governing Council of the Legion of Frontiersmen. However, when he took over as President, Loch wrote to the War Office to advise them officially. He also wrote a private letter to a personal friend of his who was Parliamentary Under-Secretary to the War Office referring to the 'anti-bolshy' side of the Legion's activities. This, officially private, letter was placed on War Office files and was to cause some concern that the Frontiersmen might be becoming political in their activities.[8] Also, another member of the Governing Council of the Legion was the right-wing conservative, Commander Oliver Locker-Lampson, who was one of the founders of the 'Clear Out the Reds Campaign'. Whilst the rank-and-file Frontiersman was a patriot and a traditional Royalist, they absolutely refused to have anything to do with any sort of party politics. It seems that little or no money was to be actually forthcoming, as in 1923 Tamplin wrote to Burchardt-Ashton to express his grateful thanks for a donation which got the Frontiersmen out of debt for a while.[9]

Burchardt-Ashton was a wealthy man, whose son had been killed, like many others in the War, and the Legion was his great interest.[10] He took over as Acting Commandant from Tamplin and, although he was to receive the complaints common among voluntary organisations about financial discrepancies, it is obvious that he was supporting the Legion personally throughout his years. It became all the more painful to him when he was eventually asked to resign. It is said that all publicity is good publicity, and in 1923 the Legion were to receive considerable bad publicity. When we last heard of the Founder, Roger Pocock, he was licking his wounds after being

27 *The S.Y.* Frontiersman.

expelled from the Legion. He had continued his writing, although his novels with a western background sold better in America than Britain. In spite of his age and infirmity, Pocock had managed to get a territorial commission and was sent to France with a Labour Company. He received a temporary captaincy, but his health forced him back to England and attachment to the R.A.F. at Chattis Hill near Andover. Although his substantive rank was Lieutenant, he was always to be known after the War as Captain Roger Pocock.[11]

At Chattis Hill, he made friends with Captain Norman MacMillan, who was instructing there following injury when flying in France. His book *Into the Blue* tells the story of his adventures in the Royal Flying Corps. In the 1920s, the first circumnavigation of the world by aeroplane was the target in all flying countries. The Americans eventually succeeded in 1924 with complete government financial backing. Britain has always relied on the great British amateur. In 1922 MacMillan was recruited by Major W.T. Blake, air correspondent of the *Daily News*, to act as pilot in an attempt at the flight. The flight attempt bordered at times on tragedy and farce and finally failed in the sea off Calcutta when MacMillan and his aerial photographer, Geoffrey Malins, nearly lost their lives in a crash into the sea. Both men blamed Blake for the delay in rescue which nearly killed them.[12] When they had recuperated and returned to London, MacMillan came to see Pocock. He and Malins were still keen to achieve the world flight, but would have nothing more to do with Blake. MacMillan wanted Pocock's advice as an experienced traveller with some knowledge of the dangerous North Pacific. He must have been a little taken aback by the response. Roger leapt from his seat. He begged to be taken into partnership. This must be a British venture and a British success.[13] Roger Pocock forgot his 56 years and that this was war-weary and subdued Britain and no longer the days of Victorian adventure and Empire-building. As usual, in his enthusiasm he ignored all the difficulties. Under such energetic pressure, MacMillan gave in. Pocock would be appointed geographer to the next expedition. That agreement was enough to send him off on a whirlwind of planning. The main problem that Pocock envisaged was that North Pacific section. He painted alarming pictures of uninhabited storm-lashed islands, some fog-bound; of hurricanes; of drift ice; of 'Bolshevists' ready to loot any passing plane that should choose to land in their area. (The 'Bolshevists' were the current hobgoblins of British society.) Pocock pointed out that for one stretch of 2,200 miles there would be no known supplies and that was far further than they could reasonably be expected to fly in one go.[14] He was right to warn that it had been folly to start out the last time without carefully prepared ground support, and it would be equally stupid to do so in the future. A seaborne expedition should go ahead and lay supplies. Money for such a project would be scarce. They would have to seek sponsorship, particularly from the newspaper industry. Malins' skilled newsreel photography would bring some limited reward. However, hard-nosed businessmen would not be enthusiastic about backing a new expedition the year after such a calamitous failure. If the expedition succeeded, everyone would want to be associated with it, but as to taking a gamble in advance, Pocock was soon to find that there were few who were prepared to risk money. In his usual way, Roger Pocock swept all these arguments to one side – that is if he ever properly listened to them. He would contact again the Legion of Frontiersmen, the most patriotic of people and seek their support. The one man who might have dissuaded him, Driscoll, was now far away in East Africa and Pocock went right to the top, to the President, Lord Loch. Pocock was highly impressed with Lord Loch, but not with the current Staff officers and Council of the Legion. Certainly, the majority of these must have backed the idea, as Lord Loch would not have been able to offer support on his own. They did cover themselves to a certain extent by renting the Expedition an office at headquarters in Adam Street, London rather than providing one free. Advertisements announcing 'Adventurers wanted, small capital essential. Those who wish to see the world and help their country apply at ...',[15] were published under the auspices of the Legion. Of course, when the expedition later failed ignominiously, none of the Legion Staff and Council accepted any responsibility, laying it all on Pocock's shoulders and saying that they had not agreed to the idea.

They needed a ship and Pocock went off on an excited tour of all seaports as far away as Rotterdam and Antwerp. He saw numbers of poor ships at the price they could afford and some good ships at a price they could not afford. When he was in Hull, Pocock saw an advertisement that caused him to take the first train to Birkenhead.

> There lay the *Vanduara*, a very dream of loveliness, a schooner-rigged steam yacht, named in honour of the famous racing clipper, and built in 1886 for the Coates people, master spinners of thread, who were very rich and were reputed to have spent three hundred thousand pounds on this little wonder ... During the War, she had been in the Liverpool Pilot Service. Running away from submarines, she had tired her engines, reducing her speed from sixteen knots to a little more than seven. We did not need high speed, which meant the gobbling of coal in regions where it could not be replaced. We did need a sound ship and, crawling the whole length of her keelsome, I could not find so much as a speck of damp. And she was going for fifteen hundred pounds. By selling out my capital I scratched up six hundred and thirty, sufficient to hold her while she was surveyed for insurance. She came out 100 A1 for hull and engines, but needed a new foremast, so our S.Y. *Frontiersman*, as she became, was left for refit.[16]

Pocock was now so deeply into the project that he was ready to risk everything. The *Vanduara*, which he called a 'dream of loveliness', was called other things by more knowledgeable people. It is quite extraordinary how she could receive '100 A1' at Lloyds for hull and engines. Although the hull was sound, she had no watertight compartments and it would have been suicidal

28 Lord Loch visits the ship, seen here talking to the Captain and Dr Thompson the publicity officer.

to take her to the North Pacific where she would encounter ice floes. One small hole would send her straight to the bottom. Surely, Roger Pocock had sailed on enough ships in his life in rough enough waters to know this? The only answer can be that, once again, he allowed his heart to rule his head. He did admit that the triple expansion engines had been worn out in the Liverpool Pilot Service running away from U-Boats, but what he did not admit was that she had been sunk and raised again once, and still had the same engines. They were worn out. Pocock thought that would not matter because the eight-knot maximum she could now produce would be plenty enough for his requirements. He intended to sail across the Atlantic, but never troubled to look at the sails that were far too small for that purpose. In any case, he never engaged a crew with sufficient experience to operate sails.

Having bought the ship, the next item was to find a crew for her. Whereas in 1898 for his Klondyke Expedition he had been able to pick and choose, he found much less interest in his latest project. He had wanted 40 men, but finished with around thirty. In any case, the ship would not have been big enough for forty. He asked them for between £200 and (optimistically) £500 each. Frank Ransley, a First War pilot with the D.F.C., and his friend Bill Heaton were early volunteers. They could only afford £100 each, but were accepted and signed on at one shilling a month to comply with Board of Trade regulations. Because their contribution was comparatively small, they were signed on as stoker and coal trimmer.[17] Pocock told prospective adventurers that they were due for dangerous adventure on perilous seas, but then suggested that profits could be made from trading after the flight had passed by. They were even taking with them a specialist salesman, Capt. Francis, although only Pocock seemed to know from where that experience came. Pocock planned to leave a man in charge of most of the dumps on uninhabited islands. He intended that up to two-thirds of the dumps could be missed, and they would still have enough supplies. MacMillan and Malins would take off in spring 1924 and ship and plane would rendezvous in Japan. The ship would then follow the aviators to Canada and the Kurils and Aleutians, picking up the stranded men on the way and then making its way home. The whole trip should take from eighteen months to two years. It all sounded very neat.

Writing in later years, Pocock said he was most satisfied with the crew he recruited. He had originally wanted Commander Andrew Downes, R.N. as skipper, but Downes was unable to get a Board of Trade Master's certificate, so he took on Lt Commander Robin Spalding; R.N. Downes signed on as Boatswain. The crew were to find Spalding far too weak and the honest ones would have preferred to serve under Downes, who they thought would have made a better skipper. We can say the 'honest' ones, for they could not all be described as such. Pocock, in his customary way, was trusting everyone and taking them at their word. He was desperately short of money, and of applicants who had some money to put into the enterprise. 'We had seven Air Force pilots as firemen to serve as advisors in preparing the depots.'[18] Actually, he had just two pilots, only one, Ransley, was a recorded air ace and the other an instructor. Nothing had been said to them about advising on depots. 'The rest of us were seamen and soldiers, all war trained men,'[19] wrote Pocock. Ransley said in his privately published autobiography that 'The rest of us were a motley lot with only about four who had seen service at sea and it was only thanks to them that we managed to get as far as we did.'[20] Frank Ransley later joined the prison service and became a noted Prison Governor. When interviewed towards the end of his long life, he said, perhaps not completely in jest, that he met so many criminals on that voyage that he joined the prison service in order to study the criminal classes more fully.[21] Although there were some gentlemen and ex-officers, the others consisted of too many characters who appeared to be using the expedition as an easy way out of the country without alerting the authorities. Also, there were a number of homosexuals in the group at a time when such activity was illegal and strictly punished when caught.[22] There was certain to be trouble with that mix of men. One condition of taking part was that everyone had to join the Legion of Frontiersmen.

29 *Lord Loch with the Captain.*

Although in the beginning all appeared on the surface to be going well, there were some warning signs. The *Frontiersman* was ready by the middle of May 1923, and some of the men who had already signed on went to Birkenhead and from there they crewed her to London. The press were starting to take an interest. *The Daily Courier* published a large photograph of the men on board at Birkenhead together with a large write-up of the story. MacMillan had travelled to Birkenhead to take possession on behalf of the expedition, although it is unlikely he knew just how much the refit had cost.[23]

Another crew member who is important to the story is Guy Eardley-Wilmot. He was the son of Rear-Admiral Sir Sidney Eardley-Wilmot and had a distinguished War record in the army. Eardley-Wilmot was one of the limited number of the crew who was exactly the type that Pocock wanted. He was a real man of adventure with considerable sea-going experience, although even that needs qualifying. Guy Eardley-Wilmot had been originally commissioned in the Navy, but had proved rather too inclined to 'bend' any cutter or small boat with which he was entrusted. He left the Navy by mutual and friendly agreement. Most of his life he was short of money as his family kept him on a very small allowance. When his mother, a member of a wealthy banking family, died, he found himself suddenly in funds for a while. He was a big man, often known as 'Tiny' to his many friends. During one of his impoverished years, his friends at his club got together and bought him one share in each of 40 different companies. They were carefully selected as the ones that gave shareholders a lunch at their annual general meeting. His friends were then satisfied that Guy was certain of at least forty good meals in a year. Eardley-Wilmot was a blunt man in dealing with anything that was not correct and would not put up with any inefficiency. He would have been one of those to be somewhat surprised by the uniform that they were expected to wear on the expedition.[24] It was different from the usual Frontiersmen uniform of navy or fawn shirt and breeches. It was to be black trousers with wide black belt, black shirt with military style pockets worn with medal ribbons and sleeves rolled to the elbow and black peaked cap with Legion of Frontiersmen badge. Perhaps it is a coincidence that it bore similarity to the uniform worn later on by Oswald Mosley's Blackshirts.

The ship sailed down to St Katherine Dock in the Port of London ready for it to be opened to the public on 16 June. MacMillan had been working hard to get support for the flight, and Pocock for the sea expedition. MacMillan was collecting many promises of support. One of the largest newspaper syndicates offered him considerable backing, so long as he could get the project – and the plane – off the ground, so it was vital that the sea-borne expedition should proceed smoothly. He was also well on the way to getting the backing of a big city with the promise of a Lord Mayor's fund.[25] Several wealthy capitalists had also shown interest, but were hesitating to be the first

30 (right)   *Captain Geoffrey Malins among the visitors to the ship.*

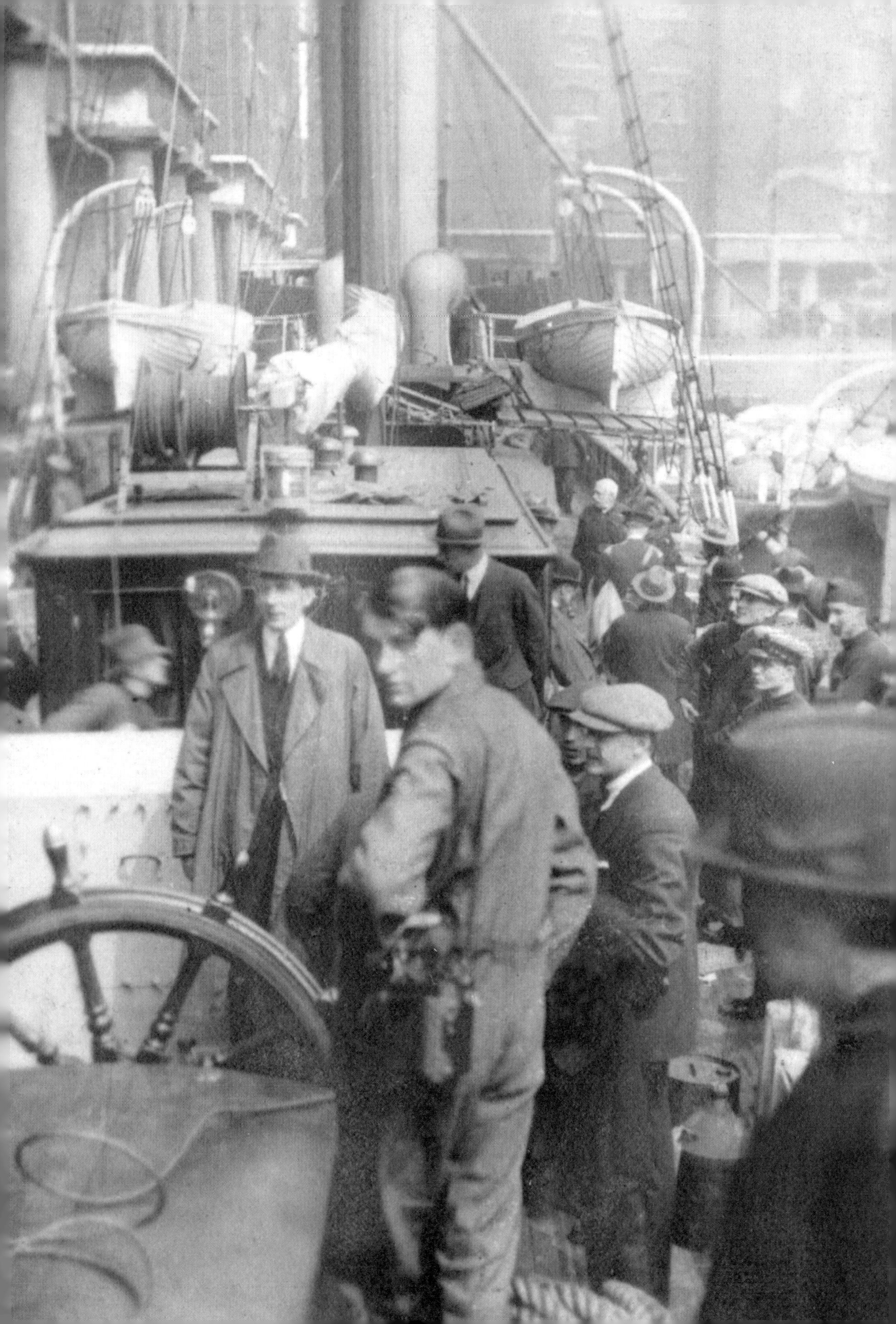

to put in real money until they were sure of some return. Pocock was having similar results, with plenty of interest but little actual money. The bills were coming in far faster than the money and he was struggling to find a crew. His usual main supporter, his sister Daisy (Lena Ashwell), could offer little. Her husband, Henry Simson, was helping finance her latest venture, the conversion of the dilapidated Bijou Theatre into the Century, and he could not be asked for too much help in financing another of his brother-in-law's schemes, however patriotic.

Pocock was doing rather better in persuading manufacturers to donate products, and by the time the *Frontiersman* sailed she was well laden with stores. Not all of these goods were of immediate use. Pains Fireworks had given £150-worth of their product and nobody ever went short of cigarettes as they had thousands.[26] There was flour by the sackful and Crosbie's Jams and Pickles sent many cases. One strange little invention, 'The Shackleton Folding Lifeboat', received a great deal of publicity in the press both in Britain and later when they arrived in America.[27] Frank Ransley wrote, 'We now learned that the volunteer crew's aggregate contribution amounted to £6,000 and that as several firms were donating supplies we should be able to complete our mission without having to raise more money.'[28] He was to be proved completely wrong in this. Pocock was not averse to the odd publicity stunt. The *Daily Mirror* reported on 8 June that six large balloons were to be sent up over London to obtain atmospheric data. Anyone securing a balloon was asked to return it to 6 Adam Street. What atmospheric data of any use they expected to collect it is impossible to imagine.[29] Mellon, the ship's cook, was something of a comedian and the next day's *Daily Mirror* showed him doing balancing tricks with a lifebelt together with a picture of Pog, who was supposed to be the ship's mascot and appeared in many press releases, although the dog never apparently sailed with the *Frontiersman*.[30]

As sailing day approached, the big problem of acquiring a Chief Engineer remained. Several men came and looked at the engines, but left hurriedly after only a glance. The Second Engineer, Pearce, was appointed apparently because of his experience as a motor-cycle mechanic, although that could hardly be regarded as the ideal qualification for the job. It was not until they had sailed and were off Gravesend that they found their Chief. He arrived on deck wearing a natty bowler hat, removed it and went to look at the engines. He took one look at them and, without a word, replaced his bowler hat and made his way back on deck. The skipper had been wise enough to order full steam ahead, so the Chief shrugged his shoulders and went down again into the engine room. Several times when they were at anchor on the journey, the Chief put on his bowler hat, but was persuaded to stay and make the best of it.[31]

June 16th was open day and crowds came to see the ship. Picture postcards of the *Frontiersman* were on sale. Sir Sefton Brancker had already visited them on 7 June and given the project his blessing and the encouragement of the Ministry of Civil Aviation, although no financial or material backing,

31 *Loading stores donated by sponsors.*

which was what was really wanted. MacMillan, Malins and Lord Loch were all on board the ship to welcome the crowd and, as could be expected, many Staff officers of the Legion turned up in full uniform and medals. Some were photographed with Roger Pocock in a group later titled by Eardley-Wilmot in his album as 'Captain Pocock and his gang'.[32] Also present was Dr Fred Thompson, a friend of Pocock. Just before the First War, the two had tried to interest the Spanish in setting up a motion picture industry in Spain. Pocock had written hopefully to Rudyard Kipling suggesting that he might care to join the venture and write the screenplays. Kipling had

32-3 *Frontiersmen on board the ship. Eardley-Wilmot disparagingly noted these photos as 'Captain Pocock and his gang'.*

THE WORLD FLIGHT EXPEDITION

refused, his letter thanking Pocock for '... offering to help me learn the mechanism and find out how it is done.'[33] The idea had been shelved with the coming of war. Thompson was still connected with the film industry and was a member of the Adventurers' Club of Los Angeles. His duty was to go ahead to California to publicise the expedition there, a job that he did with rather too much enthusiasm and imagination. The best press write-up came from *World's Pictorial News* of 23 June. Their headline was 'Rear Admiral as Odd-Job Man'. They were of course referring to Guy Eardley-Wilmot, who was actually a Rear-Admiral's son, but that would have not made anywhere near so good a headline. The reporter had enjoyed a long interview with Roger Pocock and waxed lyrical about the spirit of Frobisher and Drake. Pocock's ability to spin a yarn had captured him and the article is somewhat excessive in its praise.

> As I sat in the little chartroom of the ship and listened to Captain Roger Pocock, the famous writer and pioneer, the leader of the expedition, while, with a map of the world spread out before him, he told me in a quiet matter-of-fact way of his plans for the wonderful voyage he is embarking on, I realised easily how he has got together so splendid and enthusiastic a band of 'adventurers'.[34]

It is in this article that we find the first strong clues of how much the ship had really cost:

> The response to the call for an amateur crew, every member of which should pay to join and work his passage as well, was so satisfactory that the yacht *Vanduara*, a pilot boat tender of the Mersey Harbour Board and originally belonging to Mr Coats (of Paisley cotton fame), was purchased for £10,000 and insured for that sum; this amount having been raised by subscription in five and a half months.[35]

If this sum is only approximately correct, the original price of £1,500 had grown with the cost of a new foremast and a re-fit – and nothing spent on the engines! On the voyage, when trouble started brewing, the crew got together and worked out that they had put in altogether some £5,800, although whether some said they had invested more than they really had cannot be known. In a later interview with the press, Malins said that the total cost of dispatching the ship was about £12,000. It does not seem likely that the sums received from subscription (rather than merely promised) can have totalled more than £1,000 or £1,500, so it can be assumed that the expedition sailed with a millstone of debts of some £5,000 about its neck.

Pocock admitted knowing that they were deeply in debt when the ship sailed on the afternoon of 16 June 1923, but he kept his worries to himself. 'The solvent for worry is hard work',[36] he wrote, and so he threw himself into the tasks of charting and scrubbing decks. He excused his action in sailing without having secured a financial anchor for the expedition by saying that, had he made the financial problems public and postponed the start, those who were considering backing the expedition would have pulled out. If the ship sailed and things went well, the nervous backers would come forward with their cash and he would be able to pay the bills. It was a very large gamble indeed. Things were not going well from the start and it was very foolish – many of his critics would say almost criminal – not to get together with at least Malins and MacMillan and be honest with them about the financial problems. The expedition was run under the auspices of the Legion of Frontiersmen, which has always prided itself in its democracy. Every member of the crew was supposed to be an equal partner. Pocock did not tell his partners what the problems were, and so, when they came to find out, some were to hold a long-term bitterness and others were publicly to accuse him of nothing less than cheating. What he was guilty of was optimism of the utmost craziness. The basic flaws in his character were to land him in trouble yet again.

34 *Visitors from the public on board the ship in London, 16 June 1923.*

The ship picked up its reluctant Chief Engineer at Gravesend, but only sailed as far as Dover before the engines failed completely and the ship was left drifting helplessly in the hands of its mainly inexperienced crew. Slowly, the *Frontiersman* drifted nearer to Dover Pier until the crew's attention was drawn to the Piermaster dancing up and down on the end of his precious pier like a dervish, expecting at any minute to be sunk with his charge. Just in time, the crew regained control and the ship had to wait at anchor for spares to be sent down and the ailing engines patched up. Pocock admitted to being held up 'for a few days' due to 'some small indisposition of the engines'. It was nearer to ten days, on 28 June, before the ship was ready to set sail again.[37] The flaws in the make-up of the crew were already becoming apparent. The more criminal types were banding together and already showing signs of being anti-Roger Pocock. Spalding was not strong enough a character as Captain and the crew always puzzled as to why Downes had not been given his master's ticket. Fortunately the First Officer, the diminutive Wells, was an excellent officer and was prominent in many committee meetings that were held at every difficulty that arose. In addition to the elements of

The World Flight Expedition

35 *(above)* Mellon, who was described as the ship's comedian, juggling. The dog with him, 'Pog' supposedly the ship's mascot, apparently never sailed.

36 *(above right)* Guy Eardley-Wilmot and G.E. Heaton.

37 *(right)* Silver, the expedition photographer.

38 Mellon fooling around again on board ship.

the crew who were criminals, there were others who were unsuitable for the task. One man was permanently seasick, even on the calmest days. He always carried a pocket full of biscuits, which he constantly munched to try to settle his stomach. Some years later, Frank Ransley met him again when the man was a prisoner in Maidstone Prison. He had been ordained in the Church of England but died quite young in prison, wealthy but lonely. He left around £100,000, which was a very large amount of money in those days.[38]

The crew gradually started to enjoy the voyage through calm summer seas and to forget their growing problems. After a peaceful steaming, nursing the engines, they made their first landing at Madeira. One member of the crew decided to go ashore dressed only in a pair of 'Aertex' underpants because 'that was how the natives dressed'. He lasted five minutes before being arrested and Pocock had to bail him out.[39] After a day at Madeira, they were on their way again for more calm sailing to the West Indies. Pocock had an airy cabin in the deckhouse with much to do. As cartographer, his job was to prepare accurate charts for the harbours, synchronised to a single scale and painted to show the contours. He was also to make a sectional chart showing the compass bearings for the flight, which could be easily handled in a plane cockpit. This was to be sent to MacMillan in time for the proposed start of the actual flight in February 1924.

Pocock was still keen to do a share of scrubbing decks and polishing and, although it had been previously agreed that he would not do so, he was involving himself in the running of the ship. He would have liked to have lent a hand with the heavy work such as stoking, but although he was game, his age and infirmities prevented it. He was always about the ship, handing out cigarettes, of which they seemed to have an endless supply. As they steamed deeper into the tropics, the increasing heat was having its effect on the crew, particularly the amateur firemen. They found a use for one of the sails that had proved hopelessly inadequate for sailing, although they had

The World Flight Expedition

39 *Silver the photographer, Heaton and Captain Spalding.*

40 *Heaton at work trimming coal.*

one very expensive new mast. They rigged up a sail bath on deck, which was very much appreciated, until some fool cut one of the supporting ropes as a practical joke and the bathers crashed down on the deck. As many gallons of bath water flooded immediately down into the engine room, that incident was no help at all to the sick and struggling engines.[40] Eventually, the ship made landfall at the tiny island of St Lucia in the West Indies. The crew agreed that this was the nearest place to Paradise they had ever seen. They anchored off the tiny capital town of Castries and enjoyed bathing in the small surf in the secluded coves, while some took trips up into the forested hills. The Governor and his wife, Colonel and Mrs Houston, invited Pocock and a few of the crew to dine at the Residency. After dinner the guests went out on the verandah with Colonel and Mrs Houston to look down over the lights of the little town. They were surprised to hear the sound of exploding fireworks and see a most exceptional display coming from the ship and illuminating the tropical night. One hundred and fifty pounds of Pains fireworks at 1923 values made an unforgettable show. Every inhabitant of Castries crowded down on the beach to watch in open-mouthed amazement as the rainbow flares from many fireworks lit up the tropical sky. The next morning, a contrite

41 *The sail bath.*

member of the crew with a bad hangover, who had broached the liquor stores the previous night as well as the fireworks, reported to Capt. Spalding. He was sent home, having already spent the value of his investment in the expedition. The inhabitants of the tiny island were dreadfully disappointed when the *Frontiersman* sailed out of the bay. They had never before seen such a firework display and were unlikely to see one like it again.[41]

The crew's diet was helped by flying fish, which would land on the ship's deck to be transferred with alacrity to the frying pan. On 31 July they reached the Panama Canal where there was a problem over the payment of canal dues and this held them up for a time until the authorities agreed to accept payment by cheque. This was one of many that were passed by the expedition, but were apparently seldom honoured due to the absence of funds. By now they were running short of coal and the journey from the Panama Canal to California would be against strong head winds. The ship looked in at Acapulco in Mexico where there was no coal to be had, but they anchored off Manzanillo to find some 20 tons on the quay that could be purchased. It was time to open the emergency cash box, which contained £350 for use in such eventualities. Early the next morning, 10 August, Pocock requested the whole Ship's company to assemble on deck. Frank Ransley never forgot the scene on that morning. Pocock stood in front of them looking tired and drawn as if he had slept very little during the night. Tears were running down his usually cheerful cheeks. 'Gentlemen', he said, 'we have a thief aboard. Someone has opened the cash box and taken our complete reserve of cash. I ask the thief to "do the right thing" and own up.'[42] The men looked at him, a few feet shifting uncomfortably on the deck but, apart from the normal sounds of the breeze at the mastheads and a few unconsidered noises coming on the wind from Manzanillo, there was silence. After a long minute, Roger Pocock the dreamer, Roger Pocock the idealist who trusted easily, turned and made his slow way back to his cabin with bowed head. With embarrassed murmurs, the company broke up and went about their duties.

By now it was obvious to all that the expedition was failing. Some did not care, they had journeyed almost as far as they wished to go. Others were getting increasingly furious with Pocock for landing them in such a mess, although on that particular morning there could have been only a few men who did not have some sympathy for him. They needed that coal to get to California where Pocock expected some help and their mail with, hopefully, a letter from Legion Headquarters to say that enough money had come in to relieve their problems. Pocock went to see the British Consul, but he was away. 'I saw the American Consul and got him to back the bill, which I endorsed, which made it my personal obligation to pay. Afterwards it was paid.'[43] That sounds as if his long-suffering brother-in-law had to help him out again because he does not say that he paid it himself. They had samples of the coal, which showed it to be of good quality. When they got it on board, it turned out that they had been defrauded, as very little of it would burn. Much of it was shale and was more likely to put out the ancient engines than actually burn. The ship visited a small island in the hope of cutting some wood to burn, but there was none to be had and in any case they had no practical way of cutting and hauling it. In the end, they eked out what coal would burn by burning any spare wood they could find around the ship. They were even looking at the expensively made and beautiful mahogany fittings in the cabins when they arrived at San Pedro, the port of Los Angeles, on just about their last shovel of coal.

They were in for some surprises.

Seven

UPSETTING THE AMERICANS

Dr Fred Thompson had gone to Los Angeles ahead of the ship as publicity officer and had been rather busy among his friends, particularly in the motion picture industry. He had told everyone that each member of the crew was a scion of the British nobility, all sons of Dukes and Earls. Consequently, the welcome waiting for the harassed crew when they arrived on 24 August completely overwhelmed and amazed them. The exclusive California Yacht Club had offered them moorings. Although the *Frontiersman* was by no means a large ship, she took up virtually the whole of those moorings. All right for a day or two, but when things continued to go wrong, the millionaire yacht owners had things to say. The hospitality waiting for them was boundless. The crew were invited to the ranch of a millionaire Mr Wooden, at Beverley Hills, where they admired his thoroughbred horses and his thoroughbred daughters. They were conducted to see an oil well at Signal Hill.[1] The mail waiting for them offered no comfort to Pocock. The funds promised to MacMillan had not materialised. There might hopefully be enough money to pay for the building of the plane but that was all. MacMillan was sorry but firm, Pocock had spent enough already. The World Flight Expedition must fend for itself and fund itself in Canada. The ship was once again in need of repair. They had no money and no coal. They were broke and yet were being welcomed as wealthy adventuring aristocrats.

The highlight of the hospitality was a dinner given at the Thos. Ince Motion Picture Studios in Culver City. Ince, who could have been one of the first rank of film-makers had he not died comparatively young, was making a film *Anna Christie* and during the dinner filmed the flooding of the ship's engine room. This was quite a spectacle, but rather discouraging to the engineers of the *Frontiersman*.[2] The magnificent and expensively printed menu for the dinner gives an idea of the lavishness of the occasion. It also awarded Roger Pocock a new rank, as it announced:

> A dinner in honor of Commander Roger Pocock and the personnel of the British Steam Yacht *Frontiersman* who are surveying the course for the World Flight by Captain G.H. Malins and Captain Norman MacMillan of the Royal British Air Force. Given by the Adventurers Club of Los Angeles

UPSETTING THE AMERICANS   117

42 *Eardley-Wilmot in chair. Clockwise from bottom left, crew members Bromley, O'Dell, Mellon, Pearce, Masterson, Perry.*

at the Thos. H. Ince Motion Picture Studios, Culver City, California. August 29, 1923 6.30 p.m.³

The Legion of Frontiersmen was not an unknown organisation in California at the time. The Canadian Division has a photograph of half a dozen ex-patriot British in the distinctive uniform of the Frontiersmen who rode in the Disabled American Veterans' Parade in San Francisco in 1923.⁴ There must have been some puzzlement among the members of the Adventurers Club about what had happened to all the grand titles they had been

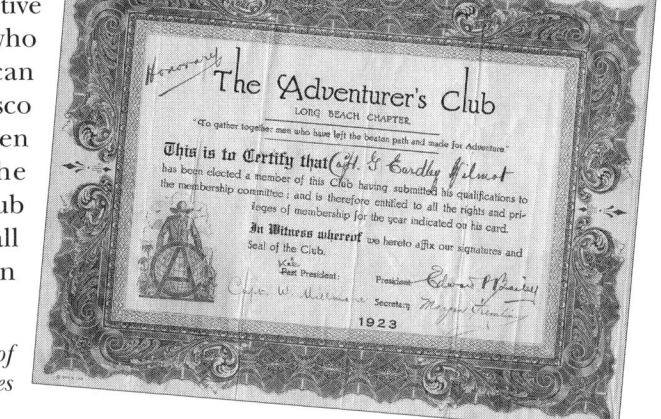

43 *The membership certificate of the Adventurers Club of Los Angeles presented to Eardley-Wilmot.*

44 *The party at Mr Wooden's ranch at Beverley Hills, California.*

45 *Mr Wooden with his thoroughbred horses and his daughters.*

told were borne by the members of the crew. No expense had been spared to put on this dinner in honour of these noble British adventurers and the menu went into great detail: 'It is especially noteworthy that every section of the Pacific Slope, from Alaska to Mexico, has contributed some characteristic article of food or drink to this dinner ... The dinner is composed of materials brought by sea, land and air over an aggregate of approximately 10,000 miles ...'[4]

The dinner was served 'by the Elite Catering Company' on the largest stage of Thomas Ince's studio, and the entertainment included the shooting of actual scenes from *Anna Christie*: 'By courtesy of the International Film Service, a film showing the genesis of the flying machine will be shown.'[5] The meal was of many courses, including Columbia River salmon and roast Alaska reindeer. It is doubtful whether the Californians could, or would, have put on a better show had British Royalty been present. Some of the crew must have felt very uncomfortable knowing they were in fact penniless. Pocock kept quiet about their troubles, partly to save face and partly in the hope that he might find a backer among the wealthy Americans. He would have been quite prepared to swallow his patriotism for a while if American money could get the ship to Canada. It was an amazing banquet for men who had come from a foundering expedition tottering on the brink of abject failure to find themselves treated almost as if they were kings. So many cities and states were involved in preparing the banquet that Dr Thompson must have excelled himself with his advance publicity. One would think by the nature of the banquet and the menu that the hosts expected the noble crew to arrive wearing coronets with ermine trimmings on baronial robes. The banquet was not the end of the evening. Speech followed speech by eminent and wealthy Californians welcoming and praising the adventurers and members of the crew had to answer as best they could. Their menus were all signed by Mr Ince and by various others. One of Ince's colleagues wrote such comments as 'I am surely glad to have met you and your real nice friends and hope to see you in your country soon.' and 'I think you could have played my part of Mate Burke in *Anna Christie*. I am sure you would have been ideal. With every good wish for your adventure.'[6] By the time the dinner and the entertainment were over, it was two o'clock in the morning and the crew reeled back to the ship in a dazed state.

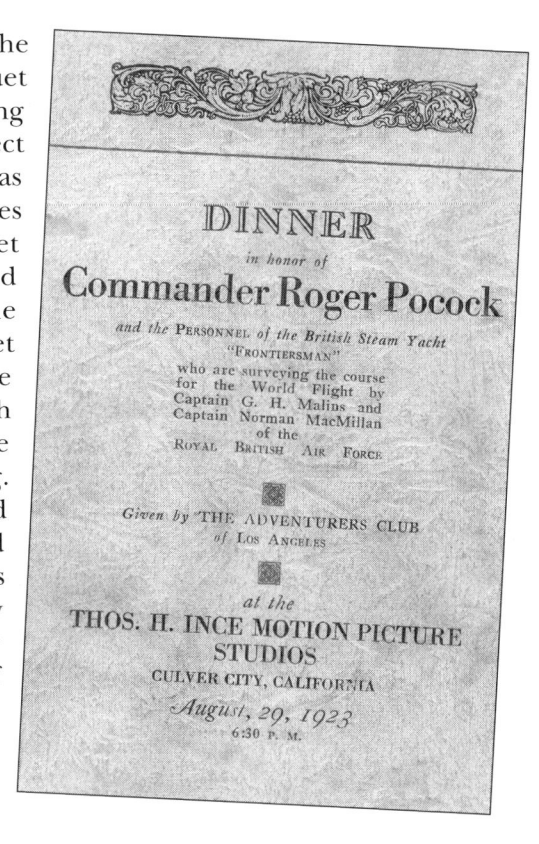

46 *The menu of the Dinner given for the crew at the Thos. Ince Motion Picture Studios, 29 August 1923.*

Although they could not hope to match the opulence of the banquet provided in their honour, the crew of the *Frontiersman* had to return the hospitality. So, the most important members of the Adventurers Club and other dignitaries from Los Angeles and surrounding cities were invited to a lunch on board the *Frontiersman* two days later on Friday 31st. With the cramped conditions it was only possible to provide a cold lunch of such things as cold salmon, cold pork, cold sirloin of beef and fruit salad. Although they were able to supply some of the food from their own stores, they had to send out for many other items. No-one had any money to pay the bills that they were gradually incurring.[7] Something of an emergency committee grew up whose main members were Downes, Wells, Spalding, Eardley-Wilmot and Pocock. They got together for daily meetings to discuss what could be done and we can be sure that Eardley-Wilmot was telling Pocock in no uncertain terms what he thought of his actions. It is quite possible that, had Pocock taken Eardley-Wilmot into his confidence back in England, he was just the

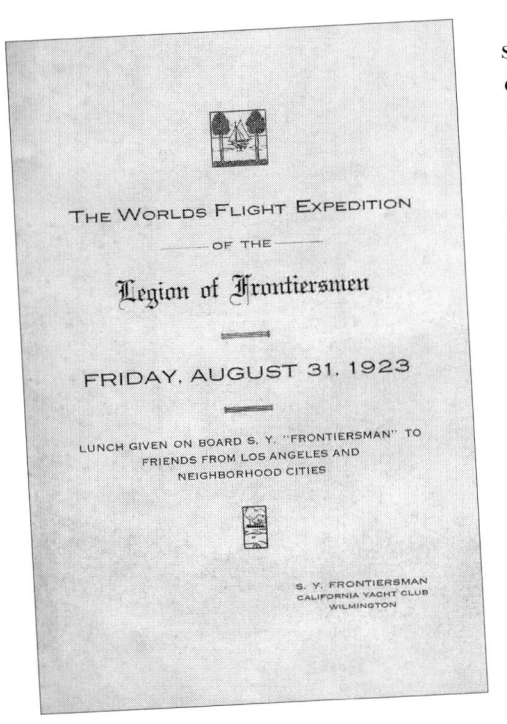

47 Menu of the lunch given on board the S.Y. Frontiersman *to notable Los Angeles citizens.*

sort of man to have got something done which could have ensured a real chance of success for the expedition. Meanwhile, the crew had invitations to all the local film studios, which they were pleased to accept. The ship was graced by lovely young stars such as Claire Windsor and Pauline Fredericks, and Pocock made sure he stood next to one young star when group photographs were taken, even managing a surreptitious arm round her. He was still not too old to be attracted to a pretty face.[8]

Rumours started to spread about the problems of the crew. After all, why were they stopping so long? Surely, they wanted to be well ahead with their journey before winter took hold in Canada and the North Pacific. Also, the activities of some of the crew were not what should be expected of English gentlemen. Then, a ray of hope shone out to Pocock. Into the bay sailed a yacht belonging to William B. Leeds Jnr. He was a friend of Eardley-Wilmot and remained so throughout their lives. Eardley-Wilmot became a regular member of the crew of Leeds' yachts. Leeds was the epitome of the eccentric American millionaire. His first wife, whom he married in October 1921 when he was 19, was Princess Xenia of Greece. In later years he would come to England and take over the old *South Western Hotel* in Southampton to entertain his friends. Once during 1927 he arrived at Southampton after crossing the Atlantic in a small boat. He had no luggage with him and immediately ordered 16 suits. On another occasion he came over on the *Queen Mary*, presented every member of the hotel staff with an inscribed gold watch and left again for France the same evening on the *Queen Mary*. Princess Xenia divorced Leeds in 1930, and that same year he rescued a former telephone operator whose rowing boat had been swamped off Atlantic City and married her five years later. He shot himself at the age of 69 when seriously ill from cancer, almost exactly six years after Eardley-Wilmot's death in an English chest hospital.[9]

Eardley-Wilmot introduced Pocock to Leeds and for several days the three men could be seen walking along deep in earnest conversation. Could Leeds be persuaded to finance them as far as Canada? Unfortunately he could not. The mud was sticking and the rough elements of the crew were blacking Pocock's name to anyone who would listen to them. The heady welcome of the first week or so was evaporating and it became evident to Pocock that he was not going to get the backing he needed to take the ship

48-49 *Goldwyn stars on board the ship.*

to Canada, where he believed Canadian friends could even take over the whole project. The final blow to the expedition came on Wednesday, 12 September. The ship was raided by L.J. Tyson, Harbour Prohibition Officer, and Earl Beach, Deputy Collector of Customs. They demanded to see the ship's rum casks. According to the strict prohibition laws current at that time, these had been sealed by customs when the ship arrived. They broke the seals and took samples from the casks to find that they contained nothing but water. Some person or persons had cleverly broached the casks without damaging the seals, drawn off the rum and re-filled them with water. Pocock was thunderstruck. Here was further evidence that he had not been careful enough in selecting his crew. He contented himself with an attack on the prohibition agents, accusing these Americans in his writings of searching cabins and trampling on valuable possessions, although other crew members made no accusations against the Americans.[10] Pocock would never accept that he had been mistaken in his choice of crew members. That was far from the end of the day's troubles. On to the ship strode Deputy U.S. Marshal Bill Finn, not one bit like the film version of a U.S. Marshal. He was resplendent in shirtsleeves, light coloured braces, cloth cap and large evil smelling pipe. He made himself known to Capt. Spalding and then nailed up a writ attaching the ship for debt on behalf of the Los Angeles Shipbuilding and Dry Dock Company, claiming 250 dollars for labour, materials and equipment. After posing proudly by the nailed up writ for his photograph to be taken, he strode off the ship.[11]

50 *Marshal Bill Finn poses by the writ for debt that he has just attached to the ship.*

Pocock immediately cabled to London for help, but newspaper reporters had got to Malins first. The story the British press had was that the prohibition authorities had found 65 gallons of Scotch whisky on board the *Frontiersman* and had confiscated it. Malins received the news from a *Daily Telegraph* reporter firstly with astonishment, secondly amusement, and finally not a little indignation. Malins thought the whisky referred to was just about the quantity the ship left London with – not an excessive amount for a crew of 38 officers and gentlemen. It was necessary also to leave small quantities at the proposed dumps. Whisky had been most useful in the 1922 flight, used for everything from antiseptic to local anaesthetic. Malins concluded 'If the authorities have held her up for a thing like that they ought to be ashamed of themselves.'[12] Later, the full facts of the writ for debt became public and Malins and MacMillan heard the truth about the missing rum. The cable from Pocock, added to the press publicity, brought two separate and different results. MacMillan and Malins changed their earlier hard line and told Pocock to hang on while they did all they could to raise more money. To try to give him more time at the American end also, a statement was filed to the Federal Court in California that the owners promised to pay all outstanding debts by 10 October.[13] The second result was that the Legion of Frontiersmen washed

51 *Eardley-Wilmot in later years crewing for American millionaire William B. Leeds.*

their hands of the whole affair, terminated the relationship between the Legion and the World-Flight Expedition and even refused to forward any mail that came into their office in Adam Street to the crew of the *Frontiersman*.[14]

In San Pedro, the California Yacht Club, by now incensed that all their moorings had been taken up for so long, told the Captain of the *Frontiersman* in no uncertain terms to vacate them, and Spalding was forced to move the ship out into the bay where it became very difficult for the crew to come and go. To get back on board from the shore they had to attract the attention of someone on the ship and get him to row over. This was a most unsuitable arrangement and not good for the tempers of all concerned. Pocock's pride was very badly hurt. Although he would not admit it, in private moments he must have pondered who were the crooks in the crew. Suspicion falls on one man as their leader; one man who had access to the cash box; one man who always had a different, expensive, painted woman in tow at every port at which they docked; one man with the ability to organise a few others. Frank Ransley could have put a name to this man, but was not prepared to do so when interviewed.[15] The antipathy to Pocock was carefully orchestrated behind the scenes. It is virtually certain that some of the crew had travelled as far as they wished on the journey and had no stomach for being marooned on a cold uninhabited island in the Arctic Circle for several months. Pocock was given a job for a few days as a film extra by a director, Harold Shaw, whom he had

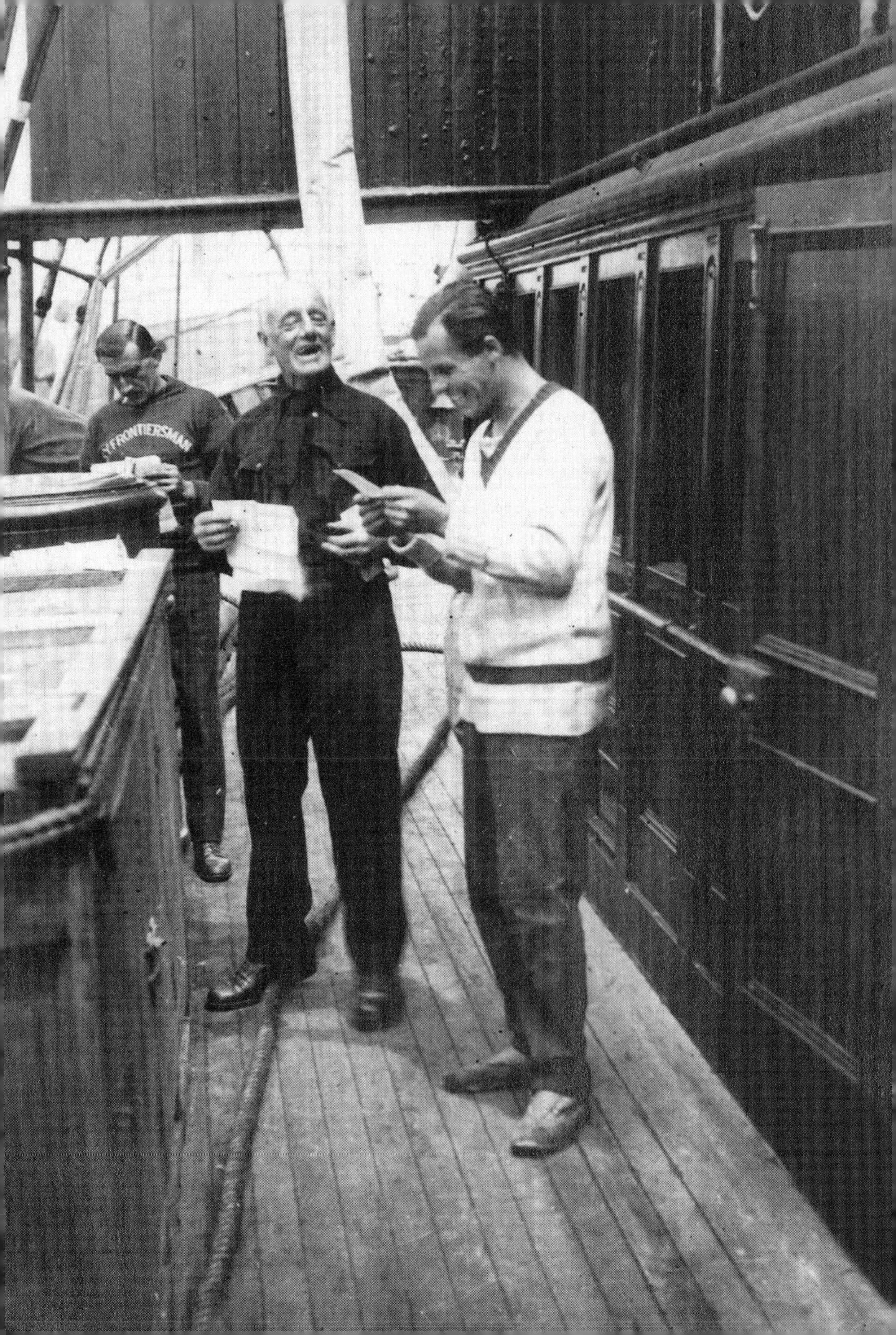
FRONTIERSMAN

known in London. For this he was paid 75 dollars, which he brought back and gave to Spalding to help pay for provisions for the crew. Some of them commented on his absence and construed it as desertion, but the majority of the men had decided to make the best of a bad job and look for employment.[16] After all, California was a booming area and the climate was glorious. The manager of the Los Angeles Labour Exchange was an expatriate Scot with the very Scottish name of Robert Burns. He was exceptionally helpful, and found some sort of job for every man of the crew who went to him. Some men took jobs on a nearby oil terminal and pay was generally very good.[17] Some English newspapers were painting word pictures of the adventurers starving on a California beach, but this was far from the case.

As the days turned into weeks it became certain that there was no hope of enough money being raised to save the expedition. The majority of the crew drifted away, not even bothering to sleep on the ship or even return to her. They were still invited to visit film studios and some of them went to meet Douglas Fairbanks and Mary Pickford who were filming *The Thief of Baghdad*. The crew knew the expedition was over. The ship was auctioned and Pocock watched his treasured *Frontiersman* go under the hammer with much private bitterness. He claimed that the auction was not very public with only a couple of men looking like clerks attending. The ship with its contents was sold for the equivalent of about £100, just a mere fraction of its value. Pocock wrote of reading in a California newspaper some months later that the ship had been bought by bootleggers who took her to the West Indies, loaded her with liquor and brought her back through the Panama Canal. His account reported that she lay off San Francisco waiting for a boat to come out and unload the cargo when a sudden storm blew up. The ship was blown well out to sea and there was a fight among the crew who raided the cargo. They then scuttled the ship to hide the bloodshed and bodies and took to the boats. When they reached the coast they were arrested by Federal officials. We therefore assume that the S.Y. *Frontiersman* now lies somewhere in deep water off the coast of California.[18]

The British Press continued a mild interest in the story for some months and paragraphs on it kept appearing. The *Daily Chronicle* reported on 6 November that a new British attempt at the world flight would be made the following spring.[19] The Government wanted nothing to do with the remnants of earlier expeditions and it was announced that Squadron Leader Stuart MacLaren, the first man to fly from England to India, which he achieved in a Handley-Page bomber in 1919, was to make the flight. Once again, no Government money was to be made available, but MacLaren was to be given leave and 'all possible assistance by the R.A.F.'.[20] Air Chief Marshal Sir Hugh Trenchard was to give the project his personal attention. The MacLaren expedition proved no more successful than the 1922 MacMillan one, and the Americans achieved the feat in 1924 with full Government support.[21]

52 (left)   *The first mail received at anchor in California.*

By Christmas 1923, only four of the crew had returned to England. Many were having a very enjoyable time in California and in no hurry to get home. Some had no intention of coming back. One of the four back in England was Guy Eardley-Wilmot, and he had every intention of stirring things up and getting all the reasons for the failure aired publicly. He started by writing to Sir Sefton Brancker, who had given the Air Ministry's blessing to the whole venture. Brancker replied in a most conciliatory tone:

> ... I saw Lord Loch and Mr Christmas [the accountant to the expedition] this morning. They exonerate MacMillan from blame and say he actually has been trying to get in touch with you. I gave him your address and those of the other members of the crew who have returned to England, and suggested that he should get you and MacMillan to meet with him and discuss the whole situation before anything further was done. He will be writing to you, so please hold your hand regarding publicity until you have talked matters over. In any case I doubt if paper agitation is going to do anybody any good. Naturally, the Air Ministry moral support of the Legion of Frontiersmen World Flight has been withdrawn.[22]

Eardley-Wilmot replied by return, but I have found no copy of what he said. No doubt he pointed out that the withdrawal of moral support was a useless act because the expedition had collapsed long ago. Brancker wrote back, again by return:

> ... I quite see your point and have done so all along. I hope perhaps that your meeting with Lord Loch and MacMillan may bring forward a suggestion as to what we could do to restore our loss of prestige involved by this unfortunate incident. Anyway, you can be sure that the Air Ministry is not going to support any further funds being collected by the existing organisation. I am awaiting the results of your meeting before doing anything further.[23]

No record has been found of the meeting between Eardley-Wilmot, MacMillan and Lord Loch, but Eardley-Wilmot, Heaton and the others had called on Col H.T. Tamplin, Commandant of the Legion of Frontiersmen on 20 November. Tamplin wrote on 21 November to Arthur Burchardt-Ashton, then Treasurer, later to be Tamplin's successor. He wrote to thank Burchardt-Ashton for a donation (one of many by this man) of £20 to solve one of the Legion's constant financial problems. Tamplin also told him about the visit:

> A number of the crew of S.Y. *Frontiersman* called yesterday, all gentlemen, asking what we were going to do. They denounced Pocock in un-measured terms and said he is now a fugitive from the fury of the law somewhere in Los Angeles. The gentlemen who came here were very indignant and hotly resented that they should be the victims of Pocock's fraud and deceit. They described Pocock's grandiloquent orations at the several Dinners of Welcome of a public character, at which they were entertained, in which he appears to have posed as the Representative of the Legion of

Frontiersmen. I must say they were speedily convinced of the real position and we parted on excellent terms.[24]

Although there can be some sympathy for Pocock, he actually brought much of the trouble upon himself. The Legion of Frontiersmen were being most unfair by denying all responsibility. They had wanted any credit for success, but after their early enthusiasm did their best to distance themselves from the whole affair. Pocock was probably sensible in lying low in America and he did not return for several years. He managed to earn a living in the film industry either as an extra, or writing, with John P. McCarthy, short western films such as *Brand of Cowardice*. Eardley-Wilmot's comments to Lord Loch must have been blistering, but the meeting was inconclusive. In a letter written in 1965 shortly before he died, Eardley-Wilmot said, 'I tried most unsuccessfully to write an account [of the expedition] for various magazines but I found it quite impossible to dodge the laws of libel.' He also said, 'I remember when I eventually returned home that I crossed swords with his sister Lena Ashwell.'[25] Lena Ashwell would, as usual, have been working in the background to help her brother and the redoubtable lady would have rushed to his defence. Any meeting between her and Eardley-Wilmot would surely have seen many sparks fly.

The *Daily Mail* interviewed MacMillan and raised the story again on 6 December. They reported his statement to them:

> To finance the ship's expedition about £7,000 was raised including money contributed by the crew. When the ship left England, there was about £2,000 in the bank. Later, bills for repairs began to come in, and to our great surprise we learnt that we had a deficit of £5,000. This was partly because the outfitting of the ship cost more than had been estimated and because the ship steamed to the Panama Canal instead of sailing as had been arranged. In the ship's safe at the beginning of the voyage was £350. This was spent on the journey in food charges, Panama Canal dues and other items, and when the *Frontiersman* got to California it had no money. Repairs had to be carried out, and as money which it was expected would be forthcoming did not arrive, the boat was seized for debt and most of the crew obtained employment ashore. Since then, I hear, the ship has been sold for about £450.[26]

Eardley-Wilmot was not happy about this carefully worded statement which did not admit the theft of the £350 and which said the minimum about the troubles in California. He wanted his own version made public and so a letter in response to this article was published in the *Daily Mail* on 13 December, signed by Eardley-Wilmot and Herbert Heaton, a friend who had returned with him. The letter was written from Eardley-Wilmot's address in Marlow:

> ... We think it only fair that you should know the facts with regard to the 'volunteer crew seeking adventure', and would be grateful if you could publish them to clear the crew's good name. We are sending this to you with the

full consent of other members who have got back and also of those who are still stranded in California and elsewhere. We did not set out for the sole reason of adventure, but entirely in a patriotic spirit to help in gaining for our country the honour of providing the first men to fly round the world. This expedition was started by Captains Pocock, Malins and MacMillan, under the auspices of the Legion of Frontiersmen, backed by the moral support of Lord Loch ... and General Brancker ... With these well known bodies behind us we set off having subscribed some £5,400 between us for the cause. The rest of the story is becoming Notorious – how we were all made fools of in the eyes of America and stranded in California, either to find work out there or to struggle home as best we could. Only four of us have succeeded in doing the latter, and on our arrival in town, we find that the Legion of Frontiersmen now disown us, although every member of the crew wore their uniform and was compelled to become a member of the Legion before sailing. The Air Ministry have also backed out of any and all responsibility, and have withdrawn their moral support. We would point out that it was only through these public organisations backing the expedition that the crew felt quite secure in investing their capital and in giving their services. That is the way in which 38 ex-service men of all branches have been treated. Can you wonder at discontent? We are sure that neither the public nor the expedition's numerous creditors can blame us for the fiasco.[27]

Perhaps Eardley-Wilmot was exaggerating about the poor chaps 'stranded in California', but he had taken on the mantle of crusader for laying the blame where it belonged. Unfortunately for Eardley-Wilmot, Pocock was still lying low in America. Although he felt unable to risk the laws of libel by writing the whole of what he believed, we can be certain that he spoke to as many newspapers as he could. The popular journal *John Bull* attacked the Legion of Frontiersmen and most particularly Lord Loch even before Eardley-Wilmot arrived back in Britain. Under the heading 'Who Will rescue Them?' it enquired: 'What is Lord Loch going to do about the still unsolved scandal of the British pioneers stranded in America as a result of the ill-fated voyage of the Steam Yacht *Frontiersman.*'[28] They also strongly criticised Col Tamplin who

> ... has written to us to say that the World's Flight was a completely independent and separate undertaking, in no way initiated, conducted or financed by the Legion. How then does he account for the World's Flight appeals for money issued from the Frontiersmen's office, describing Lord Loch as President, and bearing the symbol and motto of the Frontiersmen 'God Guard Thee'.[29]

By 29 December, it looks as if Eardley-Wilmot had been talking to *John Bull* because another article appeared headed 'Blot on a Great Name'. The article put the blame entirely on the Legion of Frontiersmen and Lord Loch as its President.

> ... Before they started, the Frontiersmen and the two airmen subscribed nearly £6,000 between them towards the Air Flight Fund, and in order to do so scraped together all the money they could spare. They did not take the funds with them but arranged with the headquarters of the Legion to send sums out to them as required. They were somewhat astounded when the money they had written for did not turn up. Their troubles increased when repeated cables to Adam Street asking for aid were not answered ...[30]

John Bull continued their attack and then turned their attention to the Air Ministry: 'The Air Ministry, which through General Brancker lent its support to this ill-fated expedition, has also shown its generosity by backing out of it. It is a grave scandal ...'[31]

After this, interest in the matter seems to have died away. The Americans, backed to the hilt by their Government, were the first to achieve the flight in 1924. A British amateur attempt by MacLaren and Plenderleith came to grief at a similar place to the MacMillan expedition of two years earlier.[32] Very few of those who helped organise the Frontiersmen World Flight Expedition come out of it with any credit. MacMillan and Malins were intelligent officers who should surely have been too worldly-wise to be swept along by Pocock's enthusiasm. The Air Ministry followed the regular path of politicians by giving 'moral backing' but nothing of substance, and then retreating as soon as things went wrong. The Legion of Frontiersmen's behaviour was nothing short of disgraceful. They had seen a chance for good publicity in the Expedition, but soon denied everything and washed their hands of the matter leaving men stranded in America. The Legion had no money. This can be proved by letters from Tamplin to the Treasurer, Burchardt-Ashton, thanking him for his financial support saving the Legion from insolvency. However, Lord Loch and other members of the Governing Council were wealthy and influential men, but apparently unwilling to use either in support of the men in America. The worst culprit was Roger Pocock, not for being dishonest, but for being foolish, a dupe and for letting his heart rule his head over the purchase of an unsuitable ship and recruiting unsuitable men for the crew. Nobody appears to have had the confidence to warn Pocock about some of the crew members – but if they had, would he have listened? Pocock took too much responsibility on himself. Some good did come out of the expedition. Frank Ransley was one who said it was the best £100 he had ever spent. He and a friend made enough money working to buy an old car and see something of America before they returned to England by working their passage. For years afterwards he was in demand to give talks about the expedition and reckoned he was so fascinated by the criminal minds he encountered in the crew that he decided to make his successful career in the Prison Service.[33]

Had Pocock succeeded in getting the expedition to Canada, it is doubtful whether he could have drummed up much support there. His most powerful contact, General Sir Sam Steele, had died in 1919, and Steele's son Harwood

53 *Vancouver Command outside the Armoury which is still in use.*

Steele would not have had the same influence as his father. The strong pre-war Frontiersmen units had dwindled away; very many had been killed in the War and people in general wanted to get away from anything military. There was certainly a Victoria and Vancouver Island Squadron there at the time of the ill-fated expedition, commanded by Major Seymour Rowlinson, but they were not of any great significance. Between 1905 and the early days of the First War, the Legion of Frontiersmen had gradually become quite strong and influential in the Dominion. Historian for the Legion in Canada, Will Shandro writes:

> The earliest documentation of the Legion of Frontiersmen being activated in Canada is Roger Pocock's four-page letter to The Hon. Fred White, RNWMP, of Ottawa and dated 15 April 1905. The letter is stamped 'OFFICE OF THE COMPTROLLER RNWMP APR 29 1905'. This is followed by another letter dated 25 June 1905 to the RNWMP in which Albert D. Willcocks (or Albert Dean-Willcocks) of 519 Sherbrooke St. Montreal introduces himself as 'Organizer for Canada'. These and other early letters to and from the RNWMP state a willingness to assist Pocock, and state that members of the Royal North-West Mounted Police would not be in conflict of duties by joining the Legion of Frontiersmen.[34]

54 *The Mayor of Vancouver inspecting the Frontiersmen in the Vancouver Armoury. At that time they were carrying side arms.*

This can be contrasted with the attitude of the British Police at the same time when the Legion of Frontiersmen wrote to Scotland Yard with a request from a police constable to join and the reply was (as we have seen) that there were 'substantial objections ... difficulty in adjusting duties ... impossible to spare more than a limited number of men in time of war ... it is a purely private organisation and, that being so, it is perhaps undesirable to recognise it by granting permission.'[35] By early in the First War, the British police had changed their mind, and they welcomed the uniformed Frontiersmen as mounted auxiliaries to the City of London Police. This was an official duty they retained right through the 1920s, and including the period of the General Strike.

Shandro continues: 'Based upon information contained in the *Regina Morning Leader* of 1917, Captain C.H. Dunn (of Lake Wabamun, Alberta) recruiting for the 210th Frontiersmen Battalion, identifies Stanley Winther Caws (of Lac St Anne, Alberta) as the first Commandant of the Legion of Frontiersmen in Canada.' Pocock claimed in his *Chorus to Adventurers* that Sam Steele was Canadian Commandant '... as O.C. Legion of Frontiersmen in Canada he [Steele] obtained for us official sanction from the Dominion Government.'[36] Probably Steele did his best to aid Pocock and agreed to some form of honorary title to please the younger man, but his name is not listed in Canadian Legion records. Pocock's diary records one brief meeting with Steele in London for supper in February 1907.

55 *Taken in Stanley Park during the First World War. Behind the men is the look position.*

Records from Nelson, British Columbia also document that a very active Nelson Command under E.C. Wragge as established by 1907. Wragge's correspondence indicates contacts with Roger Pocock, London H.Q., S.W. Caws at Lac St. Anne, and other Frontiersmen units in Vancouver, Victoria, Calgary, Yukon Territory, and likely Saskatoon. As well, 1909 letters stamped by the RNWMP discuss the agreement to use 'machine guns' for training by the 'White Horse' [today 'Whitehorse'] camp of the Legion of Frontiersmen.[37]

Perhaps this suggests Steele's influence behind the scenes. Shandro has confirmed early units also in Edmonton, Asquith, Moose Jaw, Regina, Winnipeg, Toronto, Hamilton, Montreal and other places. Shandro continues:

> When the hostilities of 1914 erupted on the European continent, the Legion of Frontiersmen answered the call to arms. Canada's Imperial rough riders, scouts, veterans and patriots enrolled in local Canadian Expeditionary Force Battalions and militia home front regiments. Those that could not qualify for military service became active in home front Legion of Frontiersmen units and patriotic endeavours. The intensity of the Great War, the demands for manpower, and the horrendous losses caused by it, brought an end to activities of the Legion of Frontiersmen by war's end. Commands of the Legion of Frontiersmen withered and faded. It would be more than a decade before an 'original Patricia' [member of Princess Patricia's Canadian Light Infantry] would revitalize Canada's Legion of Frontiersmen.[38]

There were few Frontiersmen in Canada to help Pocock's expedition in 1923, had he succeeded in reaching there.

Eight
SUCCESS, THEN FAILURE AGAIN

There has always been dispute in Canada over the number of Frontiersmen who joined the Princess Patricia's Canadian Light Infantry. The Frontiersmen have claimed anything from 600 to 5,000 men, however, the PPCLI curator told Robert H. MacDonald when researching his *Sons of the Empire* that only 83 claimed any connection with the Legion.[1] Will Shandro is convinced that many more were Frontiersmen. 'Upon enlistment in PPCLI or any other regiment, was it not likely that a "Frontiersman" with previous military experience would proclaim service of his regular army unit … [rather than] the irregular Legion of Frontiersmen?'[2] In 1914 Justus Duncan Willson was local Edmonton Commandant of the Legion and a member of the RNWMP. He was actively recruiting Frontiersmen for the Princess Patricia's. Lt Col Stevens' 1964 account of Edmonton Frontiersmen in the First War, *A City Goes to War*, records that:

56   Badge of 210th (Frontiersmen) Bn. C.E.F.

> In Edmonton the Legion of Frontiersmen were the first to go. They mobilized in their regalia (bushranger hats, khaki shirts and neckerchiefs) … they fetched up at Lansdowne Park, Ottawa, where a Montreal millionaire was exercising the ancient privilege of raising a private fighting force for the crown. Thus began Edmonton's long association with Princess Patricia's Canadian Light Infantry.[3]

Stevens also wrote regarding Willson that, 'As local commandant of the Legion of Frontiersmen he had been responsible for the dispatch of three hundred recruits to Princess Patricia's Canadian Light Infantry.'[4] Without clear evidence, we cannot claim that all these recruits were in fact Frontiersmen. However, there is strong circumstantial evidence in support of that argument. Certainly the then officers of the Legion of Frontiersmen were of paramount assistance in the raising of the PPCLI and no other organisation in Canada at the time had access to the large numbers of veteran volunteers demanded

57 210 (Frontiersmen) Battalion Canadian Expeditionary Force leaving Moose Jaw, 1915.

by the PPCLI. The usually reliable Driscoll wrote in a bulletin to all members on 1 March 1915 before the formation of the 25th Fusiliers that: '... nearly 50 per cent of Princess Patricia's Canadian Light Infantry are members of the Legion.'[5] Louis Scott who was responsible for re-building the Legion in the 1930s was a decorated 'Patricia'. He would not have tolerated the Legion consistently making this claim had it been incorrect. It can be asked why the PPCLI wished to play down the input of the Legion of Frontiersmen. Much of the blame for this must lie with the Legion itself as, in Shandro's words: '... over the years some people claiming to be authentic Legion of Frontiersmen members have represented the authentic organisation badly, and any regiment would naturally distance themselves from such persons.'[6] The Legion can only blame this distancing by military bodies on the unacceptable behaviour of those claiming the name of the Legion of Frontiersmen during subsequent years. Shandro also writes that: 'Willson had also served in the South African War and remained for a while in the South African Constabulary. In 1915 he became the officer commanding "Steady D" Company of the 49th Battalion, Canadian Expeditionary Force – after designated the Edmonton Regiment, and finally the Loyal Edmonton Regiment (4 PPCLI)'.[7] Moose Jaw Frontiersmen were also keen to join the PPCLI. J. Wilson, in *First in the Field, Gault of the Patricias* (1995), described their typical Frontiersmen method of joining:

> ... hearing that the PPCLI contingent from Calgary would be passing through Regina, wired Gault for authority to join the train, though it was

obvious he could not reply in time. They persuaded an American C.P.R. employee, 'Smoke' Thompson, to place two coaches on a siding close to its junction with the main line. When the train from the West arrived, they bluffed the night operator at the Regina station that official arrangements had been made to hitch their carriages to it.

The train conductor was less willing to co-operate. A drawn Smith & Wesson persuaded him to take them to the next divisional point. There they again were obliged to convince a new conductor to allow them to proceed. At Winnipeg a telegram from Gault guaranteed their transportation to Ottawa.'[8]

In Calgary, a Command was established in 1912. Calgary was a former North-West Mounted Police outpost and in 1913 the patriotic citizens, concerned that London was at risk of bombing by German airships, started a fund to purchase an airship *The Calgarian* to be used for the defence of the motherland. Shandro takes the story further in one of his articles:

Not to be outdone, the Legion of Frontiersmen took the proposal further, advocating the building of airships in Calgary and training of 'aerial scouts'. No doubt the construction of an airship was soon judged to be beyond the capabilities of an emerging pioneer community. At a time when strategists were preoccupied with horses ... the Legion of Frontiersmen was thinking about aerial reconnaissance and an aircrew training programme![9]

Shandro also tells us what happened to Stanley Winther Caws:

Coincidentally, Stanley Winther Caws the 'Frontiersman Commandant' of Lac St Anne, Alberta (a South African War veteran and a sergeant in the 19th Alberta Dragoons of Edmonton) transferred to the Royal Flying Corps and flew aerial scouting missions until he was killed in action. Caws and his observer downed two of three enemy aircraft before Lt Caws was killed by gunfire from the third aircraft. The observer, Lt Wilson, was forced to land the aircraft behind enemy lines and was subsequently taken prisoner. The Germans buried the former Legion of Frontiersmen commandant with full military honours in 1915.[10]

In addition to the 25th Fusiliers (Frontiersmen), the Legion also had a named Canadian unit, the 210th (Frontiersmen) Battalion. This was raised in Moose Jaw apparently in response to the need for skilled men for remount duties. We have seen how the Frontiersmen were performing these in England and it seems that with the loss of some of these to the 25th, it was anticipated that Canada could replace them.

According to Battalion veteran C.S. Taylor, British and Canadian authorities detailed an 'original Patricia' who had recovered from wounds to recruit Canadian cowboys for remount duties in England. This objective seems to have become somewhat diminished as the new battalion took on a wide variety of tradesmen, outdoor workers, homesteaders, war veterans and former soldiers. The more rugged individual and the experienced veterans were being encouraged to enlist. These men were added to the nucleus of this new battalion, the already existing quasi-military Legion of Frontiersmen.[11]

However, when it reached England, the unit was broken up and 'the officers and men were re-assigned. The true cowboys went to remount duties, some men to forestry units, others were assigned as railways troops, a few officers to the flying corps, and most men to units at the front.' (Shandro)[12]

The Frontiersmen were also active in Eastern Canada. In 1911 Dr A.W. Wakefield, who had been a U.K. member, established a unit in Labrador. In 1912, he established a second troop at St Anthony and other troops soon followed. In 1912, a troop was formed in St John, Newfoundland, under Lt E.W. Vere Holloway attaching to it such religious groups as the Church Lads Brigade. Australian Frontiersmen historian, Jeff. Henley, wrote: 'On the outbreak of war, Dr Wakefield wrote to the Canadian Prime Minister Sir Edward Morris offering the Newfoundland Frontiersmen for active service. However this offer was declined by the Government but they were free to enlist in the Canadian Army then being formed.'[13] Right up to the present day, authorities in all countries refuse any offer of help from the independent thinking and often troublesome Frontiersmen.

> Thus 150 members of the Newfoundland Command of the Legion of Frontiersmen became part of the Newfoundland Regiment ... During the War these members served in Egypt, Gallipoli, France and Belgium ... Not all members of the Newfoundland Command of the Legion of Frontiersmen served with the Battalion; some served in the Royal Naval Reserve! The lookout area to the sea near St Johns was first named Signal Hill in 1762. Fortifications were first built here called Queens, Wallace, Duke of York, Quidi Vidi Pass, Carronade and Waldegrave Batteries ... With the outbreak of war in 1914 the Waldegrave Battery was re-activated and in July 1916 responsibility for manning the Battery was given to the Legion of Frontiersmen. They were paid by the Canadian Government and made a 'temporary attachment' of the RNR under HMS Brition (ex-HMS Calypso). A gun from the Brition/Calypso was mounted at Fort Waldegrave and the gun Frontiersmen/RNR crew were recruited by Lt Vere Holloway. Evidence of their occupation of the Battery can be seen from a shield carved in the rock face. This shield contains the dates 1868 and 1916. After the war the barracks buildings at Fort Waldegrave were sold but fell into disrepair and were torn down.[14]

It may be thought that the Frontiersmen were only a quasi-military style organisation, but there is much evidence of other naval links and proposed naval links. In August 1933, one of the earliest Legion members, Robert Smith an engineer, wrote to the then Commandant, Burchardt-Ashton, 'I am much interested to know that you have restarted a Maritime Section at Leigh.' (Leigh-on-Sea, Essex.)[15] This was formed by one of the Legion eccentrics 'Count' Johnston-Noad, who was in fact a Count of Montenegro, a title also enjoyed by that other eccentric and early Frontiersman, William Le Queux. Frontiersmen have always liked to have titles and ranks. Even in recent years they don't seem to have changed; some, mainly from outside groups, using variations of the name of the Legion, finding themselves titles from some ex-communist states.

58 *Maritime Division, Portsmouth, c.1930.*

An author did ask the writer once whether the Frontiersmen 'still parade on Wimbledon Common giving each other medals'. Johnston-Noad made the national papers for a scandal when he got into an argument with his 'landlady' and discharged his gun in her direction.[16] There was also a very active Maritime Section at that great naval port, Portsmouth, in the 1930s. Smith started the original Maritime Section and got excellent support from all round the country and a Command was formed at Ipswich. The Member of Parliament, E.G. Pretyman, who had been a Government Navy minister, appears to have got the credit, although Smith did much of the hard work as Secretary and a draft constitution and plan was placed before the Admiralty. 'The one point we were determined upon was: that before we enrolled more men or took any definite steps, we should obtain true recognition by the Admiralty as, in my opinion, the lack of proper military recognition was the great stumbling block in the way of the L[egion of] F[rontiersmen].'[17] As on many future occasions, he and others were to find that no Government Department would be prepared to take official notice of the Legion. Because of this rejection, it was decided to separate the Maritime Section from the Legion, although the authorities still counted them as linked.

> Our programme was not too ambitious, we were prepared to enrol coastwise people, yachtsmen, bargemen and fishermen, who were not eligible for the R.N.R., train them in signalling and for use in time of war in (1) Relief Coastguards, (2) Shore boating, (3) Local Pilotage, (4) Examinations, (5) Minesweeping. The latter was Mr Pretyman's idea, and he was so well known to the Grimsby men they took up the idea with enthusiasm. We undertook to be self-supporting, asked for nothing but the recognition of our badge and officers so that we should be an Auxiliary Force under whatever safeguards the Admiralty liked to impose.
>
> Well! We had interview after interview with officers sent by the Admiralty. First, they could not see what good we could do and when that was well rubbed in they talked of the difficulties they were going to have, of the Naval Enlistment Act, of how we should interfere with the R.N.R. ...[18]

As well as Pretyman and Smith, the first Maritime Section included Linton Hope, who designed yachts and who had been a prospector in the Transvaal, J. St A. Jewell who had a reputation as a writer on sea and yachting subjects and Erskine Childers, whose name is still remembered today, and who was a prominent Frontiersman serving on their Governing Council. His later involvement in Irish nationalism caused the Legion to feel it wise to remove his name from its publicity list of early members. The Legion has attracted supporters from many sides of the political spectrum and it had a great Welsh nationalist, Owen Vaughan, or Owen Rhoscomyl as he was also known, as an enthusiastic early member.[19]

This reaction from the Admiralty is basically a repeat of what has always been said about the Frontiersmen from founding until the present day, that they seek official recognition without responsibility to any official authority while energetically retaining their independence. Smith continued,

59 *Captain E.C. Edwards-Carter.*

So it happened that, when War was declared, our organisation was not in being and the Admiralty had hurried to recognise Boy Scouts to replace Coastguards [and] improvise at huge cost all the other services we offered to perform. The War was half over before they got examinations done by practical cargo men and so began to find contraband in any quantity. Lastly, Minesweeping had to be taught while war was on. Is it any wonder that our failure is a sore point with me? We were beaten by lack of imagination in the official mind! I do not know if it learnt anything from the War or whether our scheme could be put forward again with any possibility of success. The need for it would still appear to exist.[20]

Smith had put into writing the opinions that many Frontiersmen before and since had expressed about the 'official mind'. The Legion of Frontiersmen had many ideas in advance of its time and these, added to the organisation's desire for independence and its eccentricity, meant that throughout its history it would be distrusted by the majority of those holding official positions. The recipient of the letter, Arthur Burchardt-Ashton, had progressed from organising remounts during the War through being treasurer and adjutant to succeeding Col Tamplin as Commandant in 1925. He was born in 1854 and in 1878 went to Hawaii sugar planting with his brothers. There he built his own house and also became an expert in breaking the horses they needed for hauling goods across a country without roads. The enterprise was obviously a success because he was able virtually to retire to Britain in 1890 successfully breeding horses and sailing. He purchased a substantial estate in Hampshire, near Farnham where he was able to enjoy riding and allow his land to be used by the Legion. He was one of many who lost their only sons in the War, a sadness which never left him. His son, as a cavalry officer, was one of the first military pilots, but decided one day, after rather too much whisky, to take up a plane without permission. He proceeded to 'buzz' a demonstration by a noted French pilot and the ensuing fuss meant he had to resign his commission.[21] He joined up in the War as a private soldier in the Royal Fusiliers and was killed in action as a lance-corporal while attached to the Durham Light Infantry.[22] Burchardt-Ashton senior had desperately wanted to go with Driscoll to East Africa, but at 61, with no relevant military experience for the area, and being vital to the Remount Service, he had to spend most of the War in Britain, although his connection with the Boy Scout movement did allow him to spend some time in France.[23] In 1925 he returned the Frontiersmen to their City of London Mounted Police Reserve duties, which they carried out throughout the General Strike.[24]

It is possible to wonder about Burchardt-Ashton's judgement of men, as his Adjutant, and eventually 'Chief of Staff', was a Captain Edwards-Carter. Burchardt-Ashton was forced more than once to defend his adjutant as rumours about him constantly surfaced. Edwards-Carter had enjoyed a varied career in South Africa, finishing as a Captain, apparently on the staff of the High Commissioner, Lord Gladstone. In 1914, while on holiday, according to him, Edwards-Carter, armed with a recommendation from Lord Gladstone, was commissioned as Captain in the Royal Warwickshire Regt. Edwards-Carter always claimed that the English climate affected his health and he had to resign his commission. In fact, War Office files show that he had been bouncing cheques and resigned his commission to avoid an unfortunate court martial.[25] In a letter written in Edwards-Carter's defence to a complainant, Burchardt-Ashton wrote: 'He then organised a group of munition factories in the Midlands, and in 1918 sought to return to the forces. Eventually he was successful and was given his commission as Lieutenant in the Royal Volunteer Reserve, in which he served till December 1919, when he was invalided on demobilisation.'[26] One of Driscoll's officers in East Africa, Major Hazzledine, was most suspicious of Edwards-Carter. Many after the First War were upset by anyone who had not served but had been connected with munitions, believing that they had profited while others risked their lives. His mistrust of Edwards-Carter was increased by the fact that as soon as hostilities were ended Edwards-Carter's health had recovered sufficiently for him to acquire a Naval commission and go to France. In addition, although he did not let it become officially known, Edwards-Carter had committed the inexcusable act of petitioning the King for war medals.[27] As he was connected with the Frontiersmen this was another black mark for them from the officers at the

60 *Harborne Troop in camp, South Midlands, 1936.*

War Office. The black marks were remembered and recorded, but the times when the Frontiersmen were useful tended to be forgotten.

The Frontiersmen were useful to the Government in the General Strike. Burchardt-Ashton had written in January 1926 to Col Curre to try to persuade him to start new Squadrons in the West Country. He told Curre about his Mounted Police Reserve: 'We can get no assistance and I have to hire the horses myself, but from what I can hear it is very likely that we shall be wanted. I am told at Scotland Yard that Mounted Police are far the best way of dealing with the mob; also I am told privately that the Government dare not turn out the troops, not even the Guards.'[28] The Commissioner of the City of London Police, Sir Hugh Turnbull, served for many years on the Governing Council of the Legion. In 1922 the Frontiersmen in South Africa had earned the praise of Smuts when they turned out to help quell what they called the 'Rand Rebellion'. In fact their duties here had also been against strikers. Crafford's biography of Smuts noted that '… overseas newspapers had convinced the British people that the Bolsheviks had been at the bottom of the trouble; that, in fact, Smuts had smashed a Red revolution'. The truth was that the Frontiersmen had assisted when '… they had broken the might of organised labour'.[29] Legion Orders for April 1922 published Smuts' commendation of the Frontiersmen: 'General Smuts has further honoured us by sending an Application Form for Membership duly filled in, in the usual way.' Smuts rejected any rank, saying that to be a Frontiersman was honour enough, but he was appointed Legion of Frontiersmen Commissioner for South Africa, another powerful ally for the Frontiersmen, thus making it more difficult for the War Office to reject them diplomatically as they always wished.

In June 1926 Burchardt-Ashton wrote to the Director of Naval Intelligence to request an interview. A Frontiersman, Tom Cushny, stationed in the Dutch East Indies, had sent in information that should be of use to Naval Intelligence:

Success, then Failure Again

61 *March-past, Horse Guards Parade, 1935 with General Sir John Shea taking salute.*

> I became aware of the danger to the new Naval Base then under construction in the Straits of Johore being outflanked by the simple manoeuvre of establishing an enemy base in Coconut Bay, 150 miles due south. Here lay a vast anchorage in a commanding position, cutting the sea route to Australia and sealing off Singapore. It was well stocked in coal, fuel oil, fresh water and foodstuffs.[30]

The Navy usually had a higher opinion of the Frontiersmen than the War Office. In 1929, the Legion of Frontiersmen were used officially by Lord Lloyd, the High Commissioner for Egypt, but by then the Frontiersmen were again aggravating the War Office. Needless to say, Roger Pocock was back in England after his spell in Hollywood and after the fuss over the World Flight Expedition had mainly died down. Every time he took interest in the Frontiersmen, trouble was seldom far behind. Instigated in the main by Major Hazzledine and 'Kaid' Belton, the disquiet about Edwards-Carter and, to a lesser extent, Burchardt-Ashton had come to a head. Some of the Frontiersmen of the old 'range' type who were unhappy at the apparently almost political leanings of the official Legion had formed a breakaway organisation, the 'Independent Overseas Legion of Frontiersmen'. These were men who yearned even more for the good old days and the wide open spaces of the frontier. They had also seen genuine active service in the First War. Pocock, who had been found a home as a Brother at Charterhouse, was delighted to be brought back to be at its head alongside the ageing Driscoll, who was scraping a living in Kenya, and who had been persuaded of the unsuitability of those currently leading the official Legion. In 1931, the name was changed to the 'Imperial Overseas Legion of Frontiersmen'. This was to

62 *A Frontiersmen event of the 1930s started by the founder, Captain Roger Pocock.*

be the first of a number of breakaways that have riven the Frontiersmen to the present day. As the Legion has never been sufficiently well off to employ permanent lawyers to protect the name, several 'Legions of Frontiersmen' of many variations, often run by the most unsuitable types, have sprung up and then usually died off. These have upset the official Legion and have confirmed War Office opinion that any organisation containing the term 'Legion of Frontiersmen' was seldom to be trusted. The War Office were soon to hear of the squabble between the two groups. Choosing words carefully, they expressed the thought that the Legion's military value was 'problematical'.[31] Burchardt-Ashton had spent much time and his own money promoting the Legion, but Pocock's 'Independent Legion' were keen to rubbish him, writing that he was a 'Commandant-General who would not pretend to have had the advantage of any military training' and pointed out that he was

> supported by certain members of his administrative staff claiming titles not sufficiently warranted and not traceable in such rank as conferred by His Majesty's Commission. Long experience has shown that under such guidance units tend to drift into an incompetent independence or relapse into undesirable groups in uniform, or fade out.[32]

This complaint by 'Captain' Roger Pocock is rather an ironic one coming from a man whose substantive rank had only been Lieutenant, and who was only a temporary acting Captain for a few months during the War. Records

63 *Mounted camp, south Midlands area, November 1935.*

also show that during the early years of the Legion Pocock was at times referred to 'Captain', although he had been no more than a corporal in the army in South Africa.

These arguments came to the War Office after a problem with the Frontiersmen regarding Egypt. The Legion was still yearning for official recognition and Edwards-Carter, who apparently had learnt nothing from his failed application to the King for medals, decided to do something about recognition on his own. This was strictly against orders, as Lord Loch had insisted that all correspondence with Government officials should be seen by him first. Edwards-Carter ignored this and wrote direct to General Sir W. Braithwaite, who had inspected the Legion on its last annual parade. He wrote on 3 January 1929 to request recognition by the War Office and adding,

> I may say that on the Gold Coast the Legion is recognised as a part of the Defence Force and the Government has supplied it with arms and machine guns. We have just formed a large unit in Cairo which has been approved by Lord Lloyd, the High Commissioner. An officer from Army G.H.Q. will sit on the Legion Executive as liaison officer.

64 *Inspection of legion of frontiersmen by Major General Sir Edward Perceval, Horse Guards Parade, 17 May 1936.*

65 *The Legion of Frontiersmen on Horse Guards Parade.*

He also enclosed a Legion recruiting leaflet which, although it said, 'We can not accept and do not want the young man who is eligible for and should join the Territorials', clearly stated '… recognised by the War Office'.[33]

This letter caused a minor uproar in official circles. The section in King's Regulations aimed specifically at the Legion had been renewed in 1925 and the War Office wanted to know what the Colonies were doing in officially recognising the Legion. The Colonial Office was to be informed that the Gold Coast authorities had been 'indiscreet'. Officials in the Gold Coast back-pedalled furiously and only admitted to supplying the Legion with 'twenty old rifles no longer accurate and some machine guns.'[34] The biggest furore came from Egypt and Lord Lloyd himself, who was most upset by the attitude of the War Office. He wrote back to them pointing out that the Frontiersmen in Egypt paraded in uniform only on Armistice Day and Empire Day, and their behaviour had been exemplary. In a letter dated 20 March 1929 he wrote to Sir Austen Chamberlain, then Foreign Secretary, and expressed his fury: '… the Army Council maintain that they "do not recognise but express sympathy and take cognisance of it." I find it hard to seize the distinction, especially since I am aware a member of the Cabinet is

66 *Coronation Parade, 15 May 1937, Bombay. Guard of Honour to Lady Brabourne who was the mother-in-law of the current Patron, The Countess Mountbatten of Burma.*

67 *Lord Derby with the Liverpool Legion of Frontiersmen.*

on the central organisation of the Legion and there was a recent inspection on Horse Guards Parade by the Adjutant-General.'[35] Lord Lloyd was not the first, nor the last, person to have been unable to 'seize the distinction'. The Cabinet member referred to by Lord Lloyd was the Rt Hon. Leo Amery, who was the Secretary of State for the Colonies as well as being an influential member of the Governing Council of the Legion. Amery was a fervent anti-appeaser in the 1930s and is remembered for administering the *coup de grace* to the Chamberlain Government by quoting Cromwell's command to the Long Parliament. It has also been said that Amery might have been Prime Minister had he been half a head taller and his speeches half an hour shorter. Sir Austen Chamberlain passed Lord Lloyd's letter to the War Office who appear to have decided to calm matters down as they had become far too heated for comfort. They told Lord Lloyd that they were in the habit of inspecting the Boy Scout movement and giving them the same encouragement and, of course, they meant no criticism of Lord Lloyd. It seems that the first that Lord Loch heard of the whole matter was when he received a letter from the War Office dated 28 March to complain about Edwards-Carter's action. C.H. Wybrow, who commanded and had re-formed the Egypt and Sudan Command of the Legion, wrote to Edwards-Carter to complain about the upset he had caused. Wybrow had served in East Africa in the First War before being transferred to Intelligence work due to his command of seven languages, including Turkish and Arabic. After distinguished and adventurous service, which included escape from the Turks while under sentence of death, he had joined the Egyptian Civil Service.[36] The Legion had been of great assistance to the British authorities during the riots in Egypt and their help had been appreciated in non-military duties by General Sir Peter Strickland, G.O.C. Egypt.

Lord Loch admitted to the War Office that Edwards-Carter had taken a very great liberty. He agreed that the Legion would remove the offending phrase 'recognised by the War Office' from its pamphlets and Edwards-Carter was to be admonished. The strong and constant support of Burchardt-Ashton saved Edwards-Carter, but his retention in a senior position in the Legion was to say the very least unwise. In July 1929, when the new Labour Government came to power, Lord Lloyd was recalled to Britain and British troops were withdrawn from all of Egypt other than the Canal Zone. In June 1930, confidential letters between Lord Loch and Burchardt-Ashton show that, possibly again due to the influence of Amery, informal discussions were being held about the possibility of some Frontiersmen going to India to help with the problems of civil disobedience there. Not only were the Frontiersmen involved in the City of London Police, but also in the 1930s they had strong representation in the Bombay City Police. Lord Loch wrote to Burchardt-Ashton, 'I will be going to London tomorrow and will see what I can do at the War Office and India Office on Friday morning. If by any chance a contingent of Frontiersmen is accepted for India what pay would they expect to get? For how long would they be prepared to enlist?'[37] This again came to nothing, as the power of the War Office would have dissuaded the India Office from using the Frontiersmen.

The War Office were not to be free of the Frontiersmen who between 1931 and 1933 were petitioning for a Charter of Incorporation. They brought forward some big names in their support, their petition being signed by, among others, Governing Council members the Duke of Portland, the Earl of Derby and Major-General Sir Cecil Lowther. The Earl of Derby was known to hold similar right-wing views to Amery. The Imperial Legion had no such great supporters but on their behalf Pocock protested that 'Lord Loch is assisted by a staff of incomplete competence'.[38] The petition ploughed its slow path through official channels but in 1933 was rejected with no official explanation or comment. Much agitation against the official Legion could be blamed on the 'Kaid', Andrew Belton, a strange and complex character. Belton is another who appears to weave his way through the first forty years of the Legion and not always to their benefit. He told great stories about his adventures but the much quieter and more reliable pioneer Frontiersman Robert Smith, who claimed to be number 5 on the Legion records although he does not

Success, then Failure Again

appear in Pocock's diaries until 1908. Smith is not in Pocock's list of the first 25 members, but that list was not written until 1930 when Pocock's memory might have been faulty. Smith called Belton a 'human kaleidoscope', and wrote that Belton was 'not invariably accurate in his facts'.[39] Belton gave an account of some of his adventures to *Southern Cross*, a South African newspaper, in 1959. Belton was born in 1882 and at the age of 17 ran away to join the Imperial Yeomanry in South Africa, rising to the rank of Captain. In March 1908 he arrived back in England 'full of malaria and knowing that I would have to get out of the country straight away'. He claimed that he saw in the newspapers that rebellion had broken out in Morocco. 'I made up my mind immediately and was away that night without saying a word to anybody.' He told his version of events to the newspaper which reported:

68 *This spoof advertisement appeared in* The Frontiersman *magazine between the wars. It shows the Frontiersmen humour, although this would have disturbed the authorities.*

> He arrived in Tangier, but found that the gate of the city were locked and that he could not get out to join the rebel leader 220 miles away in the interior. Eventually he got through the gates disguised as a Moorish woman, his face veiled, and walked the 220 miles to Fez. There he declared himself and was received by the rebel leader, Mulay el Hafid, tested in the command of the troops then in Fez (about 8,000 men) and finally appointed Commander-in-Chief of all Mulay's forces with absolute power and the military title of Kaid. He was then 25 years old. Kaid Belton reorganised Mulay el Hafid's army and commanded it to such good effect that, five months later, he defeated the forces of the reigning Sultan Abdul Aziz (which was commanded by another white soldier of fortune, the Kaid McLean, a Scotsman). Kaid Belton dethroned Abdul Aziz and put Mulay Hafid on the throne of Morocco.

Belton's story seems a typical fanciful Frontiersman yarn, and while Kaid McLean is recorded, Belton seems to get no mention in records.[40] His War Office file is a brief one, but the index strangely adds 'The Kaid' to his military rank and this is how he always liked to be known.[41] Before the First War he had found his way to Canada where he claimed to have learned to fly in 1911. After the War, he was back in the Cape, where he became a successful organising officer for the Legion and acted as deputy to the ageing Col Driscoll. Smith wrote that Driscoll wisely did not consider either Belton or Pocock suitable to be Commandant-General of the breakaway I.O.L. of F., but wished the post to remain vacant until a suitable senior officer could be found. Belton seems to have been back in England in 1932 and, supported by Pocock and without Driscoll's knowledge, managed to get himself elected as Commandant-General. According to Smith, Belton then surprised everyone in March 1933 by announcing that he was disbanding the I.O.L. of F. without any reference to Driscoll and forming the Imperial Legion of Frontiersmen 'into which he proposed to enrol untrained youths as an unarmed force to withstand Communists when they attack the seat of Government'.[42] This apparent politicising of the organisation not only upset the War Office again when they came to hear of it, but also many loyal Frontiersmen. 'The corpse however was less dead than it looked and, when he discovered he was not quite a Hitler as yet, I heard that he proposed to offer the I[mperial] L[egion] as a going concern to the L[egion of] F[rontiersmen].'[43]

Smith's quiet diplomacy and friendly contacts in both camps helped the two organisations come back together in 1934, while Belton's Imperial Legion continued in Britain and Canada, although they soon got tired of Belton's politics and he left them. Burchardt-Ashton was eventually persuaded to retire as Commandant-General to be replaced by a retired Brigadier, Edward Morton, whose military career made him acceptable to both organisations. In summer 1934, in probably the last official letter he wrote before his death, Driscoll commended the new amalgamation to everyone with the words, 'Let there be one flock and one shepherd'.[44] His words have been either forgotten or ignored as, to this day, the Legion has a history of groups breaking away or setting themselves up as their own sort of Legion of Frontiersmen whilst claiming descent from the early Legion. Often, these have been headed by the most unsuitable characters who could never be accepted into the official Legion.

Within a couple of months, Pocock had come up with another of his Good Ideas. He was now officially in charge of recruitment. He suggested that he undertook a world tour of all Frontiersmen units, giving newspaper interviews and drumming up recruits. Headquarters probably thought it would be a good idea to get him out of the way for many months. He was still highly respected around the Commonwealth. Headquarters then would not have him around all the time trying to meddle in everything, as he was often tempted to do when in London. Pocock had to get leave of absence from Charterhouse, which involved letters to the Archbishop of Canterbury and Jan Smuts. Charterhouse were concerned about him undertaking such a massive trip at his age, but eventually they agreed, although he would not receive his Charterhouse pension during his absence.[45] Fortunately his popularity was such around the Commonwealth that his expenses were minimal. In the story of the journey he wrote for *The Frontiersman* magazine he wrote, 'To the friends who helped to finance the journey, I tender my heartfelt gratitude'.[46] Pocock may have been an annoyance to Commonwealth Headquarters, but he was welcomed wherever he visited around the world and as Director of Recruiting did a grand job. He was a well-enough known personality to attract newspaper coverage wherever he went. Mindful of the problems that Pocock had caused in the past, Lt Col Wybrow, who had succeeded Edwards-Carter, wrote to some of the Commands and particularly to Col Louis Scott in Canada that Pocock's tour was in no way official and that,

> ... while it is hoped that all Frontiersmen throughout the world will welcome him in a manner worthy of his age and past association with the great body he created, everything he might say, both in public and in private conversation, must be accepted as an expression of his PRIVATE opinion, and in no way official or binding on the Legion in any way.[47]

Wybrow had worked in Canada in his youth. The Legion were hoping that Pocock's trip would be a success, which it was, but were afraid that he might land the Legion in trouble once again. This was an extraordinary trip for a man who celebrated his 70th birthday in Canada on the journey in the more difficult travelling conditions of those days. He started in South Africa, visiting Durban, Johannesburg, Pretoria and Capetown. From there he sailed to Australia for Perth, Adelaide, Melbourne and Sydney. Australia had always had numbers of Frontiersmen, but due to the great size of that country they seem to have been spread over the country in ones and twos, although when the need came, as in both Wars, the Frontiersmen were always ready to get involved in action. Next came 26 very strenuous days in New Zealand, by air, road and rail, holding 23 squadron meetings. Pocock was pleased to visit the home that his parents had lived in during their brief period in New Zealand before he was born. He wrote to his elder brother in America when he returned, 'Moreover, as a son of

69 *The 1935 World Tour, New Zealand. Roger Pocock with New Zealand Commandant Colonel J. Findlater and Captain W. Palmer.*

70 *Hong Kong Squadron in camp, 12 October 1935.*

a pioneer settler, I was welcomed as an "Old Identity". There was a certain amount of fun in being given civil receptions by local Mayors, red carpet being laid as if I was the Royal family, guards of honour and all kinds of fuss.'[48] There can be no doubt that Pocock was a well known person around the world, and his recruiting drive was bringing results. He returned to Australia, to Brisbane, Townesville, Cairns and Thursday Island. He reported a Legion strength in New Zealand of over one thousand. The next stop was Manila and on for a week in Hong Kong, which his report said was one of the best squadrons. Here he had to get on a horse and hold a mounted parade. Then to Shanghai, Nagasaki, Kobe, Yokohama and Tokyo. He sailed on the *Empress of Russia* to arrive in Vancouver in time to celebrate his birthday there.[49] Canada had become one of the strongest arms of the Legion. After the First War, as in Britain, the Legion had crumbled away. A large number of pre-war members had perished and it was not until 1929 that the Legion began to attract substantial numbers again. The man responsible for that revival, and to whom much credit must go, was Col Louis Scott. Towards the end of 1929, a Louis B. Blain emigrated to Canada from England. He had been a Frontiersman in England and carried a Letter of Authority from Headquarters to try to re-organise and re-vitalise the Legion in Canada. His attempts aroused little interest until a Col Wheeler suggested that Blain contact Col Scott.

Scott had a brilliant record with Princess Patricia's Canadian Light Infantry. He had won the D.C.M. and had been commissioned in the field and he had many valuable personal contacts in the Canadian Government. He saw that such an organisation would have a great potential. He soon became deeply involved, having received permission from London Headquarters to take over reorganisation of the Legion in Canada. His great strength was that he picked his staff with great care. Firstly in Edmonton and then in other parts of the Canadian West and then into the East, he built up the Legion. On 5 June 1930, London Headquarters wrote, 'The Council is quite prepared to regard Edmonton as the Headquarters of the Legion in Canada, as this is the centre from which the revival of the Legion is taking place.'[50] On 19 April 1933 Headquarters granted Divisional status to Canada, Canadian Headquarters to be in Edmonton under the command of Louis Scott, D.C.M., with the rank of Commissioner-General. A constitution was drawn up governing Canadian Frontiersmen and a copy sent to Headquarters for approval. The reply came back,

> A splendid Constitution that you have drawn up could well be a model for the world Legion. On all matters affecting the Legion in Canada, it is natural that we first consult you, as our representative and Senior Officer in the Dominion. The Commandant-General has every confidence in your judgment, and leaves the whole question of the future of Canadian Division in your hands, it being understood that he will confirm any changes or new appointments that you might think fit to recommend in the event of any reorganisation taking place there.[51]

These two letters are very important in the light of events that were to occur a few years later. The Canadians had minor problems with breakaway groups such as the 'Canadian Frontiersmen' and the 'British Columbia Legion of Frontiersmen', but none of them had much long-term success. The Canadian Division was able to achieve something that British Headquarters could not. The Canadian Division applied for a Dominion Charter and this was granted on 9 July 1937, so the Canadians received an official recognition which the British with all their influential friends could not.[52] Louis Scott was keeping to the traditional Frontiersmen ideas on discipline. On formal parade, the strictest military discipline was upheld, but off duty all Frontiersmen mixed socially as equals. Col Scott was District Supervisor for Northern Alberta for the Soldier Settlement Board, which allocated land for soldiers at the end of their service. A soldier had been settled on a farm of about 200 acres at Hastings Lake, some 35 miles south-east of Edmonton. Although the soldier had signed to accept the farm, it turned out to be most unsuitable for farming, heavily wooded with hills, bogs and various holes. It was also on the shores of the Lake. The soldier had made a half-hearted attempt at farming but soon quit. It may have been unsuitable for farming, but it was ideal for use as a training camp for Frontiersmen. Col Scott was able to negotiate the land at a minimal price for use as a training ground, and so 'Fort Scott' came into being. The Frontiersmen worked with a will and soon a log cabin was built, which still stands today. Over the years Fort Scott has grown into a substantial property used as a summer camp for Canadian Frontiersmen. The south side of the property borders on the road and stones collected on the property were used to erect a Monument in memory of the 9,000 Frontiersmen worldwide who had given their lives in the First War. This Monument was ready for Pocock to unveil officially on Sunday 10 November. It was a thriving Canadian Division that welcomed Pocock. His reception through Canada was exceptional. He started with a banquet in his honour at the *Hotel Georgia* in Vancouver and then moved on to Edmonton where he was taken to Fort Scott to unveil the Memorial. It was a particularly cold day with plenty of snow and Pocock was taken into the log cabin so that all could 'fortify' themselves before the ceremony against the cold. It was here that Pocock met Dr Braithwaite for the first time since their involvement with the Riel Rebellion. Perhaps they fortified themselves too well, because it was reported that Pocock 'slipped on the ice' and had to be assisted to his feet.[53]

After this he went on across Canada to Camrose, Calgary, Regina, Winnipeg, Sault Ste Marie, Toronto, Kingston, Ottawa and Halifax. In a speech he made at Toronto, he recommended the Air Force to young fellows with a yen for adventure and danger. He told them, 'Always tackle the most dangerous thing you can find'.[54] At Ottawa he visited the R.C.M.P. where he received a great welcome as the Mounted Police always held him in high regard, despite his leaving them after such short service. It is certain that one of the subjects discussed was the one thing that the Canadian Division had been working towards. It can be assumed that his suggestions were listened to and respected and Canadian Frontiersmen believe that it was much to do with his intervention and influence that the following year in October 1936 *The Canadian Frontiersman* was able to report the following:

> AFFILIATION. Royal Canadian Mounted Police. The following extract from General Order No. 695, Part 1, week ending 26/9/1936 of the Royal Canadian Mounted Police, is published for the information of all members:
>
> By Authority of the Honourable, the Minister in Control of the Force, The Legion of Frontiersmen is hereby affiliated with the Royal Canadian Mounted Police in the same manner as Units of the Canadian Militia are affiliated with Regiments of His Majesty's Forces in the United Kingdom.[55]

Back in England, after '37,000 miles of sheer enjoyment',[56] Pocock was delighted that one of his greatest dreams had come true. The organisation that he had founded was now affiliated with the force he so admired and of which he had once been a member. Although Commonwealth Headquarters had denied all authority to Pocock's visit they were quick to boast of the affiliation, but due to the actions of their latest Commandant-General Morton, that affiliation was to prove tragically short. Pocock wrote an account of his travels for *The Frontiersman* magazine full of his ambitious plans for the future and was keen to use modern technology where possible. He wanted a chain of radio stations to bring Frontiersmen into speedier contact with each other. He was happy that Maritime units should be expanded and wished to see Air units in other countries than England where there were a few, '… the future of the Legion will be in the air-ways, and it will be useful if we can find photographers in our membership for aerial photography

71 Collage used in Frontiersman *magazine. At centre, King George VI inspects a Guard of Honour of Eastern Canada Command at Quebec Station on a royal visit to Canada. Top centre left, Guildford Squadron with Queen Mary at the opening of Queen's District Nurses Hospital, Guildford.*

in time of war'.[57] He repeated his regular claim that the Legion did not want youngsters who could join the Forces, but men of experience. He was concerned about the political activities of the Blackshirts and that the Legion could be mistaken for them in spite of Legion strict non-political rules. On 18 May 1936, *The Times* reported him saying that, 'rather than be mistaken for politicians in uniform we had to relinquish our shirt for the abominable tunic',[58] although the patrol tunic and breeches worn by the Frontiersmen showed great similarity to his beloved Canadian Mounted Police.

The Frontiersmen in Britain were beginning to explore other avenues of service. They were engaging in intensive anti-gas warfare training, working with St John Ambulance Brigade and there was talk of a closer relationship with that organisation. *The Times* had reported in May 1935 that jointly with St John Ambulance the Legion were to undertake a demonstration at London Air Park at Hanworth at an air-defence display. Also that month, replying to a question in the House of Commons, the Home Secretary said,

> I understand that the Legion of Frontiersmen like some other voluntary organisations is in touch with the Order of St John and the British Red Cross Society with a view to assisting those bodies for the alleviation of the consequences of air attack. I have informed the Legion that, in my opinion, assistance of this nature would be work of national importance. No specific duties have been allotted to this body at present and any drill which may have been undertaken has been arranged voluntarily.[59]

The War Office was still implacably opposed to the Legion of Frontiersmen having any official status and must have been upset at the affiliation to the R.C.M.P. All it could do was to warn against the organisation whenever asked. The War Office has a long memory and, even after 100 years, the Ministry of Defence will still advise enquirers against having anything to do with the organisation in spite of all the good things it has achieved. It has never been able to prevent senior officers lending unofficial support to the Legion, inspecting them, and even feeling that their services might be better used. One strange proposal, which is supposed to have come direct from the C.I.G.S. General Sir Archibald Montgomery-Massingberd, was reported in the *New Zealand Frontiersman*, by E.H. Rhodes Wood. In the Second World War, Rhodes Wood joined the Pioneer Corps, rising to be Major and wrote entertainingly for their magazine as 'Eddie Harwood'. He also wrote a book of anecdotes and about the history of the Pioneer Corps. Rhodes Wood had unofficially formed what he called the 'Lost Squadron', claiming that all round the world were single Frontiersmen and even twos and threes who had no representation as they were isolated on frontiers. Headquarters disapproved of Rhodes Wood's 'Lost Squadron' but, acting as New Zealand overseas liaison officer, he appears to have discovered all sorts of otherwise unpublished facts and events. In the June-July issue of the *New Zealand Frontiersman* magazine he wrote that the policy of the Legion in Britain was being directed to some form of amalgamation with St John Ambulance Brigade and the British Red Cross. He also told the New Zealanders that Montgomery-Massingberd had written to Headquarters in London a few years earlier suggesting that the Legion of Frontiersmen should train for anti-aircraft gunnery, 'provided the Corps voluntarily evinces a desire to adopt this form of training whole-heartedly, and to the exclusion of other military exercises which can be of little use to it'.[60] Rhodes Wood said that official military quarters were at that time very concerned at the scarcity of anti-aircraft artillery in the United Kingdom. It seemed that, at the time of writing, there were only two brigades, each of three batteries, in the whole country and the co-operation of the Legion

72 *This collage from the* Frontiersman *magazine shows among other things: 1935 gas warfare and anti-aircraft gun training, the Legion Air Command demonstration at London Air Park, Hanworth, signal training on the Downs above Brighton, the Farnborough Hampshire Squadron, unarmed combat training and tent pegging.*

73 *Lord Mountbatten inspecting the Rhodesia Command before its disbandment.*

would have, for once, been welcomed with open arms by the military. It would seem doubtful that the War Office would have approved.[61] Needless to say, the Frontiersmen were not interested in such a different task. Brigadier Morton was a good organiser, but was an old fashioned and traditional military man. After the War, Rhodes Wood still retained his membership of the Legion and in 1952 presented a cigar box on behalf of the Legion to Winston Churchill.[62]

In New Zealand the Frontiersmen were expanding well. They received excellent publicity when one of their number, Charles Ulm, achieved international fame. He had been co-pilot to Australian C.E. Kingsford-Smith when they were the first to fly the Pacific in their plane 'Southern Cross' from America to Australia. They had already succeeded in flying round the coast of Australia.[63] Ulm, together with another Frontiersman, 'Scotty' Allen, both members of Otago Squadron, made a pioneering flight across the Tasman Sea in their plane 'Faith in Australia'. They landed on Saturday 16 December 1933 and made headlines in all New Zealand papers, photographed either with local Frontiersmen or in their own Frontiersmen uniforms.[64] In Australia, most Frontiersmen seem to have been in small numbers spread around that large country, consequently the Legion history there is not yet fully collated. Certainly centred around the larger cities there were good numbers there who served in the First War, and many Australian Frontiersmen served and also fell at Gallipoli. March/April 1915 records of New South Wales show around 200 members still in the Sydney area. Wherever there has been British representation there have been Frontiersmen at some stage, maybe only one or two in places like Samoa and Fiji but active Squadrons in many African countries such as Nigeria and South Africa. The British East Africa and Mount Kenya Squadron Commands lasted for fifty years from 1907 to 1957. Between the Wars, as well as Driscoll living in Kenya and actively recruiting, they enjoyed the support and active membership of such well known men as Ewart Grogan the 'Cape to Cairo' man and John Boyes, another extraordinary character.

Boyes was a bluff Yorkshireman who never lost his strong Yorkshire accent. He was born in 1873, the son of a Hull boot- and shoe-maker. As a true Frontiersman, he was both eccentric and independent. He began his adventures at the age of 13 by walking across England to Liverpool and signing on as a boy on a sailing ship to South America. There he contracted yellow fever, which nearly cost him his life and damaged his eyesight. He then worked his passage to Africa, arriving in 1896. He fought in the Matabele War, meeting Baden-Powell and making friends with Selous. After this he made his way up the East Coast and in 1898 began his real adventures in the unexplored heart of Africa, where he began trading. Boyes used to say that the things that secured his success were an alarm clock, a bottle of iodoform, and a bottle of fruit salts. When he drank them when they were fizzing hard he convinced the natives that he was a magician able to drink boiling water. At the time the Kikuyu were frequently raided by the Masai, and Boyes became a blood brother, disciplined their warriors and helped maintain peace. A Government expedition disarmed Boyes and his bodyguard and he was charged with various serious offences. Fortunately, he was acquitted and became a prosperous trader. In the First War he served with the Intelligence Corps, with such other great men as Pretorius and linking up again for a while with Selous.[65] After the War, Boyes took to farming. He visited London in 1929 for the East African reunion dinner organised by Capt. Lloyd, where both Smuts and Von Lettow Vorbeck were honoured guests. In her biography of her husband, Ada Cherry Kearton wrote that, when staying with Cherry Kearton and his wife for the event, he remarked to Kearton in his strong Yorkshire accent: 'Eh! Cherry lad, it's a wunderful wurld. Its nobbut a few years sin' they were trying to heng me for two hoondred murders; an' to-neet ah's setten at table next to t'Guvnor!'[66] Boyes gave valuable evidence to the Carter Land Commission in the 1930s, although he tried to claim ownership of the whole of Mount Kenya, which he claimed had been ceded to him by his Kikuyu blood brothers! John Boyes was a very keen Frontiersman and said it was the uniform he best liked to wear, because of its association with the great frontier campaigners of the past. He was a common sight in Kenya marching around in full Frontiersman uniform. Boyes wrote two excellent books of his adventures: *King of the Wa-Kikuyu* and *Company of Adventurers*. As with most Frontiersmen, Boyes 'tells a good tale', and it is impossible to

74 *Inspection by Field Marshal Viscount Slim.*

verify many of his claims. John Boyes died in 1951, and he is buried at Forest Road Cemetery in Nairobi.[67]

One of the inaccuracies in Errol Trzebinski's *The Life and Death of Lord Erroll*[68] is to claim that Boyes had actually set up the organisation in Kenya. That honour goes to Mr Sellwood of Nairobi back in 1907. Trzebinski claims that Lord Erroll commanded the Frontiersmen in Kenya when the O.C. was, in fact, Boyes. Erroll actually commanded A Squadron and a number of the notorious Happy Valley set were Frontiersmen, including Dr Joseph

Gregory, Erroll's wife's doctor who was the Squadron M.O. with the Legion rank of Lieutenant.[69] So far, no direct link can be made with Belton who had been so successful recruiting thoughout East and South Africa, but his and Erroll's political ideas were not that far apart and there are some indirect links through mutual acquaintances. Erroll wore the Legion of Frontiersmen mess kit for the first time at the Frontiersmen dinner in Nairobi in September 1938. Erroll's influence and money meant that A Squadron could use the *Queen's Hotel* in Nairobi for their headquarters.[70] Boyes had visited London in December 1929 for an extraordinary Dinner. Over 800 ex-Service men and women who had served in the East African campaign dined at the Holborn Restaurant. The dinner was presided over by General Smuts and the guest of honour was General Von Lettow-Vorbeck who was photographed with Smuts. In his reply to Smuts' speech welcoming him, Von Lettow-Vorbeck said that he knew that, 'both in England and Germany there were people who did not quite agree to his accepting that invitation, but he had decided to accept it. He wanted to show by accepting it that he held them fair and brave, and therefore honest adversaries.'[71] The main organiser of the event was Capt. A.W. Lloyd, M.C., of the 25th Fusiliers (Frontiersmen) and now fully employed as *Punch* political cartoonist. The speeches were enthusiastic about a new sense of peace and co-operation between the two countries. So far, all researches have drawn a blank as to why Lloyd decided to organise this dinner. Following this dinner Von Lettow-Vorbeck and Smuts became life long friends and Smuts helped support him from 1945. At the time of the dinner, Von Lettow-Vorbeck was a parliamentary deputy for the German National People's Party; however, he tired of the way politics was being run in Germany and retired in disgust. He was to fall out of favour with Hitler and the Nazi party. Hitler would have liked him to become the German ambassador to Britain but he could not stand the Nazis.[72]

Nine
Dwindling Influence

During the '20s and '30s men, and some ladies, joined the Legion of Frontiersmen. Many had served in the First War and wished to continue the comradeship and maybe serve their country should the occasion arise again. There were some young men who joined, preferring the glamour of the Frontiersman uniform to the practicality of the Territorials. The Frontiersmen were wise enough in general to try to help the young men who joined them. Often a young man would be elected to command a troop, which was the best training he could ever have. One, Ernest Meacock, wrote that he was a 'young troop commander in a squadron composed of hard-bitten troopers – many of them ex-commissioned officers – all be-medalled and many decorated, most of them refusing to take rank, but all determined to have a good time in what was an incredible elite force.'[1] An example of the First War veterans was Bob Moyse, who had won the M.C. and the D.C.M. as a Sgt Major in the Essex Regiment. During the depression he founded the D.C.M. League to assist the many holders of the D.C.M. who had fallen upon hard times in the days of the depression. The Princess Royal agreed to become the Patron of the League. Bob Moyse was a real 'character'. Only 5ft 4ins tall, he had been a good boxer, swimmer, gymnast and all-round athlete. After the War he became a well-known Salford bookmaker. His story of how he came to join the Legion is that one day he saw two Frontiersmen in full uniform riding their horses down a local street until they came to the local public house. Tethering their horses outside, they disappeared inside for refreshment. Bob Moyse decided that this was the sort of organisation he should join and soon rose to be Commanding Officer of Manchester (H) Squadron.[2]

Co-operation with St John Ambulance was an important part of London Headquarters' plans but seems to have been less important elsewhere. Headquarters were working closely on protection against aerial chemical warfare and joint demonstrations were carried out. Frontiersmen were trained in anti-gas warfare and detailed two-hour examinations were being sat and certificates issued. Fortunately, the Frontiersmen were never needed to exercise their anti-gas skills.[3] The year 1938 began with things looking quite bright for the Legion of Frontiersmen. Their voluntary services were beginning to be accepted more readily and the affiliation to the Canadian Mounted

75 *This photograph of an unknown Frontiersman was found in a second-hand bookshop was taken apparently some time in the 1920s.*

76 *Captain Robert Moyse, M.C., D.C.M., B.E.M.*

77 *Manchester Frontiersmen with Robert Moyse, M.C., D.C.M., B.E.M., (front row, 4th from right), 1930s.*

Dwindling Influence

Police had been a great benefit to the Legion worldwide as well as in Canada. One man was then to take a decision that had repercussions, which are probably still having effect today.

Brigadier Morton had proved himself to be an efficient organiser and matters were now running with the military precision that could be expected with a traditional army man at the helm. The problem was that Morton was too traditional, and must have considered himself still in a military situation with the absolute power of that position reinforced by his success in commanding the amalgamated Legion. Unfortunately, the Legion always has had (and still has today) more than its fair share of ex-corporals who thought they should be Captains, and Captains who thought they should be Colonels, unwisely believing that Frontiersman rank had real meaning in the outside world. A Captain M.L. Fitzgerald of Lorreteville who was O.C. of N Squadron, Quebec City in Canada paid a private visit to London and there he sought out Brigadier Morton. Over lunch one day he gave his opinion to Morton that Canada was a vast country and far too large to be under the command of just one man who could not possibly do justice to the whole Dominion and that it should be divided into Eastern and Western Canada Command. He said that Quebec objected to being governed from Edmonton. Needless to say, in his opinion the best man to command Eastern Canada was himself. With an almost unbelievable and utterly dictatorial decision, Fitzgerald's request was granted by Morton with no consultation whatsoever. Col Scott was astounded to receive a letter from Morton dated 14 June 1938 telling him that Imperial Headquarters had decided that Canada was too vast an area to be under one Command and it had been decided to divide it in two. The two Commands were to be Western Command and Eastern Command with the boundary to be the eastern edge of the State of Manitoba. Fitzgerald was to be the new Commandant of Eastern Canada. It is not difficult to guess Scott's reaction to the letter but he replied formally referring Headquarters to the letter written to him in 1933 placing him in total charge of Canada which also said that Headquarters would first consult Scott 'on all matters affecting the Legion in Canada'. He pointed out that they had totally disregarded their own ruling.[4]

78 Brigadier Morton, C.B.E., Late Commandant General.

79 *Major General Sir John Duncan, Chief Commandant of St Johns talking to Brigadier Morton.*

Scott knew of a Canadian Frontiersman officer on holiday in England so he contacted him and asked him to investigate what was actually going on at Headquarters. The essence of the report to Scott was as follows:

> I am very pleased to be of assistance to you in this matter. In response to your directions, I went, I saw, I listened. I met Capt. Erswell (Staff Officer, Admin.) and spent all the morning with him. He informed me that neither he nor Col. Dunn (Chief of Staff) are at all pleased with this move, which was signed, sealed and delivered before the office knew anything about it. Captain Fitzgerald did not meet with I.H.Q., instead he met with Col Morton only (Brigadier Morton) at a luncheon, and Morton made the decision on his own, without consulting any of the others. The Legal Advisor is very concerned about the turn of events. He is of the opinion that Colonel Scott should have been consulted, according to existing agreements. This is also the opinion of Dunn and Erswell.
>
> I asked why, if they were not consulted, did they go along with Morton's decision, made on his own. The answer was that Morton is a stubborn ****** and to clash with him would cause trouble at I.H.Q. It appears that a certain Liaison Officer at I.H.Q. has no ****** use for Canadian Headquarters. It all came out when I suggested that Morton be asked to resign, failing that, expelled. Dirty linen came out by the basketful. No amount of soap would clean such a mess! I suggest that we would do well to break with such a mess.[5]

Although British records of events were lost in the 1940 bombing of London, Canadian records are very clear and all the original letters still exist there. It is apparent that there was some jealousy of the success achieved by the Canadian Frontiersmen. Headquarters closed ranks behind Morton and increasingly bitter letters flew each way across the Atlantic. All the letters were printed in full in the *Frontier News*, which was the magazine of Canadian Division, in their October 1938 issue. In conclusion, *Frontier News* commented,

> The above correspondence covers the entire situation up to the present time and the Advisory Council of Canadian Headquarters is not in agreement with such arbitrary action in the attempt of Imperial Headquarters to force the proposed set-up on Canada for the following reason:

(1) The proposed action is absolutely opposed to the Constitution of the Canadian Division, under which Frontiersmen in Canada have agreed to be governed.

(2) It is in direct violation of the principles set out in the Dominion Charter, which designates Edmonton as Headquarters and the governing body of Frontiersmen in the Dominion. [A full copy of the Charter was published in this issue of the magazine.]

(3) The appointment by Imperial Headquarters without reference to the Canadian Division of a junior member of our Command to the highest rank in the Legion of Frontiersmen in Canada, a rank in which the member in question does not have the complete support of Frontiersmen in the Dominion, nor in his own area.

The Canadian Advisory Council has, therefore, informed Imperial Headquarters that it cannot agree to any suggested changes but will be pleased to give the fullest consideration to any constructive policy for Canada, if constitutionally submitted to Canadian Headquarters at Edmonton, Alberta for consideration.[6]

Imperial Headquarters in London then made the almost unbelievable blunder of actually attempting to dismiss Col Scott. What made Headquarters think that, knowing the great popularity of Scott, they would succeed it is impossible to imagine. One can only assume that the senior officers at Headquarters were so taken up by their grand titles that they imagined they had the power and authority of regular army officers of rank. They ignored the fact that they were dealing with members of a voluntary civilian organisation. The letter, signed by E.G. Dunn, the Chief of Staff, was dated 27 April 1939:

... After affording you every opportunity, you have failed to carry out the undertakings made in your Declaration of Allegiance; you have also consistently flouted the authority of the Commandant-General and neglected to obey his orders. The Commandant-General has lost confidence in you as Commandant, Western Canada Command, and therefore has no alternative but to deprive you of your appointment and by virtue of the powers invested in him to order that you be dismissed from the Legion of Frontiersmen ... All units of the Western Canada Command have been informed of the action of Imperial Headquarters and have been directed to correspond direct with the Chief of Imperial Staff, pending further instructions.[7]

It goes without saying that the vast majority of Canada Frontiersmen remained loyal to Scott. That this would happen should have been obvious to Morton and Dunn before the letter of dismissal was sent. War arrived in September 1939 and this served to turn men's minds away from internal wrangles in the Legion. The younger men on both sides of the Atlantic were either called up or started to enlist. Not before time, Lord Loch was drawn into the controversy and on 19 October he wrote a hand-written and personal letter to Col Scott. He made an attempt at mediation, climbing down on the dismissal, but as he also backed Morton over the division of Canada this had no chance of success.

> ... In a letter received in London on 10th July, 1939, the Canadian Secretary of State said that you have requested that the question in dispute should be referred to the Grand Council of the Legion of Frontiersmen; this was done and a meeting was held on the 1st of August. At this meeting we had the advantage of a high official from the office of the Canadian High Commissioner in England. It was agreed that I should consult with General McNaughten who was then in England. His advice was that I should write to General Mathews, Adjutant General at Ottawa. This I did but unfortunately the war started just after I had written, which caused great delay. If it had not been for the war I should have gone to Canada myself as President of the Legion of Frontiersmen to discuss the question with you and other Frontiersmen in Canada. Unluckily this is now impossible.[8]

This hastily penned letter written personally from Lord Loch's private address to Scott throws up some interesting points. In spite of British authorities' refusal to recognise the Legion, it seems from this letter that 'high officials' were getting involved with the affairs of the Legion. It is certain that this further major problem within the Legion was well known by the War Office and was another factor taken into consideration when the Legion again requested in 1939 recognition and a named unit as they had been granted in the First War. The tone of Lord Loch's letter to Scott and the way it was written gives the impression that Lord Loch was far from happy with the affair, and yet even he was not prepared to have Morton over-ruled. Scott, with the full backing he had in Canada, was not going to accept the conditions and replied to Lord Loch on 1 December that, while His Lordship would be most welcome in Canada after the war, the Canadian Division strongly resented Headquarters' interference in their affairs. At a General Meeting, the Canadian Legion had re-affirmed their loyalty to King and Country but had voted to split from Headquarters and act as an Independent Division of the Legion.[9] However, the most serious damage possible to the Legion had been caused, and on 31 October the Commissioner of the Royal Canadian Mounted Police had written to Scott to tell him that, in view of the internal disputes in the Legion, he had no alternative but to cancel that hard-won affiliation to the Mounted Police. This was the bitterest pill of all for Canadian Frontiersmen to swallow, and was something for which they could never forgive I.H.Q. Headquarters were still not prepared to let matters lie and instigated a series of legal actions to attempt to invalidate the Canadian Charter. Although the Canadian Division held the opinion that Headquarters was using its contacts in political circles to apply pressure, Headquarters lost every one of its legal battles. The victories for the Canadians had to be hollow ones because there was to be no restoration of their prized affiliation. The loss of the affiliation was even harder to take as, when King George VI and Queen Elizabeth had visited Canada that year, the Frontiersmen were called upon by the Mounted Police to help. This was provided with great efficiency and, after the visit, Brigadier S.T. Wood, the Commissioner of the R.C.M.P., wrote to Col Scott to congratulate him. In a letter dated 22 June, Brigadier Wood said, '… The assistance of the Legion of Frontiersmen was of inestimable value and the highest praise is due its members both for the smartness of their appearance and the efficiency with which they assisted the police … '[10] In fact the King had commanded that Col Scott be presented to him when the Royal Visit reached Edmonton on 2 June. Scott had been commandant of the Central School of Instruction of the Royal Air Force when the King had reported as a Royal Navy cadet during the First War. The King was very interested in the Legion and its service to the Crown. Scott had actually ordered the future King to get his hair cut for a lapse of discipline when under Scott's command.[11] All the praise that had been heaped on the Legion was now to count for nothing, thanks to the arrogant stupidity of one man, Brigadier Morton.

The dispute had one additional result. Although Roger Pocock, whose infirmity was increasing with the advance of his seventies, had not been involved in these problems, it eventually came to his notice. Not normally one to exercise tact and discretion, he felt that with the two countries he most loved moving into another World War, he must not take any action that could damage the image of the Frontiersmen. Col Scott wrote to him and asked permission to publish his photograph in the *Canadian Frontiersman* and Pocock readily agreed. Imperial Headquarters once again acted dictatorially and wrote to Pocock to issue a severe reprimand. He felt that they were invading his personal affairs and replied with a letter that he said 'scorched the paper'. He told them that their handling of the affairs of the Canadian Division 'demonstrated incompetence and irresponsibility'.[12] He therefore resigned from all connection with the Legion of Frontiersmen. No sooner had the Canadian Division heard this than they offered him membership, which he accepted with alacrity. He was to remain with them and die in 1941 as a member of Canadian Division. Perhaps Headquarters were not too unhappy no longer to have him interfering. For some years they had been playing down his part in the founding of the Legion. Their 1938 handbook said that he was 'assisted by Driscoll', and that the Legion was based on ex-members of Driscoll's Scouts. While we know that Driscoll played a big part later on, it must have hurt Pocock to see the Legion deny the truth that he was the sole originator.

Anticipating a coming war, the Legion wrote to the War Office in 1939 offering their services as a self-contained unit. They put a memo of 25 items before the War Office. The somewhat fanciful item 22 attracts attention, 'If on looking out of a War Office window, one saw a strong and healthy flower

80 *Glasgow Troop, 1937.*

growing, one would not crush it with one's foot?'[13] To the margin of this, some official reading it has pencilled 'impossible'. The request to the War Office resulted in the following internal memo dated 1 April 1939:

> The Legion of Frontiersmen have applied for War Office recognition on several occasions. This has always been refused since they insisted on retaining their separate identities ... Moreover, there have been various internal dissentions and at least one breakaway since the war ... Further, they have rightly or wrongly the reputation of being 'tough' characters likely to have affinities to the Fascists ... The Adjutant-General thinks that the spirit behind the various efforts of the Legion of Frontiersmen to secure official recognition has always been and still remains a desire for prestige with the avoidance of control.[14]

81 *Bognor Regis Frontiersmen, 1935.*

The minutes of the Army Council of 17 April 1939 read: 'The Legion of Frontiersmen is not to be allowed to form self-contained units within the A.D.G.B. and the N.D.G. They are not to be offered any form of recognition, however they are to be invited to enlist as individuals.'[15] No error of judgment or unwise statement from within the Frontiersmen has ever been overlooked by the War Office. Leslie Hore-Belisha, the Secretary of State for War, wrote a charmingly tactful letter to the Legion to tell them that there was to be no 25th Fusiliers (Frontiersmen) in any coming hostilities. He did concede that if a National Defence Company was to be formed consisting entirely of Frontiersmen it might be possible to add a 'parenthetical addition' to its official title. Whatever the opinion of senior officers, Territorial Army units competed with each other to enlist every one of the younger Frontiersmen that they could. Ernest Meacock wrote,

82 *The South Sussex Squadron kit inspection at Arundel Park, Whitsun 1934.*

> When the Territorial Army was doubled over night, we were asked whether we could supply n.c.o.'s and officers to help with the training and there was an immediate response naturally. I vividly remember a T.A. Sgt Major whispering in my ear, 'Sir, when you call the Parade to attention, you must not address them as "Frontiersmen!", the order is "Squad".'[16]

He also said, 'When the LDV was formed [soon to be the Home Guard] the Legion melted away as our highly trained Frontiersmen were gladly embodied by whichever unit could grab them. I served as Adjutant to General Gough in 'Z' Zone until I was called into the Royal Tank Regt.'[17] Certainly the Legion of Frontiersmen had a major, but so far unacknowledged, influence in the Home Guard. Once again, the Frontiersmen were an unofficial step ahead of everyone. The Chairman of the CCCTA, Lord Cobham, noted on 9 March 1945:

> In the present war the first move in the formation of the above bodies was made in the end of November 1939 when Col Sir Francis Whitmore, Lord Lieutenant of Essex, came to see me, who then occupied the position of Under-Secretary of State for War at the War Office on a matter that was giving him some concern. It appeared that an odd formation known as the 'Legion of Frontiersmen' was carrying out rapid recruiting from men in Essex who were not liable to be called up for the Services. Sir

Francis wanted the War Office to know all about this quite unofficial undertaking particularly as he was not satisfied that the man at the head of it was the best person to run it. The following morning I had a talk with the Adjutant-General Sir R. Gordon Finlayson about this, and he agreed that if encouragement were given to the creation of a voluntary force of this nature, it was likely to meet with a very ready response all over the U.K.[18]

The very mention of the Frontiersmen's activities would have acted as a spur to the War Office to ensure that any action would be official and not the result of the Legion's recruitment. Much as they wished it, they could not exclude the Frontiersmen completely. In Salford, Bob Moyse received a telephone call from the local police. According to his family he disappeared for a few days and when he returned the LDV was in being and operational in his area.[19] Wherever there was a need for them, the Frontiersmen around the world found themselves a suitable task in the new conflict. Before the First War, the Legion had been gearing itself up for military action, whatever their age. By 1939 things had changed and the men in their 40s found themselves more suited for some kind of Civil Defence role. Leo Amery, one of the *eminences grises* behind the Legion between the Wars, exemplified their thinking. They were anti-bolshevists but, in the main, they viewed with distaste the opinions and actions of the Fascists. They shared the opinion of Amery and Churchill of Britain's lack of preparedness, as Amery said,

> In 1918 her Army, if not the most numerous, was the most effective fighting force in the Alliance. She disbanded it to a level below that of 1914, or even of 1899. Having invented armoured warfare she ignored its possibilities and left it to others to develop. Supreme in the even more potent weapon of the Air she was content to relapse to the position of fifth or sixth of the European Powers.[20]

It was the hope of the Governing Council of the Legion that the British tradition of the volunteer amateur would be there through the Legion of Frontiersmen to back up official forces. The Boy Scout movement was enjoying success, and yet the Legion of Frontiersmen continued to enjoy its internal squabbles. The Boy Scout movement had its Baden-Powell. Once their one great charismatic leader Driscoll was no longer visibly at the head, the Legion searched, and still continues to search, for a leader of that ability to rule and persuade by strength of personality. In November 1941 the Founder, Roger Pocock died at the age of 76 and so ended his 'splendid adventure'. He had been the man of ideas whose dreams were behind the Legion of Frontiersmen. Had he also had the leadership qualities of his friend Driscoll, one is led to wonder how much more success his Frontiersmen might have enjoyed. His Legion still survives after a hundred years but remains a history of what might have been. His funeral was a quiet affair as many of those of his comrades who still survived were engaged in the War. He was cremated and his ashes were scattered, but his name was added to the family memorial in Cookham Church, where Frontiersmen still commemorate him on major anniversaries. The War Office almost succeeded by their policy of denying the Frontiersmen named units in wiping out the organisation, but after the War it still bounced back, albeit in a smaller way. Anyone who has watched the British television programme *Dads Army* has commented on a certain similarity with the Frontiersmen. The Legion's most senior officer in Selsey, Sussex, where the Frontiersmen are very active in support of the community, admits that he has been somewhat affectionately known locally as 'Captain Mainwaring'.

The Canadian Frontiersmen worked consistently for the War effort. They busied themselves recruiting for the armed forces and were used in a number of towns as Auxiliary Police. They also trained in A.R.P. (Air Raid Precautions) work, making the point to the authorities that during the 1930s the Legion had specialised in anti-gas warfare training and could put this into practice should Canada be bombed. In an event reminiscent of the Legion's involvement with the territorials in England in the early days of the Legion, military authorities invited the Legion to join in an exercise in Ontario to test security measures. On 11 June 1942, members of the Guelph Squadron of the Frontiersmen were invited to act as 'German spies' and attempt to cross the Speed River over four bridges there. They were not allowed to cross by boat or swim. This sort of exercise was guaranteed to appeal to the inventive mind of a Frontiersman. A list of the 12 members taking part was supplied to the militia headquarters with age, height, weight, colour of eyes, hair and complexion; also the assumed names they would be using, and presumably carrying on them. The Frontiersmen entered fully into the spirit of the event with names such as 'Otto Behung', 'Otto B. Schott' and 'Benito Hamberger'. Ten of the 12 made it across the bridges by a number of ruses and in a number of disguises. Their Captain, Arthur Corke, walked cheerfully across a bridge dressed as a woman (Leni Belchenburp) and two went across brazenly in their Auxiliary

83 *Captain Robert Moyse, M.C., D.C.M., B.E.M.*

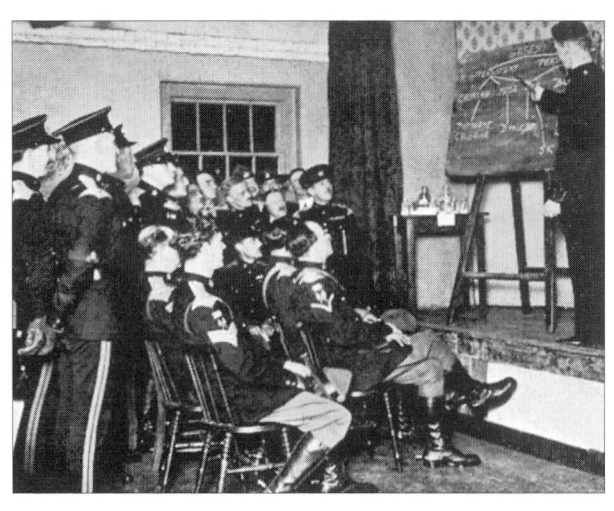

84   Gas warfare lecture on respirators.

85 (left)   Major Jack Gallagher, B.E.M., responsible for re-forming the legion in Selsey and West Sussex area in the 1960s.

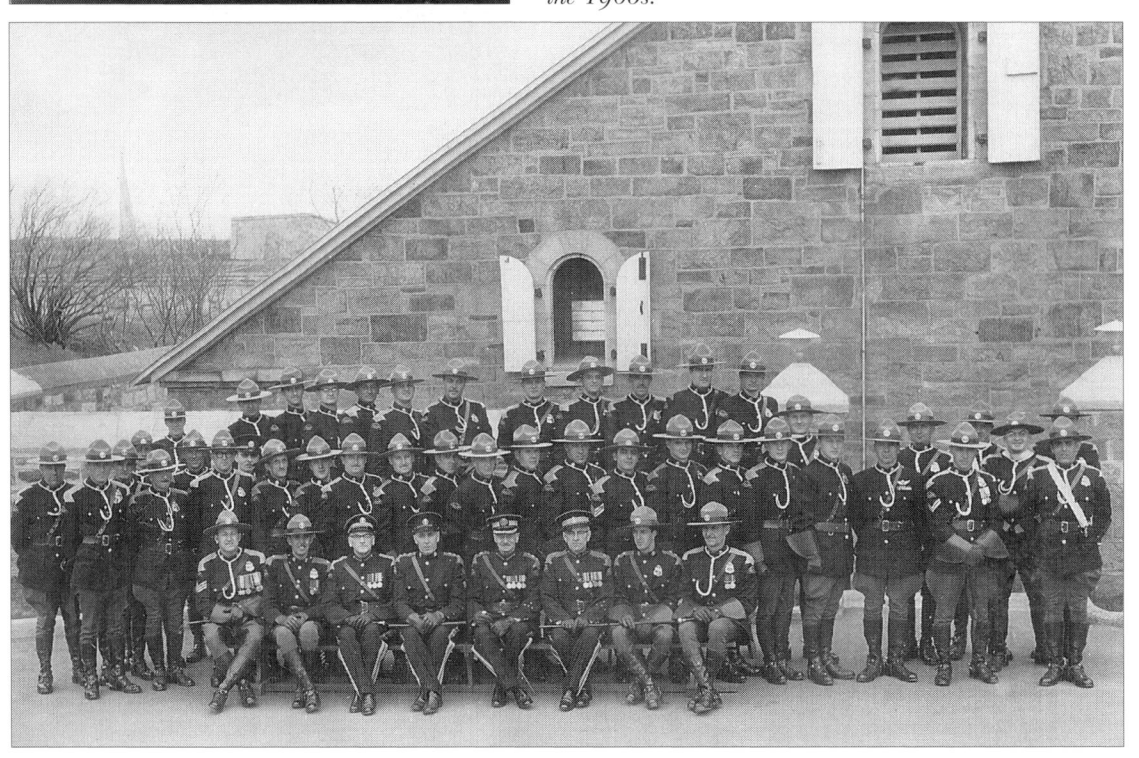

86   Quebec Frontiersmen 1950s to mid-1960s. Note the municipal police badges on the left breast on some tunics. These men worked as a form of auxiliary to the municipal police.

Dwindling Influence

Police uniform without being challenged. One of the two caught, Sgt Armstrong (Frankenstein Beerschwizzle), almost made it across as a taxi driver but was recognised by an acquaintance. He was taken to headquarters, but there he was able to seize the rifle of a careless guard and then take the entire Staff captive. It was agreed that the Frontiersmen had won by eleven to one and the spies were then invited to the officers' mess of the militia for the evening for 'generous refreshments'. The local paper, *The Guelph Mercury*, published a full account of the exercise and mentioned that several young boys had been shocked to see a 'hard looking woman boldly walking along the main street, smoking a pipe'. The whole episode could easily have featured in an episode of television's *Dad's Army*, but it does again raise a question about the poor preparedness and lack of imagination of the militia as opposed to the consistent inventiveness of the somewhat eccentric Legion of Frontiersmen.[21]

87 *Badge of the Canadian Division of the Legion of Frontiersmen (beaver replaces the mural crown).*

Pocock had referred to an Air Command on his visit to Canada and this had been started in 1932 by a retired Wing Commander, Alec Knowles-Fitton.[22] By 1936 the Command was able to put on a display, using their own aircraft, for Home Office officials. By 1939 the Command could call on seven aircraft with which they carried out mock air raids at Hanworth airfield.[23] As usual with anything proposed by the Legion of Frontiersmen, officials refused to be impressed. Early in the War, Lord Beaverbrook came up with the idea that any individual, organisation or town able to raise £5,000 would be able to present an aircraft, usually a Spitfire, to the R.A.F. By the end of the War, it is believed that around 1,500 Spitfires had been presentation models. Even if the Frontiersmen could not have a named unit, they had a way of having the name on active service. The Canadians were again at the forefront of the money raising and there were Spitfires on service called 'Corps of Imperial Frontiersmen', 'Frontiersmen' and 'Legion of Imperial Frontiersmen'.[24]

* * *

In 1946, Major Hazzledine, one of the few remaining survivors of the 25th Fusiliers (Frontiersmen), wrote to the War Office to see if they could help him find Kaid Belton, as he wished to revive the Legion. The War Office could not, or would not, help him with this.[25] It was not until 1949 that the Legion of Frontiersmen was able to hold its first General Meeting for ten years with an attendance of around a hundred with a few representatives from New Zealand also there. The new headquarters was to be in a Nissen hut on what had been a blitzed area off the Pentonville Road in London. 'The 1949 General Meeting was not a post-mortem or a court of enquiry. The fact that

88 *Roeslare, Belgium, May 1972.*

89 *The Legion Colours marching through London. Captain Philip Shoosmith leads the Legion of Frontiersmen down Whitehall to lay a wreath at the Cenotaph.*

the Legion had been knocked out was accepted and no explanation or excuses were offered or expected.'[26] This was how the New Zealanders reported back in their magazine. Major Hawkins of Worthing, who was the treasurer, was in the chair. Col Dunn still held the post of Chief of Staff and read a letter of resignation from Brigadier Morton, 'a retirement which was accepted without comment or protest'.[27] Two months later, Brigadier Morton was dead. Yet again, the Legion had lost many members who had not survived a war and others had had their fill of uniformed service. As in 1919, the Legion

90 *Frontiersmen escort the Belgian Colours on Belgian Day.*

91 *Capt. M. Warnauts of the 3rd Belgian Lancers presents a lance carried in action by Frontiersmen in Belgium in 1914 to replace those destroyed in the bombing of London H.Q.*

Dwindling Influence

92 *Colour Squadron Mounted Troop, Petts Wood, 1967.*

had to pick itself up from a very small base. Legion units were still active in African countries, serving in campaigns such as that against the Mau Mau, until these countries gained their independence, when the Frontiersmen no longer had relevance. New Zealand began to recover and found ways of serving, often similar to Special Constabulary duties, but the independent Canadian Division and Belton's Imperial Frontiersmen (without Belton) were proving successful. A few Imperial Frontiersmen units in Britain, such as in Weymouth, did not survive the War, but the successful Canadian Division began to expand to Britain, attracting expatriate Canadians to the ranks. Although Louis Scott had retired to Brighton, England, Canadian Division

93 *Major Philip Shoosmith laying a wreath at the Cenotaph in London.*

94 *Belgium Day, 1980.*

95 *Rough-rider Sgt Mike King, Peace River, British Columbia, 2003.*

96 *Members of British North America and Eastern Canada Commands now regularly take part in parachuting events.*

still wanted this charismatic man at the head, until he persuaded them it was time for them to find another leader. Col Cyril Wybrow, who had been the leading light in the Egypt Command (although not universally popular there), had held a senior position at London Headquarters on his return to Britain in the early 1930s, succeeding Edwards-Carter. He was one who had resigned in protest at Morton's treatment of Scott, although he had written the sharp letter to Scott regarding Pocock's 1935 visit. Wybrow eventually joined Canadian Division and became Scott's liaison officer in Britain. He represented Scott in a tour of Canada, where his strong character was effective until his career caused him to move to Paris.[28]

Quebec had a very strong and financially secure Corps of Imperial Frontiersmen. Scott was succeeded by Col Eric Cormack, who organised a number of meetings with the Imperials in an attempt to amalgamate the two organisations, but this eventually failed. A considerable shift from the Imperials to Canadian Division did gradually occur during the 1960s. Although the Frontiersmen were no longer affiliated to the R.C.M.P. they were regularly in demand by various city police forces to act as auxiliaries and the Imperial Frontiersmen wore a breast badge to identify their association.[29] Cormack held the position until 1964, when he was succeeded by Major Mack, who became well known round the world as Brigadier Mack. Mack was a diligent and hard-working leader who worked steadily until his death, when his wife took over the position. Will Shandro, in a paper he wrote on the Canadian

Dwindling Influence

97 *Frontiersmen march on to Horse Guards Parade, Belgian Day, 2004.*

98 *Belgian Day, 2004. Prince Philippe of Belgium takes the salute from the Frontiersmen.*

Frontiersmen in the post-war period, expressed the opinion that Cormack, as an experienced senior army officer, was able to enhance the Legion across Canada. The close association with the police forces mainly in traffic and crowd control duties were of a financial advantage to the Canadian Frontiersmen, but Will Shandro considers that the problems out-weighed the benefits. Initially it was probably perceived by the Legion of Frontiersmen as a useful public task with the added benefit of a cash honorarium to the unit. Rapidly, this disintegrated into squabbles about duty hours, individual pay for service, and the view of the Legion of Frontiersmen as a bunch of aged and over-dressed 'rent-a-cops'.[30] With the ageing of Mack, the Frontiersmen became little more than a social club for members who paraded at certain public events. It slowly declined to its present modest membership.

The Legion of Frontiersmen still survives, but as a shadow of its former self and still searching for an individual purpose. Being built on such firm foundations, it shows no signs of dying, in spite of the great dislike of it by such authorities as the Ministry of Defence. It has been helped by being accepted in the United Kingdom as a registered charity, but it is still hindered by various unsuitable types refused access to the Legion, who set up their own

99 *Cdt-General Ronald J. Potter lays a wreath at the Cenotaph, Belgian Day, 2004.*

100 *Belgian Day, 2004. The Frontiersmen on Horse Guards Parade.*

groups using the name of the Frontiersmen and at times bringing disrepute to the name. Its post-war Commandants-General have been respectable ex-officers who have served it well and it has regularly attracted a very senior retired army officer to act as President, such as Field Marshal Lord Birdwood and Major-General Raymond Briggs. The Legion of Frontiersmen has never enjoyed official royal patronage but the relationship with the Mountbatten family goes back to the May day in 1905 when Prince Louis of Battenberg agreed to join. In recent years, the Countess Mountbatten has agreed to lend her name officially to the Legion, whose badge now bears her name and coronet and which has become the Legion of Frontiersmen of the Commonwealth (Countess Mountbatten's Own). They train in basic skills of First Aid and light recovery, ready to help at any emergency until the official bodies such as police, ambulance and fire services arrive. They have instructions then to fade from the scene if no longer required. There have been numbers of occasions in recent years where the Frontiersmen have been able to do this. After one severe storm in England, the only local policeman on duty freely admitted that, had he not been able to call on the Frontiersmen for help, there would have been many more deaths.

For all its faults, many thousands of Frontiersmen have been killed or wounded in wars around the world while serving their country, and all Frontiersmen have always worked hard to be of assistance to their fellow citizens while still enjoying the original principles of 'good fellowship'. They have also always been there for 'service to the State in time of need'.

NOTES

Title page quotation:
German East, Brian Gardner, p.50.

Introduction, pp.xvii-xxii
1. Diary of Roger Pocock, 1909.
2. CO323 1221/20 Public Record Office.
3. *Collected Letters of George Bernard Shaw, 1898-1910*, Ed. Dan H. Laurence, p.720.
4. *The Yellow Earl*, Douglas Sutherland, p.185.
5. *Sons of the Empire*, Robert H. MacDonald, pp.32-3.
6. *The Times*, 15 November 1941, p.6.
7. *Ibid.*, 17 February 1931, p.10.
8. Personal letter quoted by courtesy of Tom Pocock.
9. *Chorus to Adventurers*, Roger Pocock, p.23 refers to the Legion becoming the 'eyes of the Empire'. This was expanded over the years in Legion writings to 'the eyes and ears of the Empire'.
10. *The Rules of the Game*, Roger Pocock, p.279.
11. *Ibid.*, p.278.
12. *Horses*, Roger Pocock, pub. John Murray, 1917.
13. Roger Pocock, Canada papers, family correspondence.
14. *Daily Telegraph* and other papers, letters, 26 December 1904.
15. *The Rules of the Game*, Roger Pocock, p.278.

1: Canada, pp.1-16
1. Letter from Roger Pocock to nephew Charles Wesley Kennedy Pocock, 1927.
2. *Myself a Player*, Lena Ashwell, pp.14-23.
3. *Ibid.*, pp21-2.
4. *A Frontiersman*, Roger Pocock, pub. Gay and Hancock, 1904.
5. *Ibid.*, pp.1-2.
6. *Ibid.*, p.3.
7. *Ibid.*
8. Roger Pocock, Canada papers, family correspondence.
9. *A Frontiersman*, Pocock, p.4.
10. Roger Pocock, Canada papers, family correspondence.
11. *A Frontiersman*, Pocock, p.10.
12. *Ibid.*, p.17.
13. *Lloyds Weekly Newspaper*, 3 October 1897, p.14.
14. In the manner of the time, Pocock referred to 'Indians'. These are now more correctly known as 'First Nations', or 'Native Canadians'. When quoting Pocock's writings I use his own terminology. No offence is intended.
16. *A Frontiersman*, pp.21-2 refers to this letter.
17. *Riders of the Plains*, A.L. Haydon, p.68.
18. *A Frontiersman*, Pocock, p.25.
19. *Trooper and Redskin*, J. Donkin, p.84.
20. *Ibid.*, p.85.
21. *Ibid.*, p.52.
22. Personal letter to the author from the late Lord Louis Mountbatten.
23. *A Frontiersman*, Pocock, pp.35-6.
24. *History of the Legion of Frontiersmen, Canadian Division*. Private publication, ed. Brigadier A. Mack, p.93. Quoted by kind permission of the late Brigadier Mack.
25. *Trooper and Redskin*, Donkin, p.113.
26. *A Frontiersman*, Pocock, p.53.
27. *Ibid.*, p.54.
28. *Trooper and Redskin*, Donkin, p.218.
29. *Crime in a Cold Climate*, ed. D. Skene-Martin, pp.128-37.
30. *Sons of the Empire*, MacDonald, pp.137-8.
31. *Western Avernus*, Morley Roberts. Roberts made a return journey to Canada in the 1920s noting the considerable changes in *On the Old Trail*, 1927.
32. Personal correspondence with the late Cecil Clark, British Columbia journalist.
33. Roger Pocock, Canada papers.
34. *A Frontiersman*, Pocock, p.158.

2: Accusations of Murder, pp.17-27
1. *My Long Life*, Douglas Sladen, p.163.
2. Roger Pocock, Canada papers, also *A Frontiersman*, pp.165-6.
3. *Rottenness*, Roger Pocock. Very few copies of this book survive.
4. *Baden-Powell*, Tim Jeal, p.150. Jeal points out a number of inconsistencies in Baden-Powell's claims and suggests that Baden-Powell was guilty of considerable exaggeration. In 1908 Baden-Powell warned that Germany was 'the natural enemy of this country'.
5. *Chorus to Adventurers*, Roger Pocock, pp.13-15.
6. *Ibid.*, p.11.
7. *A Frontiersman*, Pocock, p.176; also 'R.C.M.P. Quarterly', April 1948, Old-timers column, p.379, letter from ex-Sgt. R.J. Jones.
8. *Lloyds Weekly Newspaper*, 3 October 1897, p.14.
9. *A Frontiersman*, Pocock, p.178.
10. *Lloyds Weekly Newspaper*, 3 October 1897, p.14.
11. *Ibid.*, 16 January 1898.
12. *A Frontiersman*, Pocock, p.211.
13. *Ibid.*
14. *Klondike Cattle Drive*, Norman Lee, p.4.
15. *A Frontiersman*, Pocock, p.220.
16. *Ibid.*, p.221.
17. Cecil Clark had been a British Columbia policeman and a journalist. His cooperation and our correspondence helped us to find answers between us to some of the mysteries of the Curtis affair.
18. *Lloyds Weekly Newspaper*, 5 August 1900, p.14.
19. *Horses*, Roger Pocock, p.204.
20. *A Frontiersman*, Pocock, p.286.

3: Listing the Legion, pp.28-50
1. *Daily Telegraph*, and other newspapers – letters, 26 December 1904.
2. *Secret Service*, Christopher Andrew, p.25.
3. *Illustrated Mail*, 14 January 1905, p.8.
4. *Chorus to Adventurers*, Pocock, p.17.
5. *Ibid.*, p.18.
6. *Ibid.*
7. *Prince Louis of Battenberg*, Mark Kerr, p.175.
8. *Chorus to Adventurers*, Pocock, p.24.
9. *Ibid.*, pp.73-4.
10. *Ibid.*, p.63. See also *The Mysterious Mr Le Queux*, Dr Roger Stearn, article in 'Soldiers of the Queen', September 1992.
11. *Secret Service*, Andrew, p.45.
12. *Memoirs*, J.E. Edmonds,

177

typescript chapter xx, p.2, Edmonds papers Liddell Hart Archives, King's College, London, quoted by kind permission of the Trustees. See also *The Mysterious Mr Le Queux*, by Stearn.
13. *Baden-Powell*, Jeal, p.153.
14. *Ibid.*, p.375.
15. Report and Proceedings of a Sub-Committee of the Committee of Imperial Defence, pp.iii-iv, CAB16/8 in The National Archives.
16. *Secret Service*, Andrew, p.58.
17. *Chorus to Adventurers*, Pocock, pp.7-9.
18. Legion of Frontiersmen Archives.
19. *Frontier Post 1904-1984*, 80 Anniversary issue, p.8, Dr Peter Lovatt. Dr. Lovatt's biography of Driscoll is to be published shortly.
20. *Ibid.*
21. *Chorus to Adventurers*, Pocock, p.24.
22. *Ibid.*, copy of the letter is shown opp. p.27.
23. *Ibid.*, p.25.
24. The Treasury Solicitor agreed that the uniform was acceptable but pointed out that it was illegal to raise an armed force, WO32 10426/7/8 at The National Archives.
25. *Lonsdale, the authorised life of Hugh Lowther*, L. Dawson, p.154.
26. Roger Pocock pocket diary, 1905.
27. *Ibid.*
28. *Chorus to Adventurers*, Pocock, pp.29-30.
29. Pocock pocket diary, 1905.
30. Frontiersmen Archives, also note in WO32 10428, 10427, 10426 at The National Archives.
31. *Chorus to Adventurers*, Pocock, p.38.
32. Letter from War Office in Frontiersmen archives. See also the files noted above in The National Archives.
33. Legion of Frontiersmen Archives.
34. *Chorus to Adventurers*, Pocock, p.43.
35. *Ibid.*, p.74; also 'The Canadian Frontiersman', Vol.34, no.2, April-May-June, 1964, pp.6-7.
36. *Ibid.*, p.27.
37. *Ibid.*, p.28, also Pocock diaries.
38. File KV1/4, Branch memoranda. Intelligence methods in peacetime (German system).
39. *Ibid.*, p.39. This could be apocryphal. It has been the source of some discussion. It has been claimed that the saying originates with the Persian 'Khuda Hafiz e Shuma bashad' – 'May God be your Guardian'.
40. *The Times*, 27 April 1906, p.4.
41. *Ibid.*, 4 September 1906, p.8.
42. *Chorus to Adventurers*, Pocock, pp.53-4.

43. *Secret Service*, Andrew, p.49.
44. Correspondence in W.O. files October 1908, WO32/ 10428, 10427, 10426 in The National Archives.
45. *Chorus to Adventurers*, p.44-5.
46. *East Anglian Daily Times*, 10 February 1908, p.3.
47. WO32 10428 in The National Archives. See also WO32 10427 and 10429.
48. *History of the Legion of Frontiersmen*, Canadian Division, ed. Mack, p.167.
49. Pocock diary 1908.
50. *Journals and Letters of Viscount Esher*, ed. Brett, p.367.
51. Burnham wrote a first-hand account of the Shangani Patrol in *Scouting on Two Continents*. He joined the Legion of Frontiersmen at the age of 85.
52. *Chorus to Adventurers*, Pocock, pp.83-6.
53. *Ibid.*, p.90.
54. *Sixty Years of Fleet Street*, Hamilton Fyfe, p.144.
55. *All in a Lifetime*, R.D. Blumenfeld, p.189.
56. *Chorus to Adventurers*, Pocock, pp.65-6.
57. *M.I.5*, John Bulloch, p.19.
58. Vernon Kell's Diary KV 1/10 in M.I.5 files at The National Archives.
59. *The Quest for C*, Alan Judd, pp.94-5.
60. HD3/139 at The National Archives.
61. Legion of Frontiersmen Archives.
62. *Georgian Adventure*, Douglas Jerrold, p.95.
63. *The Youngest Son*, Ivor Montagu, p.31.
64. *History of the Legion of Frontiersmen, Canadian Division*, ed. Mack, p.148.
65. HD3/139 at The National Archives.

4: The Secret Government Subsidy, pp.51-74
1. HD3/139 at Public Record Office.
2. *The Times*, 10 May 1909.
3. *Ibid.*, 13 May 1909, p.9.
4. *Journals and Letters of Viscount Esher*, Vol.2, Ed. Brett p.285.
5. Reported in most major London newspapers.
6. 'Legion of Frontiersmen Northern Command', monthly gazette, Vol.1, no.4, p.25 (courtesy of Newcastle-upon Tyne public libraries).
7. *Ibid.*
8. *The Times*, 15 May 1909, p.10.
9. *Ibid.*
10. *Chorus to Adventurers*, Pocock, p.81.
11. *History of the Legion of Frontiersmen, Canadian Division*, ed. Mack, p.103.
12. *Chorus to Adventurers*, Pocock, pp.82-3.
13. *Ibid.*, p.82.
14. *Ibid.*, p.86.
15. Roger Pocock diary, 1909.
16. *Journals and Letters of Viscount Esher*, Vol.2, ed. Brett, p.390.
17. Roger Pocock diary 1909.
18. HD3/139 at Public Record Office.
19. Roger Pocock diary, 1909.
20. *Ibid.*
21. *The Mail on Sunday*, 20 August 2000, pp.38-9.
22. Roger Pocock diary, 1909.
23. MEPO2 1193 at Public Record Office.
24. Roger Pocock diary, 1909.
25. WO32 10426/7/8 at Public Record Office.
26. Roger Pocock diary, 1909; also *Chorus to Adventurers*, pp.87-8.
27. *Chorus to Adventurers*, Pocock, p.90.
28. *Baden-Powell*, Jeal, p.403.
29. *Ibid.*, p.408.
30. *The Frontiersman's Pocket Book*, ed. Roger Pocock, pp.105-108.
31. *Ibid.*, pp.148-9.
32. *The Life of Frederick Courtney Selous*, D.S.O., J.G. Millais, p.302.
33. *The Frontiersman's Pocket Book*, p.1.
34. WO32 10426/7/8.
35. 'Newsletter of the Sunbury and Shepperton Local History Society', 1983.
36. *Ibid.*
37. *Chorus to Adventurers*, Pocock, pp.287-8.
38. *Buffalo Bill's Wild West*, by A. Gallop gives his last British tour as 1904, p.268.
39. Personal reminiscences of Trooper Roberts. These were dictated from memory to his family when he was an old man.
40. *Chorus to Adventurers*, Pocock, p.54.
41. *Sam Steele, Lion of the Frontier*, R. Stewart, p.257.
42. *Ibid.*, p.266.
43. Roger Pocock diaries. Canadian archives of the Legion of Frontiersmen show the first organising officer for Canada in June 1905 as Albert D. Willcocks, and the first Commandant in Canada as Stanley Winther Caws of Lac St Anne, Alberta.
44. *History of the Legion of Frontiersmen 1904-1979, N Squadron Manawatu New Zealand*, private publication, p.56.
45. *Ibid.*, pp.56-7.
46. *Ibid.*, p.58.
47. Letters of Lt Col D.P. Driscoll in Legion of Frontiersmen Archives.
48. *Ibid.*
49. *Ibid.*; also articles on Twistleton in magazines of New Zealand Command of the Legion of Frontiersmen.
50. WO32 10426/7/8 in The National Archives.
51. *Daily Sketch*, 14 November 1914, front page.
52. Memoirs of Trooper Roberts in Legion of Frontiersmen Archives (see also notes 38 and 39).

Notes

53. Memoirs of Dr Percy McDougall in Legion of Frontiersmen Archives.
54. *Chorus to Adventurers*, Pocock, p.92.
55. Memoirs of Trooper Roberts.
56. Records of 3rd Belgian Lancers.
57. *Adventures with Animals and Men*, Cherry Kearton, pp.176-201.
58. *Ibid.*, p.203.
59. *Three Years of War in East Africa*, Angus Buchanan, p.2.
60. *Memories of Kenya*, ed. Arnold Curtis, p.27.
61. Personal file of Major Williams in WO339 at Public Record Office.
62. Correspondence with the family of Major H.H.R. White, also his personal file in WO339 at The National Archives.
63. Personal file of E. Haggas in WO339 at The National Archives.
64. Personal file of J.H. Bowles in WO339 at The National Archives.
65. Personal file of A.H. Reed in WO339 at The National Archives.
66. 'Army Diary' Richard Meinertzhagen p.131; see also 'Sketches of the East African Campaign', Dolbey.
67. Personal file of J. Pyman in WO339 at The National Archives.
68. Personal file of Capt. Welstead in WO339 at The National Archives.

5: The War in East Africa, pp.75-96
1. Personal file of J. Leitch in WO339 at The National Archives.
2. Personal file of W.N. McMillan in WO339 at The National Archives.
3. Memoirs of Frederick Turner Elliott, quoted by kind permission of his grandson, Mr. Roger Kearin of Australia.
4. *Military Operations East Africa*, from original manuscript by Major Stacke, p.135.
5. Arthur W. Lloyd was political cartoonist for *Punch* until 1952. Some of his brilliant cartoons of service life in East Africa were published in *Jambo, or with Jannie in the Jungle*, 1919.
6. Personal file of A.W. Lloyd in WO339 in The National Archives.
7. Letters and photographs in the archives of the Legion of Frontiersmen. See also WO95/5466 at The National Archives.
8. *Ibid.*
9. *From Hobo to Hunter*, C.T. Stoneham, p.165.
10. *Ibid.*, p.166.
11. Reminiscences of Pte. Clifford Hall in Legion of Frontiersmen Archives.
12. *Ibid.*
13. *From Hobo to Hunter*, Stoneham, p.167.
14. *Ibid.*
15. *Three Years of War in East Africa*, Angus Buchanan, p.6.
16. Personal file of J. Pyman in WO339 in The National Archives.
17. *Battle for the Bundu*, Charles Miller, pp.55-72.
18. Memoirs of F.T. Elliott.
19. *Adventures with Animals and Men*, Cherry Kearton, pp.205-6.
20. *My Reminiscences of East Africa*, Von Lettow-Vorbeck. Introduction to reprint by Dr Thomas Pofcansky, final page (un-numbered), also information from Mr Gerald Rilling, bookseller and student of the War in East Africa.
21. *The Life of Frederick Courtenay Selous*, by J. Millais, p.306.
22. *Ibid.*, p.307.
23. *Ibid.*, p.313.
24. *Adventures with Animals and Men*, Kearton, p.215.
25. *The Life of Frederick Courtenay Selous*, Millais, p.314.
26. *Army Diary*, Meinertzhagen, p.136.
27. *Life of Frederick Courtenay Selous*, Millais, p.315.
28. *Adventures with Animals and Men*, Kearton, p.218.
29. *Ibid.*, p.219.
30. *Military Operations East Africa*, Stacke, p.153.
31. Memoirs of D. Pedersen, New Zealand Archives, also published in various issues of *New Zealand Frontiersman* magazine.
32. Memoirs of F.T. Elliott.
33. Memoirs of D. Pedersen.
34. A short film of the 25th Fusiliers in East Africa shows Reed's experiment. The film was made by Cherry Kearton and is in the film archive at the Imperial War Museum. In his *Adventures with Animals and Men*, Kearton places the fault not in Reed's design but in the impure metal used at the local foundry where the barrel was made.
35. War Diary of 25th Fusiliers at The National Archives.
36. Memoirs of F.T. Elliott.
37. *Ibid.*
38. *Sunday Dispatch*, 6 February 1916. Darling was a former railwayman from South America and one of the first to enlist in the 25th Fusiliers.
39. *Ibid.*
40. Memoirs of F.T. Elliott.
41. Citation from *London Gazette* of 3 September 1915 quoted in the personal file of W. Dartnell in WO339 in The National Archives.
42. Memoirs of F.T. Elliott.
43. *Three Years of War in East Africa*, Buchanan, p.19.
44. Information courtesy of Eddy Reed's son Vincent Reed.
45. Newspaper cutting in Legion of Frontiersmen Archives. Interview with Driscoll by Max Pemberton.
46. Personal file of W. Dartnell in WO339 in The National Archives; also information courtesy of Driscoll's biographer, Dr Peter Lovatt.
47. Memoirs of F.T. Elliott.
48. War Diary of 25th Fusiliers at The National Archives.
49. Correspondence in Legion of Frontiersmen files.
50. *Yorkshire Evening News*, 20 June 1917.
51. *Kenya Chronicles*, Lord Cranworth.
52. *The Years of War in East Africa*, Buchanan, p.109.
53. *From Hobo to Hunter*, Stoneham, p.48.
54. *Ibid.*, p.49.
55. *Ibid.*, p.50.
56. *Three Years of War in East Africa*, Buchanan, p.110.
57. *From Hobo to Hunter*, Stoneham, p.52.
58. Personal file on A.W. Lloyd in WO339 at The National Archives.
59. *Jim Redlake*, Francis Brett Young, pp.577-8.
60. *Three Years of War in East Africa*, Buchanan, p.125-6.
61. *Ibid.*, p.163.
62. Cutting from *Yorkshire Evening Post* in Legion of Frontiersmen Archives.
63. Memoirs of Pte. Clifford Hall in Legion of Frontiersmen Archives.
64. *Ibid.*
65. *Jungle Man*, Major P.J. Pretorious, p.193.
66. Letter to *The Times*, cutting in Legion of Frontiersmen Archives.
67. *Battle for the Bundu*, Miller, p.245n.
68. War Diary of 25th Fusiliers in The National Archives.
69. Letter in archives of Yorkshire Command, Legion of Frontiersmen.
70. *Three Years of War in East Africa*, Buchanan, p.173.
71. Personal file of P. Langham in WO339 at The National Archives.
72. Personal file of H.H.R. White in WO374 at The National Archives and information by courtesy of his son and grandson in America.
73. Personal file of A.H. Reed in WO339 at The National Archives.
74. Personal file of G.D. Hazzledine in WO339 at The National Archives.
75. Personal file of A.D. Welstead in WO339 at The National Archives.
76. Personal file of J.D. Leitch in WO339 at The National Archives.
77. Cutting from *Bradford Argus and Telegraph* in Legion of Frontiersmen Archives.
78. *Three Years of War in East Africa*, Buchanan, p.182.
79. Personal file of A.W. Lloyd

in WO339 at The National Archives.
80. *Three Year of War in East Africa*, Buchanan, p.196.
81. *The Battle for the Bundu*, Miller, p.283.
82. *Ibid.*, p.284.
83. Personal file of A.W. Lloyd in The National Archives.
84. Personal file of D.P. Driscoll in WO339 at The National Archives.
85. Personal file of A.W. Lloyd at The National Archives.

6: The World Flight Expedition, pp.97-115
1. Letters in the Legion of Frontiersmen Archives.
2. Letter from Driscoll to Ernest D'Esterre of New Zealand, July 18th 1918 in Legion of Frontiersmen Archives.
3. There were regular accounts of the activities of the W.A.L.F. in the magazines of New Zealand Command.
4. Letter from Driscoll to D'Esterre, 18 July 1918.
5. Letter from Driscoll to D'Esterre, 20 February 1920.
6. Letter from Tamplin to Burchardt-Ashton, 6 December 1921.
7. Correspondence between Burchardt-Ashton and the City of London Police in Legion of Frontiersmen Archives.
8. WO32/10426/7/8 in The National Archives.
9. Letter from Tamplin to Burchardt-Ashton, 21 November 1923.
10. Burchardt-Ashton's son was killed in action in France as a Lance-Corporal. See also Chapter 8.
11. Personal file on Roger Pocock in WO339 in The National Archives.
12. MacMillan's account of the attempt is to be found in his *Freelance Pilot* and Blake's version is in his *Flying Round the World*. Contemporary newspaper reports make MacMillan and Malins' view of Blake quite clear.
13. *Chorus to Adventurers*, Pocock, p.266.
14. *Ibid.*
15. This advertisement appeared in the *Daily Mail* and a number of national newspapers.
16. *Chorus to Adventurers*, Pocock, p.269.
17. *Soldier, Sailor, Airman, Gaoler*, the privately published autobiography of Frank Ransley, O.B.E., D.F.C. p.26. I was able to interview the late Frank Ransley towards the end of his long life and discuss the expedition with him.
18. *Chorus to Adventurers*, Pocock, p.271.
19. *History of the Legion of Frontiersmen, Canadian Division*, ed. A. Mack, p.148.
20. *Soldier, Sailor, Airman, Gaoler*, Ransley, p.27.
21. Personal interview with Frank Ransley. He also made this point when he gave public talks.
22. Personal interview with Frank Ransley.
23. *Daily Courier*, 18 May 1923.
24. Telephone discussion with, and letters to the author from, the executor of the late Guy Eardley-Wilmot and his family.
25. *Chorus to Adventurers*, Pocock, p.272.
26. Personal interview with Frank Ransley.
27. Untitled newspaper cutting in the scrapbook of G.H. Heaton.
28. *Soldier, Sailor, Airman, Gaoler*, Ransley, p.26.
29. *Daily Mirror*, 8 June 1923.
30. *Daily Mirror*, 9 June 1923.
31. *Soldier, Sailor, Airman, Gaoler*, Ransley, pp.27-8.
32. Guy Eardley-Wilmot's photograph album of the Expedition.
33. Roger Pocock, Canada papers.
34. *World's Pictorial News*, 23 June 1923.
35. *Ibid.*
36. *Chorus to Adventurers*, Pocock, p.273.
37. *Ibid.*, pp.270-1; also *Soldier, Sailor, Airman, Gaoler*, p.28 and interview with Frank Ransley.
38. Interview with Frank Ransley.
39. *Ibid.*
40. *Ibid.*; also *Chorus to Adventurers*, Pocock, p.273.
41. *Ibid.*; also *Soldier, Sailor, Airman Gaoler*, Ransley, p.29.
42. *Ibid.*; also *Soldier, Sailor, Airman, Gaoler*, Ransley, p.30.
43. *Chorus to Adventurers*, Pocock, p.274.

7: Upsetting the Americans, pp.116-32
1. *Soldier, Sailor, Airman, Gaoler*, Ransley, p.32.
2. *Ibid.*; also interview with Frank Ransley and *Chorus to Adventurers*, Pocock, p.276.
3. Menu in albums of Eardley-Wilmot and Heaton.
4. *Ibid.*
5. *Ibid.*
6. *Ibid.*
7. *Soldier, Sailor, Airman, Gaoler*, p.33; also *Chorus to Adventurers*, Pocock, p.275.
8. *Ibid.*, also photographs in albums of Eardley-Wilmot and Heaton.
9. Obituary to Leeds in *New York Times*, 3 January 1972; also information from Eardley-Wilmot family and friends.
10. *Chorus to Adventurers*, Pocock, p.278; also interview with Frank Ransley.
11. *Soldier, Sailor, Airman, Gaoler*, Ransley, pp.33-4.
12. *Daily Telegraph*, 14 September 1923.
13. Cutting from un-recorded American newspaper dated 5 October 1923 in Eardley-Wilmot album.
14. Interview with Frank Ransley.
15. *Ibid.*
16. *Chorus to Adventurers*, Pocock, p.277.
17. *Soldier, Sailor, Airman, Gaoler*, Ransley, pp.34-6.
18. *Chorus to Adventurers*, Pocock, pp.278-9.
19. *Daily Chronicle*, 6 November 1923.
20. *Ibid.*
21. The MacLaren Expedition was carried out under the auspices of *The Times*. An account of the successful American effort is to be found in *The First World Flight* by Lowell Thomas.
22. Letters from Brancker to Eardley-Wilmot in his album.
23. *Ibid.*
24. Letter, 21 November 1923 from Tamplin to Burchardt-Ashton in Legion of Frontiersmen files.
25. Letter from Eardley-Wilmot to Tom Pocock, quoted by kind permission of Tom Pocock.
26. *Daily Mail*, 6 December, 1923.
27. Letter in *Daily Mail*, 13 December, 1923.
28. Undated cutting in from *John Bull* in Heaton album.
29. *Ibid.*
30. *John Bull*, 29 December 1923.
31. *Ibid.*
32. An account of this attempt was serialised in *The Times*.
33. *Soldier, Sailor, Airman, Gaoler*, Ransley, pp.39-43; also interview with Frank Ransley.
34. *Legion of Frontiersmen in Formation, Canada* paper by B.W. Shandro, M.Ed., April 2002, p.9 (copies of papers by B.W. Shandro are lodged at the Cameron Library, University of Alberta, Edmonton).
35. MEPO 2 1193 at The National Archives.
36. *Chorus to Adventurers*, Pocock, p.146.
37. *Legion of Frontiersmen in Formation, Canada*, Shandro, p.9.
38. *Ibid.*, p.10.

8: Success, then Failure Again, pp.133-58
1. *Sons of the Empire*, MacDonald, p.58n.
2. *Legion of Frontiersmen in Formation, Canada*, Shandro, p.62.
3. *A City Goes to War*, G.R. Stevens, p.12
4. *Ibid.*, p.15.
5. Legion of Frontiersmen Archives, also *Daily Malta Chronicle*, 24 March 1915.
6. 'Legion of Frontiersmen assist in PPCLI formation 1914', paper by Shandro, June 2004.
7. *Ibid.*, p.57.
8. *First in the Field*, Gault of the Patricias, J. Williams, p.64.
9. *Legion of Frontiersmen in Formation, Canada*, Shandro, p.51.
10. *Stanley Winther Caws*, a brief paper by B.W. Shandro.
11. *Legion of Frontiersmen in*

NOTES

12. *Formation, Canada*, Shandro, p.67.
12. *Ibid.*, p.68.
13. *Legion of Frontiersmen: Newfoundland, Canada 1914-18* by Jeff Henley, Australian historian of the Legion of Frontiersmen.
14. *Ibid.*
15. Letter from Robert Arthur Smith to Burchardt-Ashton, Legion of Frontiersmen Archives.
16. *The Other Mr Churchill*, MacDonald Hastings, pp.220-22.
17. Letter from R.A. Smith to Burchardt-Ashton, Legion of Frontiersmen Archives.
18. *Ibid.*
19. *Owen Roscomyl and the Welsh Horse*, Bryn Owen.
20. Letter from R.A. Smith to Burchardt-Ashton, Legion of Frontiersmen files.
21. Personal file on Arthur Burchardt-Ashton Jnr. in The National Archives.
22. *Ibid.*, also information in the Burchardt-Ashton scrapbook in Legion of Frontiersmen Archives.
23. Burchardt-Ashton scrapbook in Legion of Frontiersmen Archives.
24. Legion of Frontiersmen Archives.
25. Personal file of H.C. Edwards-Carter in The National Archives.
26. Letter in Legion of Frontiersmen Archives.
27. Personal file of Edwards-Carter in The National Archives.
28. Letter in Legion of Frontiersmen Archives.
29. *Jan Smuts*, F.S. Crafford, p.196.
30. Legion of Frontiersmen Archives, also item by Cushny in *The Frontiersman*, June 1954, pp.7-8.
31. *Ibid.*
32. WO32/10427 in The National Archives.
33. *Ibid.*
34. *Ibid.*
35. *Ibid.*
36. *History of the Legion of Frontiersmen, Canadian Division*, ed. Mack, p.105.
37. Letter in Legion of Frontiersmen Archives.
38. WO32/10427 in Public Record Office.
39. Letter in Legion of Frontiersmen Archives.
40. *Southern Cross* newspaper cutting in Legion of Frontiersmen Archives.
41. Personal file of Andrew Belton in WO339 at The National Archives.
42. Letter in Legion of Frontiersmen Archives.
43. *Ibid.*
44. *Ibid.* It is likely that this is the last letter Driscoll wrote to the Legion of Frontiersmen before his death.
45. Archives of Charterhouse, quoted by kind permission of the Registrar and Clerk to the Governors.
46. Legion of Frontiersmen Archives.
47. *History of the Legion of Frontiersmen, Canadian Division*, ed. Mack, p.108.
48. Letter from Roger Pocock to Francis Pocock.
49. Cutting from *The Province* in Legion of Frontiersmen files, undated, believed 7 November 1935.
50. *History of the Legion of Frontiersmen, Canadian Division*, ed. Mack p.70.
51. *Ibid.*
52. *Ibid.*
53. *Ibid.*, p.94.
54. Cutting from *Toronto* newspaper in Legion of Frontiersmen Archives, 27 November 1935.
55. *History of the Legion of Frontiersmen, Canadian Division*, ed. Mack, p.94.
56. Letter from Roger Pocock to Francis Pocock.
57. Open letter to Frontiersmen members, published in all Legion of Frontiersmen magazines around the Commonwealth, varying dates.
58. *The Times*, 18 May 1936, p.16.
59. *The Times*, 24 May 1936, p.8.
60. *New Zealand Frontiersman*, June/July 1935.
61. Comments in WO32/10427-8 in Public Record Office confirm this.
62. A photograph of the presentation to Prime Minister Winston Churchill on 26 February 1953 on behalf of the Frontiersmen of New Zealand appeared in a summer 1953 issue of *The Frontiersman* magazine.
63. A full account is in *The Great Trans-Pacific Flight*, C.E. Kingsford-Smith and C.T. Ulm.
64. Newspaper cuttings in Legion of Frontiersmen New Zealand archives.
65. 'John Boyes, King of the Wa-Kikuyu', article by Harry Leigh-Pink published in various Frontiersmen magazines and re-printed in *History of the Legion of Frontiersmen, Canadian Division* ed. Mack, pp.191-2. Obituary in *The Frontiersman*, October 1951, pp.3-5.
66. *On Safari*, Ada Cherry Kearton, p.69.
67. Obituary in *The Frontiersman*, October 1951.
68. *The Life and Death of Lord Erroll*, E. Trzebinski, p.142.
69. *Ibid.*, p.164, also archives of the Legion of Frontiersmen.
70. *Ibid.*, p.143.
71. *The Times*, 3 December 1929.
72. *Duel for Kilimanjaro*, Leonard Mosley, p.228.

9: Dwindling Influence, pp.159-76
1. Letter to author from E.F. Meacock.
2. Information courtesy of Bob Moyse Junior, Robert Moyse's grandson.
3. *The Times*, 18 May 1935, p.16 gave details of the Legion of Frontiersmen plans for protection against air gas attacks. Legion of Frontiersmen Archives contain a number of documents on the subject.
4. *The Frontier News*, October 1938, pp.3-4, re-printed in *History of the Legion of Frontiersmen, Canadian Division*, ed. Mack, pp.122-3.
5. *History of the Legion of Frontiersmen, Canadian Division*, ed. Mack, pp.118-9.
6. *Frontier News*, October 1938, p.8, reprinted in *History of the Legion of Frontiersmen, Canadian Division*, p.127.
7. *History of the Legion of Frontiersmen, Canadian Division*, ed. Mack, p.134.
8. *Ibid.*, p.128.
9. *Ibid.*, p.132.
10. *Ibid.*, p.115.
11. Undated newspaper cutting in the archives of the Legion of Frontiersmen.
12. *History of the Legion of Frontiersmen, Canadian Division*, ed. Mack, p.144.
13. WO32/10428 at Public Record Office.
14. *Ibid.*
15. *Ibid.*
16. Personal letter to the author from E.F. Meacock.
17. *Ibid.*
18. CAB106/1188 at Public Record Office.
19. Information courtesy of Bob Moyse Jnr.
20. *My Political Life, Volume Three, 1929-40*, L.C.S. Amery, p.378.
21. *History of the Legion of Frontiersmen, Canadian Division*, ed. Mack, pp.156-7.
22. Legion of Frontiersmen Archives.
23. *Ibid.*
24. 'The Spitfires of the Legion of Frontiersmen 1939-45', paper by Jeff Henley, Australian historian of the Legion of Frontiersmen, 2001.
25. Personal file of G.D. Hazzledine in The National Archives.
26. Report of the General Meeting in *The New Zealand Frontiersman*, December 1949.
27. *Ibid.*
28. *History of the Legion of Frontiersmen, Canadian Division*, ed. Mack, pp.201-9.
29. Information from Roger Tremblay of Quebec to B.W. Shandro.
30. 'Legion of Frontiersmen Commands in Canada, the 1960s', paper by B.W. Shandro, April 2003.

Bibliography

The works listed below are the major sources consulted. References to newspaper and magazine articles, files in the National Archives (Public Record Office), and the various archives of the Legion of Frontiersmen appear only in the reference notes. Scanned copies of the Roger Pocock diaries 1905-17 are lodged at the Cameron Library of the University of Alberta, Edmonton, as are copies of all the papers by B.W. (Will) Shandro regarding the early history of the Legion of Frontiersmen in Canada.

Amery, L.S., CH, *My Political Life, Vol.3*, London, 1955
Andrew, Christopher, *Secret Service*, London, 1985
Ashwell, Lena, *Myself a Player*, London, 1936
Blumenfeld, R.D., *All in a Lifetime*, London, 1931
Brett, Maurice (Ed.), *The Journals and Letters of Viscount Esher, volume 2*, London, 1934
Buchanan, Angus, *Three Years of War in East Africa*, London, 1919
Bulloch, John, *M.I.5*, London, 1963
Crafford, F.S., *Jan Smuts*, New York, 1944
Cranworth, Lord, *Kenya Chronicles*, London, 1939
Curtis, Arnold (Ed.), *Memories of Kenya*, Nairobi, 1986
Dawson, Capt. Lionel, *Lonsdale, the authorised life*, London, 1946
Donkin, J., *Trooper and Redskin*, London, 1889
Funnell, D.S. (Ed.), *History of the Legion of Frontiersmen 1904-1979, N Squadron*, Manawatu, New Zealand, private publication, 1979
Fyfe, Hamilton, *Sixty Years of Fleet Street*, London, 1949
Gallop, A., *Buffalo Bill's British Wild West*, Stroud, 2001
Hastings, MacDonald, *The Other Mr Churchill*, London, 1963
Haydon, A.L., *Riders of the Plains*, London, 1910
Hordern, Lt. Col. Charles (Ed.), *Military Operations East Africa, Vol.1*, from draft by Major Stacke, London, 1941
Jeal, Tim, *Baden-Powell*, London, 1989
Jerrold, Douglas, *Georgian Adventure*, London, 1937
Judd, Alan, *The Quest for C*, London, 1999
Kearton, Ada Cherry, *On Safari*, London, 1956
Kearton, Cherry, *Adventures with Animals and Men*, London, 1935
Kerr, Mark, *Prince Louis of Battenberg*, London, 1934
Laurence, Dan H. (Ed.), *Collected Letters of George Bernard Shaw, 1898-1910*, London, 1946
Lee, Norman, *Klondike Cattle Drive*, Vancouver, 1960
Lloyd, A.W., MC, *Jambo, or with Jannie in the Jungle*, Woodchester, England, n.d

MacDonald, Robert H., *Sons of the Empire*, Toronto, 1993
Mack, Brigadier A. (Ed.), *History of the Legion of Frontiersmen, Canadian Division*, Regina, Canada, n.d., private publication
Meinertzhagen, Richard, *Army Diary 1899-1926*, London, 1960
Millais, J.G., *The Life of Frederick Courtenay Selous*, London, 1918
Miller, Charles, *Battle for the Bundu*, London, 1974
Montagu, Ivor, *The Youngest Son*, London, 1970
Owen, Bryn, *Owen Roscomyl and the Welsh Horse*, Caernarfon, 1990
Pocock, Roger (Ed.), *The Frontiersman's Pocket Book*, London, 1909
Pocock, Roger, *Chorus to Adventurers*, London, 1931
Pocock, Roger, *Horses*, London, 1917
Pocock, Roger, *The Rules of the Game*, London, 1896
Pocock, Roger, *A Frontiersman*, London, 1904
Pocock, Roger, *Rottennness*, London, 1896
Pretorius, Major P.J., *Jungle Man*, New York, 1948
Ransley, Frank, OBE, DFC, *Soldier, Sailor, Airman, Gaoler*, private publication, n.d
Roberts, Morley, *Western Avernus*, London, 1887
Skene-Martin, David (Ed.), *Crime in a Cold Climate*, Toronto, 1994
Sladen, Douglas, *My Long Life*, London, 1939
Stevens, G.R., *A City Goes to War*, Brampton, Ontario, Canada, 1964
Stewart, R., *Sam Steele, Lion of the Frontiers*, Scarborough, Canada, 1981
Stoneham, C.T., *From Hobo to Hunter*, London, 1956
Sutherland, Douglas, *The Yellow Earl*, London, 1965
Trzebinski, Errol, *The Life and Death of Lord Erroll*, London, 2000
Vorbeck, General Von Lettow, *My Reminiscences of East Africa*, Battery Press, Nashville reprint of original 1920 book
Williams, Jeffery, *First in the Field, Gault of the Patricias*, London, 1995
Young, Francis Brett, *Jim Redlake*, London, 1930

INDEX

References which relate to illustrations only are given in **bold**.

Aitken, Brigadier, 80
Albert, King of Belgium, 71
Allen, 'Scotty', 155
Amery, Rt Hon. Leopold, xviii, 145, 168
Armstrong, Sgt, 171
Ashwell, Lena (Daisy), xviii, 1, 17, 27, 38, 51-4, 61, 106, 126

Baden-Powell, Robert, xviii, 30, 34, 43, 59-61, 64, 156, 168
Banning, F.W., 76
Barrington, Sir Eric, 58
Bate, R., 50
Battenberg, Prince Louis of, xviii, 30, **30**, 43, 58, 176
Beaverbrook, Lord, 171
Belton, Andrew, 'The Kaid', 141, 146-8, 158, 171
Bidduph-Pinchard, 'Jungle Jim', 34
Birdwood, Lord, 176
Blain, Larry B., 149
Blake, W.T., 100
Blumenfeld, R.D., 31, 46
Bodkin, Doctor, 35
Bottomley, Sgt Major, 79, 82
Bowles, John Handel, 73
Boyes, John, 156-8
Braithwaite, A.E. (later Doctor), 10-11, 152
Braithwaite, Gen. Sir W., 143
Brancker, Sir Sefton, 106, 126, 129
Briggs, Major-General Raymond, 176
Bromley (*Frontiersman* crew), **117**
Brotherton, Jack, 30
Buchan, John, xix
Buchanan, Angus, 72, 80, 82, 85, 88-91, 93, 95
Bukoba, Battle of, 81-4
Bull, Capt., 94
Burchardt-Ashton, Arthur, 98-9, 126, 129, 136, 138-40, 142, 146, 148

Burnham, Viscount, xviii
Burnham, F.R., 45
Burns, Robert, 125

Canterbury, Archbishop of (Cosmo Lang), 148
Carter, Pte, 95
Cassidy, Butch, xix, 26
Caws, Stanley Winther, 131, 135
Cecil, Randle, 67
Chamberlain, Sir Austen, 144
Chandler, Edmund, 31
Chevalier, Albert, 52
Childers, Erskine, xviii, 33, 60, 138
Clark, Cecil, 25-6
Cody, 'Buffalo Bill', 63
Conan Doyle, Arthur, xviii
Cook, John, Commandant, New Zealand, 64
Corke, Arthur, 169
Cormack, Eric, 174-5
Cowan, Pat, 70
Cranworth, Lord, 87
Cumming, Mansfield, 47-8, 56
Curre, Col, 140
Currey, Hamilton, 57
Curtis, Sir Arthur, xviii, 22-6
Curtis, Lady, 26
Cushny, Tom, 140

Danby, Major, 94, 96
Darling, Pte, 84
Dartnell, Wilbur, V.C., 77, 83-6
Davis, Cpl, 91
de Crespigny, Sir Claude Champion, 58
de Hora, Manoel Herreira, 40-41
de la Warr, Lady, 38
de Soveral, Marquis, 45
de Windt, Harry, 31
Denniss, E. Bartley, 61
Derby, Earl of, **145**, 146
D'Esterre, Ernest, 97

Dickens, Inspector Francis, 8
Donkin, John, 7, 8, 11, 12
Downes, Commander Andrew, 103, 110, 119
Driscoll, Lt Col D.P., D.S.O., **frontispiece**, 32, 36, **41**, 46, 54-6, 62, 66, 67, 71-4, 77, 80, 82, 88, 95-6, 97-8, 101, 134, 148, 156, 164, 168
Duncan, Major-General Sir John, **162**
Dunn, Capt. C.H., 131
Dunn, E.G., 163, 172

Eardley-Wilmot, Guy, 104, 109, **111**, **117**, 119-20, **123**, 126-9
Edge, S.F., 60
Edmonds, Lt-Col James, 33, 42
Edward VII, King, xix, 38
Edwards-Carter, H.C., **138**, 139, 143, 145-6, 149, 174
'El Desperadoes', 62
Elliott, Frederick, T., 81, 83-5
Ellison, Capt., 94
Elphinstone, Rt Hon. Lord, 58
Else, Edward, 50
Erroll, Earl of, xviii, 157-8
Esher, Viscount, xvii, 45-6, 51, 55, 58
Evans, Mabel (Dartnell's 'fiancee'), 86
Ewart, Major-General, 33, 42

Fairbanks, Douglas, 125
ffrench, Evelyn (a.k.a. 'Jeffrey Silant'), **2**, 62-3
Filibusters Club, 22-3
Findlater, Col J., **149**
Finn, Bill (U.S. Marshal), 122, **122**
Fisher, Admiral, 30
Fitzgerald, Capt. M.L., 161
Forbes, Major Patrick, 43-5, 56
Francis, Capt., 102
Fredericks, Pauline, 120, **121**
Frittell, Sir Francis, 57
Fyfe, Hamilton, 46

Gallagher, Major Jack, B.E.M., **170**
George VI, King, 165
Grahame, Kenneth (re 'Toad of Toad Hall'), 57
Gregory, Dr Joseph, 158
Grenfell, 2/Lt, 76
Grinlington, F.H., C.M.G., 42
Grogan, Ewart, 156
Gwynne, H.A., 31, 46

Haggard, H. Rider, xviii, 58
Haggas, Elverie, 73, 94
Haldane, Viscount, 32
Haldon, Lord, 32

Hall, Clifford, 79, 91
Hansen, Capt. C.E., 15
Hargreaves, Lt., 75
Hawkins, Major, 172
Hazzledine, Major, 93-4, 141, 171
Heaton, G.H., 102, 111, **113**, 126-7
Henley, Jeff, 136
Hildyard, General Sir Henry, 55
Hollis, Charles, 73
Holloway, Lt E.W. Vere, 136
Home Guard, xxi
Hope, Capt. Graham, 53
Hope, Linton, 138
Hore-Belisha, Leslie, 167
Hoskins, Brigadier, 93
House, Legion Lieut., 92
Houston, Col and Mrs (Governor of St Lucia), 113
Hutton, Major-General, 33
Hutton, Capt. Alfred, 53
Hyne, Cutcliffe, 22, 31, 42, 58

Ince, Thos (Motion Picture Studios), 116, 118-19
Ivrea, Marquis, 50

James, Henry, 61
Jenkin, 2/Lt, 76
Jenkins, Private, 87, 91
Jerrold, Douglas, 48
Jewell, J. St A., 138
Johnston-Noad, 'Count', 137
Jones, Capt., 88

Kearton, Ada Cherry, 156
Kearton, Cherry, xviii, 71, 73, 79-83, 94
Kell, Capt. Vernon, 42, 46-8, 56
Kemp, William D., **52**
Kemsley, Capt., 94
Kent, Prince George, Duke of, **xix**
King, Sgt Mike, **174**
Kingsford-Smith, C.E., 155
Kipling, Rudyard, xix, 18-19, 107
Kirton, Walter, 31
Kitchener, Earl, 68-9
Klondyke Expedition, 22-6
Knowles-Fitton, Alec, 171
Koekkoek, W., 62

L.D.V., *see* Home Guard
Langham, Percy, 93
Lansdowne, Marquis of, 58
Le Queux, William, 18, 33-5, 42, 46, 137
Lee, Norman, 24
Leeds, William B., Jnr., 120
Leitch, Major John, 75, 93

Index

Lettow-Vorbeck, Paul von, 71, 80, 81, 92, 156, 158
Lloyd, Arthur W., 77, 94-6, 156, 158
Lloyd, Lord, 143-5
Loch, Major-General Lord, 98-9, 101, **102**, **103**, 107, 126-8, 146, 164
Locker-Lampson, Oliver, 99
Lonsdale, Lord, xix, 35, 37-8
Lowther, Sir Cecil, 146
Lubbock, Basil, 39-40
Lyttelton, Sir Neville, 38

Mack, Brigadier A., 174-5
MacKenzie, F.A., 31
MacLaren, Sqn-Ldr Stuart, 125
MacMillan, Norman, 100, 102, 107, 110, 112, 116, 123, 125, 126-7
Malins, Geoffrey, 100, 102, **105**, 107, 109-10, 122-3
Manchester Troop, Legion of Frontiersmen, xxi, 67-71
Margaret, Princess, 51
Marlowe, Thomas, 37, 46
Mason, Charles, 22
Masterson, *Frontiersman* crew, **117**
M'Carty, Captain, 26
McCarthy, John P., 127
McDougall, Dr Percy, 68-71
McMillan, William Northrup, 75-6, 86
McNabb, Alex, 26
Meacock, Ernest, 159, 167
Meath, Earl of, 58
Meinertzhagen, Richard, 74, 82-4
Mellon (Ship's cook on *Frontiersman*), 106, **111**, **112**
Montagu of Beaulieu, Lord, 60
Montgomery, Bishop, 61
Montgomery-Massingberd, Gen. Sir A. (C.I.G.S.), 154
Moore, Frederick, 31
Morgan, Cecil, 62-3
Morris, Sir Edward, 136
Morton, Brigadier Edward, 148, **161**, 161-5, 172
Mountbatten of Burma, Countess, **xv**, 176
Mountbatten of Burma, Earl, **155**
Mountmorres, Viscount, 58
Moyse, Robert, M.C., D.C.M., B.E.M., 159, **160**, 168, **169**
Mucklow, Pte, 82

Northcliffe, Lord, 33
North-West Mounted Police, 6-13

O'Dell, *Frontiersman* crew, **117**
Onslow, Earl of, 58

Orde, H.S., 42, 58
Outram, George, 73, 80

P.P.C.L.I. Canada, 133-5
Palk, *see* Haldon
Palmer, Sir Charles, 42
Palmer, Capt. Lionel, 42
Palmer, Capt. W., **149**
Pearce (Second Engineer on *Frontiersman*), 106, **117**
Pedersen, D., 83
Perry, Supt A. Bowen, 11, 20
Perry, *Frontiersman* crew, **117**
Pickford, Mary, 125
Playfair, Arthur W., 17
Pocock, Charles A.B., 1-4, 17; Hilda, 2, 17; Lena, *see* Ashwell, Lena; Lillian, 1; Roger: xvii-xxii, **142**; early life, 1-27; founds Legion of Frontiersmen, **29**, 28-62, **41**; World Flight Expedition, 100-29; World Tour, 1935, 148-53, **149**; death in 1941, 165; Rosalie (Mrs Keefer), 1-4; Sarah M. (née Stevens), 1-3
Pollard, Hugh, 48-50
Poole, C.S.M., 90
Portland, Duke of, 146
Potter, Cdt Gen. R.J., **175**
Pownall, Col H.R., xviii
Pretorius, Major, 91
Pretyman, E.G., 31, 43, 137-8
Pyman, John, 74, 80

Quinn, Supt (Special Branch), 48, 50

Ramazani (Gunbearer to Selous), 82, 92
Ransley, Frank, 102-3, 106, 112, 114, 123, 129
Reading, Dick, 68-9
Reed, A. Harold (Baby), 73, 84, 93
Reed, C.S.M. Eddy, 85
Repington, Col, 51
Rhodes-Wood, E.H., 154-5
Rhoscomyl *see* Vaughan, Owen
Ricardo, Col, 56-7
Riel, Louis (Riel Rebellion) 9-11
Roberts, Morley, 31
Roberts, Lord, 33, 40, 56
Roberts, Trooper, 63, 67-9
Robins, Elizabeth, 61
Robinson, Lt, 94
Roosevelt, U.S. President, Teddy, 75
Rowlinson, Major Seymour, 130
Rundle, Gen. Sir Leslie, 58
Russia, Pocock's visit, 1904, 28-30
Ryan, Martin, 73, 94-6

Salisbury, Lord, 58, 67
'Savage Club', 31
Scott, Harry Fife, 58
Scott, Louis, 134, 149-51, 161-5, 174
Seely, Col J., 61
Sellwood, Mr, 157
Selous, F.C., xviii, 45, 61, 73, 77, 80, 82, **83**, **88**, 90-2, 156
Serjeant, Sir E., 42, 58
Service, Robert, xix
Seton, Ernest Thompson, 61
Seton-Kerr, Sir Henry, 31, 43, 53, 55
Shandro, B.W., 130-2, 134-6, 174
Shangani Patrol, 45
Shaw, George Bernard, xviii
Shaw, Harold, 123
Sheppard, Brigadier, 87
'Shepperton Cowboys', 62-3
Shoosmith, Brigadier P., **172**, **173**
Silant, Jeffrey, *see* ffrench Evelyn
Silver, *Frontiersman* photographer, **111**, **112**
Simson, Sir Henry, xviii, 51, 106
Sladen, Douglas, 18
Slim, Viscount, **157**
Smith, Robert A., 53, 87, 136, 138, 146-8
Smuts, General Jan, xviii, 35, 86, 92-3, 140, 148, 156, 158
Spalding, Lt Cdr Robin, 103, 110, 113, 114, 119, 122-3, 125
Steele, Harwood, 64, 130
Steele, Sir Sam, 64, 129, 131-2
Stevens, L/Cpl, 90
Stewart, General, 81-2
Stoneham, Charles, 78-9, 88-90
Strickland, Gen. Sir Peter, 146
Sutton-Page, Parker, 72, 94

Tamplin, Col H.T., 98-9, 126, 128-9, 138
'Texas Bob', 27
Thompson, Charles, 71

Thompson, Dr Fred, 107, 116, 119
Tighe, J.B., 50
Tighe, General, 81, 83
Traill, Stanley, 84-5
Trenchard, Sir Hugh, 125
Turnbull, Sir Hugh, 140
Twistleton, Frank (Francis), 66
Tyson, L.J., 122

Ulm, Charles, 155

Van Deventer, General, 86, 93
Vane, Sir Francis, 58-9
Vaughan, Owen, 138

Wakefield, A.W., 136
Wallace, Edgar, xviii, 31
Warde, Lt Col Henry (Senior Chief Constable), 57
Wavell, Major, 75
Wells (First Officer on *Frontiersman*), 110, 119
Welstead, Capt. A.D., 74, 93
Wheeler, Col, 149
White, Major H.H.R., 72, 88-90, 93
'Wild Bunch', 26
Willard, Legion Bandmaster, 41
Williams, Major E.B.B., 72
Willson, Justus Duncan, 133
Wilson, William Reginald, **80**
Windsor, Claire, 120, **121**
Wood, Brigadier S.T., 165
Wooden, Mr, 116, **118**
Wybrow, C.H., 146, 149, 174

Xenia, Princess, 120

York, Duchess of (Queen Elizabeth), 51
Young, Francis Brett, 90